The PARLIAMENT of PAKISTAN

A HISTORY OF INSTITUTION-BUILDING
AND (UN)DEMOCRATIC PRACTICES, 1971–1977

The PARLIAMENT of PAKISTAN

A HISTORY OF INSTITUTION-BUILDING AND (UN)DEMOCRATIC PRACTICES, 1971–1977

MAHBOOB HUSSAIN

Foreword by
Matthew McCartney

Introduction by
Mian Raza Rabbani

OXFORD
UNIVERSITY PRESS

OXFORD
UNIVERSITY PRESS

Oxford University Press is a department of the University of Oxford.
It furthers the University's objective of excellence in research, scholarship,
and education by publishing worldwide. Oxford is a registered trade mark of
Oxford University Press in the UK and in certain other countries

Published in Pakistan by
Oxford University Press
No. 38, Sector 15, Korangi Industrial Area,
PO Box 8214, Karachi-74900, Pakistan

ISBN 978-0-19-940556-5

Typeset in Adobe Caslon Pro
Printed on 55gsm Book Paper

Printed by Delta Dot Technologies (Pvt.) Ltd., Karachi

Acknowledgements
Cover photograph courtesy Associated Press of Pakistan (APP)
Photographer: Mr Afzaal Chaudhry (APP)

To
MY FAMILY
in particular,
MY MOTHER AND FATHER

Contents

Foreword

In the UK, some dates are instantly recognisable, 1066 and 1945 for big political events, and 1966 for sporting fans. We often structure our thinking about the contemporary world in terms of before and after 9/11. For Pakistan, the period from 1971 to 1977 is one of the most significant, influential, and recognisable interludes in its contemporary history. We recognise these as the 'Bhutto Years' in a way we would be more hard pressed to recall exactly the dates in which Ayub, Zia, or Musharraf served in office. The Bhutto Years are also perhaps the most personalised interlude of Pakistan's own history. Ayub and Zia serve as national emblems to Pakistan's wider participation in the US–Soviet Cold War and Musharraf as an emblem to the US's War on Terror campaign. When Musharraf reported that Pakistan had been told it would be bombed back into the Stone Age if it did not join the US-led War on Terror, it was a clear indication that his personality was a distant second to wider global forces. The Bhutto Years are just that, Bhutto is not just a convenient label, his personality tends to dominate those years. The story of 1971–1977, gives some notable guest appearances; the French and Americans in Pakistan's nuclear project; the Gulf countries in Bhutto's diplomacy; and Indira Gandhi in international peace talks among others. These years belong to Bhutto. That is what makes this book by Professor Mahboob Hussain so refreshing. Hussain steps away from this dominant narrative and lets the parliament of Pakistan take centre stage. Hussain's iconoclasm does not stop there. Any political scientist in Pakistan inevitably acknowledges Hamza Alavi, and seldom critically. Hussain by contrast takes on Hamza Alavi and his dominant paradigm. Alavi stylised the state of Pakistan as being 'over-developed', that it was relatively autonomous and was dominated by a bureaucratic-military elite. Hussain does not debate Alavi at length, however, he prioritises institutions and in doing so we see a new generation of contemporary-historical scholarship breaking free from ritual homage to older scholarship.

This book is not the story of Bhutto's rise and fall but that of a great experiment in multi-party parliamentary democracy—an experiment that worked for a while. Between 1971 and 1973, 'the parliament remained highly successful and sovereign in carrying out its responsibilities, and members of the parliament performed, as parliamentarians are expected to in a democratic parliamentary system' (p. 205). An important contribution of this book is the assertion that parliamentary democracy can be made to work in Pakistan. In the end, the person and personality of Bhutto forced his way back into the spotlight. The ultimate failure of parliament was tied into the bigger narrative of Bhutto's rise and fall. Telling the story of parliament ultimately reinforces another story, that of one of the most remarkable and controversial personalities of post-1947 Pakistan. We do come away from this book with a saddened feeling of lost opportunity, how locking in the democratic gains of 1973 could have spared Pakistan so much future trauma.

Bhutto was instrumental in creating space for the vigorous parliamentary sovereignty that captured the commanding heights of Pakistan's polity between 1971 and 1973. He was equally culpable in the subsequent weakening of parliament during his reign. While looking back, Hussain argues, 'The 1973 constitution of was a lasting achievement for this parliament, which was framed after twenty-six years of the creation of Pakistan' (p. 212). Looking forward from Hussain's narrative, we can argue, it took the removal of Bhutto and more than thirty years, for Bhutto's positive parliamentary legacy to bear its real promise.

As promised, this book tells a new story. Vast swathes of Pakistani political scientists, in other words, are wrong. The failure of parliament is ultimately a failure of its own making; we need to seek the causes of failure internal to the parliamentary process.

The 1950s are surveyed briefly here as a background to the main event, this is a familiar ground but Hussain has added new depth to our appreciation of parliament during these years. The parliamentary system as we know 'failed to establish firm roots' (p. 29) but I got to know more about the representation of women, the role of parliamentary questions, the ability of the MPs (members of parliament) to move resolutions, and the particular system of voting on financial bills. It is interesting stuff.

The conventional story of the 1970s starts with the formation of the Pakistan Peoples Party (PPP); Bhutto's rise to prominence in the 1960s; the 1970 election and ensuing civil war; and Bhutto's eventual assumption of the role of the Prime Minister. The policy reforms of these years—nationalisation of banks and heavy industry, labour reforms, and land reform—are usually told as if they emanate only from the Prime Minister's office and from the radical 1960s mobilisation of the PPP. Hussain takes us back inside the parliament, to the debates, arguments, votes, and political manoeuvrings by which campaign promises became concrete legislation. The parliamentary response to the 1972 Shimla Agreement between Bhutto and Indira Gandhi is an inspiring one. Parliament subjected the agreement to vigorous debate about every aspect of the agreement (p. 140), the debates were marked by a notable freedom of speech (p. 140), and Bhutto ultimately had to use the full and markedly democratic weight of his parliamentary brilliance in a three-and-a-half-hour speech to persuade his parliamentary colleagues to ratify the agreement. This was parliamentary democracy at its best. This process reached its apogee, argues Hussain, in the creation of the 1973 constitution. This process witnessed again, a free and open debate, the vigorous participation of all parties, and ultimately Bhutto's acceptance of the authority of parliament, but his skilful domination of proceedings were also seen. Bhutto neatly wrong-footed his opponents and during one of their periodic walkouts, he was conveniently left alone to declare an end to martial law, return Pakistan to democracy, and gain all the plaudits for himself. This represented a brilliant success (p. 106). By strengthening the democratic functioning of parliament, which in 1973, Hussain declares to have attained a sovereign status and was to become the primary institution of the state, Bhutto had been elevated to the ranks of a true statesman and his opponents were left seeming small, parochial, and petty by comparison.

From the outset, there were niggling indications that parliament was being undermined from within. Much of the very significant social and economic reforms (nationalisation, labour, education etc.) had been pushed through by decree, during martial law. In 1973, the state government of Balochistan had been dismissed and efforts by parliamentarians to debate the issue were skilfully (if not yet coercively)

side-lined by the government. Bhutto retained a privileged domination
of foreign policy and international issues (after Simla) which were rarely
discussed in depth within parliament. For example, Bhutto withdrew
from the Commonwealth with no discussion in parliament.

Parliament began to stumble after 1973. The much-vaunted
1973 constitution had, argues Hussain, created the world's strongest
Prime Minister in a parliamentary system. The constitution made
impeachment all but impossible. Bhutto with an already dominating
personality became gradually more authoritarian and by 1976, seemed
to have backing of the army, control of his party, and faced a much
weakened parliament. The vigorous debates of earlier years had given
way to a shambolic neglect by MPs, whereby parliament often had to be
adjourned because of insufficient attendance. The cabinet of educated
professionals that marked the early years of Bhutto's government, which
worked with 'zeal and dedication', was gradually replaced with figures
from the civil service and military (p. 166). Whereas Bhutto had earlier
spent hours persuading parliament to back the Shimla Agreement, as
early as 1974, the speaker of parliament was being summoned to attend
a cabinet meeting.

In later chapters, Hussain steps outside parliament and notes
that a similar process was occurring elsewhere. The army had been
side-lined after 1971 when forty-three officers were forced to retire;
General Yahya Khan was declared retrospectively guilty for actions
under martial law before 1971; and after 1973, declared participation
in a military coup would henceforth be regarded as treason. Rather
than institutionalising the subservience of the army to a democratic
parliament, Bhutto personalised the relationship. Bhutto endeavoured
to intervene himself in decisions about promotions and tried to use the
military to combat domestic strikes. He did the same with the judiciary.
Rather than empowering the judiciary to protect a democratic and
parliamentary constitution, Bhutto further amended the constitution
to reduce judicial power and strengthen executive control over judicial
appointments. We see the same story with the media; editors were
arrested, stories were influenced by the government; the media
became a showcase for Bhutto which scarcely mentioned the facts of
a democratic opposition.

It was a Greek tragedy. By 1973, parliament had become a sovereign authority and the dominant institution of Pakistan. In attaining these heights, parliament pulled up Bhutto as the master parliamentarian, to new heights of prestige and power. Hubris followed. Bhutto, the authoritarian, had free reign and few inhibitions in using this power to systematically undermine the institutions of the state, political parties, parliament, the army, the media, and the judiciary. When his nemesis came with the military coup of 1977, there was not a single institution of the state to hide behind. He personalised power to such an extent that by 1977 he was *the* person with power and the only element of the state necessary for the army to confront, remove, and assume power for itself.

This is the story of parliament through which Hussain has made a wonderfully welcome addition to our understanding of recent history, and through that of contemporary Pakistan. The scenes of celebration that greeted the passing of the Eighteenth Amendment in 2010, were an echo and demonstration of the importance of the parliamentary story in the 1970s. We can look afresh at Pakistan today and think carefully about the military, the civil service, and foreign influences (particularly China and CPEC). We can return to Hussain's lesson and paraphrase Bill Clinton 'it's the parliament, stupid'. There has been much recent debate about the need for a well-thought-out industrial policy to make sure that Pakistan benefits from the China-Pakistan Economic Corridor (CPEC). What we can take away from Hussain, is that a well-functioning parliament should be the institution to provide debate, question, and force into the democratic light, regarding CPEC policy-making, to maximise parliament's benefits to the populace of Pakistan.

MATTHEW McCARTNEY
University of Oxford

Introduction

Pakistan is one among such democracies where the history of institutions, especially the parliament, has not received the attention it deserves. This book is a research on the history of the most significant institution, i.e. parliament. It analyses the establishment, composition, development, and performance of the first directly elected parliament of Pakistan.

The book tries to answer the question, whether external forces or internal shortcomings were the main determinants on the performance of parliament. While seeking an answer to this question, the author traces the history of institutionalisation in Pakistan from 1971 to 1977.

In the book, Dr Mahboob Hussain, covers issues such as the circumstances under which the controversial 'law of necessity' was used in Pakistan; how the governor general dissolved the first assembly by excessive use of his powers, and how the ripples of this conflict reached other institutions of the state. Consequently, the institution of parliament was weakened in this institutional infight.

Moreover, this book talks about the circumstances in which the people of Pakistan waited for twenty-three years to elect their representatives through direct vote. It analyses the first directly elected assembly through many prisms and takes you through the number of candidates, their party affiliations, their educational qualifications, and their economic and social backgrounds. The statistical analysis of the age groups of members of the assembly will also prove to be interesting for the readers.

Additionally, the composition of the newly introduced upper house (the senate) and its role has been discussed. It traces as to how the foundations of the senate were laid with votes of the members of national assembly and the type of members who founded the new house. The aforementioned discussion makes the narrative engaging.

The analysis of the constitution-making process in the National Assembly of Pakistan, during the first two years of its life, helps in laying bare the assembly's sovereignty, i.e. its power in making independent decisions free from external influence. The readers of the book will benefit by finding the reasons that led to the assembly's success in passing a consensus constitution in proper time. This book also explains how the parliament coped with the challenges that confronted the nation, during the Zulfikar Ali Bhutto era.

Taking up the case of parliament, the book examines extensive debates and their effects on decision-making on crucial issues at the national level: parliament debated the Shimla Agreement, the recognition of Bangladesh, and the return of prisoners of war from India. In addressing these issues, the author relies on the proceedings of the assembly. The role of the parliament in tackling the very sensitive Qadiani issue, where religious feelings of a large number of Pakistanis were involved, is also highlighted. This study also explores the institutional relationship between parliament and other state institutions such as the military, judiciary, and bureaucracy.

Dr Mahboob Hussain is a social scientist who explores the history of parliament, scientifically, through detailed empirical scholarship. *The Parliament of Pakistan* is a good addition to the existing literature, which is limited on the subject, and one hopes that the book merits a wide academic audience.

MIAN RAZA RABBANI
Senator

Acknowledgements

I opened my eyes in a country where democracy and democratic institutions are supported in public rhetoric, but authoritarian attitudes and power-mongers hover in the very houses of parliament. Just a year before I was born, the first directly elected assemblies emerged. As a student of history and political science, I developed an interest in the evolution of democratic institutions in the postcolonial democracies. In this regard, the directly elected assembly in Pakistan became the first object of my scholarly enquiry. To test this question in the laboratory of history, I selected the first directly elected parliament as a case study.

This time-span is significant in many ways. Firstly, the people of Pakistan were enfranchised to elect an assembly commissioned with the dual task of constitution-making and legislation. Secondly, it started from the presidential form of government and turned to a parliamentary system; it also turned from unicameral to bicameral parliament. Such unique references were there in the luggage of this phase of parliamentary history of the country. It drew my attention towards the issue that till today remains a site of political debate and contestation in Pakistan.

That how this assembly functioned and fulfilled its role amid the dark shadows of doubts in the presence of powerful executive and other forces; this book is the outcome of the effort to answer these questions.

How far I succeeded in my effort to address the research questions will be decided by the readers, however, this book is a step towards highlighting the significance of the parliament, that is the basic institution of a democratic state. The progress of Pakistan, that came into existence in the result of a public struggle, is also linked with due regard to the will of the people. People should be given opportunity to decide their matters on their own and the forum of effective expression of public will is the parliament. Institutions in Pakistan are evolving in the presence of romantic charm of personalities.

When I took a step to understand this institution building, I found the guidance from my mentor Prof. Dr Massarrat Abid, former Director

Pakistan Study Centre, University of the Punjab, Lahore. I wish to express my gratitude to her wisdom and scholarly rigor that inspired and sustained me throughout this research.

A conducive atmosphere is the *beta noire* of any research endeavour. I consider it my good luck that former and present chairmen of Department of History & Pakistan Studies, as well as former and present Deans of Faculty of Arts & Humanities, University of the Punjab, Dr Qalb-i-Abid and Dr Muhammad Iqbal Chawla, fully supported me. I am equally indebted to other revered colleagues who encouraged me in this work.

A special thanks to the Higher Education Commission that granted initial funding whereby I was able to visit London and learn from the eminent historian, Professor Francis Robinson (CBE), Royal Holloway University of London, UK; I extend my heartiest gratitude to him, who commented on this work in the following words:

> … as a historian he was not used to considering the political science literature in his field. We had fruitful early discussions about the literature on institutionalisation. I have been pleased to see the way in which the insights he has derived from this literature have influenced the questions he has asked in his research and its written outcomes, as they have been produced.

Such beneficial meetings with some other prominent scholars also took place in England, including political scientist Dr Matthew J. Nelson (School of Oriental and African Studies), whose guidance and support was beneficial. During my visit to UK, I also received valuable guidance from Dr Ian Talbot (University of Southampton) and Dr Sarah Ansari (Department of History, Royal Holloway University of London). Moreover, prior to the publication of this work, I got the opportunity to meet Prof. Matthew McCartney (School of Global and Area Studies, University of Oxford) and Prof. Iftikhar A. Malik (Bath Spa University, UK); I learned a great deal from them, for which I am grateful.

It is said that good friends are a special blessing. For me, this has been Dr Rizwan Ullah Kokab whose persistent, brotherly suggestions accompanied me at every turn of the journey of my research.

I have dedicated this book to my late parents. Although, they did not receive much formal education, they guided me at every step of life and encouraged me to move forward. My thanks are also due to my wife, who displayed tremendous patience and fortitude during this research.

It would be unjust on my part if I do not offer thanks to the staff of National Assembly Library, Islamabad; Punjab Assembly Library, Lahore; Punjab University Libraries; British Library; The National Archives, Kew Gardens; and Bodleian Library, Oxford. The staff of these libraries were always willing to locate the required material for me.

Likewise, I am grateful to Oxford University Press. Their cooperation made the publication of this book possible.

List of Abbreviations

ANP	Awami National Party
BDs	Basic Democrats
CBE	Commander of the Order of the British Empire
CID	Criminal Investigation Department
CML	Council Muslim League
COP	Combined Opposition Parties
CPEC	China-Pakistan Economic Corridor
CSP	Civil Service of Pakistan
DAC	Democratic Action Committee
DO	Dominion Office
FATA	Federally Administered Tribal Areas
FCO	Foreign and Commonwealth Office
FSF	Federal Security Force
ICS	Indian Civil Service
IGD	Islami Gantantari Dal
JGMD	Jatiya Gana Mukti Dal
JIP	Jamaat-i-Islami Pakistan
JUI (H)	Jamiat Ulema-e-Islam (Hazarvi)
JUI	Jamiat Ulema-e-Islam
JUP	Jamiat Ulema-e-Pakistan
KSP	Krishak Sramik Party
KT	Khaksar Tehreek
MJAH	Markazi Jamiat-e-Ahle-Hadees
MNA	Member National Assembly
MPA	Member Provincial Assembly
MPs	Members of Parliament
NAD	National Assembly Debates
NAP (B)	National Awami Party (Bhashani Group)
NAP	National Awami Party
NDF	National Democratic Front
NIP	Nizam-i-Islam Party

NWFP	North West Frontier Province
PBUH	Peace Be Upon Him
PDP	Pakistan Democratic Party
PLD	Pakistan Legal Decisions
PML (Conv.)	Pakistan Muslim League (Convention)
PNC	Pakistan National Congress
PNL	Pakistan National League
POW	Prisoner of War
PPA	Political Parties Act
PPP	Pakistan Peoples Party
PTV	Pakistan Television
QML	Qayyum Muslim League or Pakistan Muslim League (Qayyum)
SKMPPMM	Sindh-Karachi Mohajir Punjabi-Pathan Mutahida Mahaz
SUF	Sind United Front
TNA	The National Archives (London)
UDF	United Democratic Front

Chapter One

Institution Building in Pakistan
A Conceptual Framework

This study focuses on the working of the parliament as an institution in Pakistan from 1947–77—especially the Zulfikar Ali Bhutto period (1971–77). The six years of Bhutto's regime are crucial in the political history of Pakistan, owing to multiple developments which shaped the future of the country. In fact, the era began with the emergence of a 'new' Pakistan—just as the nation was demoralised owing to the tragic separation of East Pakistan in 1971 and the consequential trauma. Pakistan, at that time, lacked strong political institutions because most of the political parties were either weak or not institutionalised. During this era, Pakistan lost its eastern wing; in this scenario, the first directly elected parliament came into existence and Pakistan's third constitution was formulated, which for the first time in its history, provided for two houses, i.e. the senate and the national assembly. The new assembly was confronted with the task to re-establish the state of Pakistan on democratic lines and to save the state from the dangers of disintegration. It also had to boost the morale of the nation after the loss of 1971.

INSTITUTION OF PARLIAMENT—HISTORICAL CONTEXT

The parliament is one of the oldest and most honoured organs of the British government. In general, parliaments are elected assemblies with the duty of checking, controlling, and sometimes electing the executive power. Their structures can vary, but most are either bicameral or unicameral. Historically, in Europe, the development of democracy over the centuries has been largely the growth of power of the parliament over the monarchy, and consequently, the sovereignty of this institution.

1

The word 'parliament' is derived from the French word *Parler* (to talk) that was given to the meetings of the English King's Council in the mid-thirteenth century. Soon after its first known use in the old French epic poem, *La Chanson de Roland*, the term 'parliament' came to acquire a more specialised meaning than its original 'conversational' connotation. In several English sources *c*. 1240, it appears in its Latinised or French forms of *Parliamentum* and *Parliament* to describe important assemblies during which the king discussed affairs of the state and conferred with his tenants-in-chief. The concept of a meeting or confrontation between the authority and magnates was already present in those early 'parliaments', whether it was to debate the great issues of war and peace, or to discuss more localised matters of the royal administration and the exercise of judicial powers.[1]

The origins of parliament lie in Saxon times[2] when monarchs consulted their 'wise men'—the Witenagemot, which included the archbishops, bishops and abbots, earls, thegns, and knights, and was later known as the Great Council. This was the foundation of the House of Lords. The barons' grievances against the monarch, including the excessive levying of taxes, formed the basis of the barons' protest which led to the Magna Carta in 1215.

The second period of the parliament's development, from the late fifteenth to seventeenth century, covers the period when it was engaged in a definitive struggle with British monarchs over the exercise of ultimate sovereignty. During this period, the parliament won the right to punish royal officials who broke rules in the collection of taxes. The third period, dating from 1688 to 1832, witnessed the beginning of the party system in the parliament, the establishment of the doctrines of ministerial responsibilities, and the foundations of the cabinet system. New institutions appeared within the parliament—parties, the prime minister, and the cabinet, and with them, the gradual decline of the power and political functions of the monarchy. The final period was from 1832 until present day, when the relationships between the parliament and the government, and the commons and the lords, were established to ensure legal sovereignty of the parliament in conformity with the wishes of the people as expressed at the ballot box.[3]

The parliament does not embrace the complete sphere of governmental activity. The vast and powerful civil service (or its equivalent administrative organisation abroad) is outside the parliament, and parliament itself does not govern but is rather the meeting-place of the government—whether personified in an individual or in a group of persons holding executive powers and of represented democratic interests. The description of parliament as a meeting-place is deliberate, for it implies that the two concepts of government and democracy confront and influence each other there.

The parliament has three main functions wherever the parliamentary system functions: making laws, scrutinising and controlling the executive, and representing the people. These functions in turn give rise to certain subsidiary functions, including debate and deliberation, controlling government finance, and acting as channels of communication between the government and the electorate.[4]

It is not the function of the parliament to govern the country. That responsibility rests with the executive, i.e. the prime minister and the cabinet. In 'presidential' systems, the executive and legislature are separate bodies. However, in parliamentary systems, they are overlapping bodies; the members of the executive are drawn from within the parliament and remain within it.[5]

The institutionalisation of parliament, like 'democracies', differs from country to country. The Indian system of government that has preceded Pakistan's political system through the ages, has been based on the role of elected representatives in the social system and the equality and wealth of all men and women.[6] The Pakistani parliamentary system is unmatched in many ways and has developed within the country in the context of its own cultural and political background, and the national and historical evolution of a responsible government.

POLITICAL INSTITUTIONALISATION UNDER COLONIAL RULE

The growth of the parliament in Pakistan was the direct outcome of the British parliamentary system in India. The governor general's council evolved and took the shape of a parliament in the course of time. The origin of the British parliamentary system in India can be traced back to the Charter Act 1833, which was a landmark in the history of legislative institutions in India. The Act of 1833 differentiated the law-making meetings of the council of officials from its executive meetings. The charter also increased the size of the council as legislature, and legislative meetings were made public and the proceedings published.[7] The Act of 1861, passed within three years of the end of the East India Company rule and its replacement by the direct responsibility of the British Crown, enlarged the council with the beginning of representation of the Indian public.[8]

Although the councils were not envisaged as parliaments in an embryonic stage, the disclaimer by Lord Dufferin in 1892 itself testified that the councils were regarded by some circles of Indians as similar to the British parliament. The Indian Councils Act 1892 further enlarged the councils, and their functions were extended in such a way as to permit members to ask questions and to discuss the budget. In the Act of 1909, the much-enlarged councils were given greater powers, including the right to move resolutions and ask supplementary questions. The reforms schemes and the Act of 1919 entailed a process of the developing parliamentary institutions.[9] In place of the small legislative council, there was now a bicameral legislature consisting of a legislative assembly and a council of the state.

In the view of the Simon Commission 1928, the central legislature in India was proposed to be refashioned on explicitly federal lines, both the lower houses, federal assembly, and the council of the states, were chosen indirectly by provincial councils.[10] The evolutionary process took its final shape in the Government of India Act 1935. After the establishment of Pakistan, its first two parliaments worked according to the Government of India Act 1935, which was adopted as the interim constitution of Pakistan with some amendments.

The Government of India Act 1935 envisaged a bicameral legislature consisting of the king, represented by the governor general and the two chambers: the council of states and the house of assembly.[11] The council of states was to consist of 156 representatives of British India—the area that was directly administered by the British government—and not more than 104 representatives of the Indian princely states, which were ruled by the local rulers and were connected with the British government through various arrangements.[12] There were seventy-five general seats—six for scheduled castes, four in Punjab for Sikhs, forty-nine for Muslims, six for women, seven for Europeans, two for Indian Christians, and one for Anglo-Indians. Six seats were to be filled by persons chosen by the governor general at his discretion. The council of states was to be a permanent body, not subjected to dissolution, but one-third of its members were to retire every third year. The house of assembly was to consist of 250 representatives of British India and not more than 125 representatives of the Indian states. The life of the house of assembly was five years, unless dissolved sooner.[13]

The federal parliament was to function as federal legislature and after the adoption of a method of distribution of powers between the central and provincial legislatures, the three legislative lists—the federal, the provincial, and the concurrent—were made. The first list belonged to the competence of the federal legislature and both the federal and provincial legislatures were competent to legislate on matters covered by List III.[14]

The federal legislature, as envisaged in the Government of India Act 1935, had not practically taken place in India because of the disagreement of two major political parties in the country—the Muslim League and the Indian National Congress.[15] There were two different types of elections. The elections to the legislative assembly of India took place in December 1945. The All-India Muslim League won all thirty seats reserved for the Muslims, and the Indian National Congress bagged fifty-seven seats.[16] The elections to the constituent assembly were held in July 1946, according to the British Cabinet Mission Plan.[17] The Indian National Congress won most of the seats for the Hindus (out of 210 seats, the Congress won 199) and similarly, the All-India Muslim League captured almost all the Muslim seats (out of 78 Muslim seats, it won 73).[18]

From 1947 to 1973, Pakistan had a unicameral system of legislature. Though not very strong, the institution of the parliament had been working effectively during the first parliamentary phase (1947–58). The military takeovers by Ayub Khan and Yahya Khan (1958–71) weakened the roots of democracy in Pakistan.

Consequently, the state of Pakistan lacked strong political institutions, and political parties remained weak, as did the political culture. However, the first general election held in 1970 brought about the directly elected parliament consisting of two houses, namely the senate and the national assembly. This parliament worked for six years and passed a number of bills and acts concerning contemporary issues of political, social, economic, and religious significance. Most importantly, the parliament formulated and enacted the third constitution of Pakistan in 1973, which is still in force. This seemingly strong parliament, under one of the most popular leaders in the history of Pakistan, Z.A. Bhutto, was suddenly overthrown by General Ziaul Haq in 1977. Once again, parliamentary democracy was not allowed to flourish in Pakistan. One major query still remains; was the military responsible for the dismissal of the Bhutto government or political parties? Many historians have ignored the weaknesses of the democratic system and its main vehicle (the parliament). Therefore, it is of immense importance to revisit the working of the parliament as an institution in Pakistan to understand its weaknesses and strengths, and also to probe into the causes of its failure to carry on the process of democracy in Pakistan.

Under the 1973 constitution, Pakistan adopted a bicameral system at the parliament at its centre, composing of the president, the national assembly, and the senate. Other organs of the parliament were: the prime minister, the speaker of the national assembly, and the chairman of the senate.

A number of challenges were faced by this new bicameral parliament during its life. This included:

- negotiating with a victorious India in the perilous times of the war of 1971,
- the task of constitution-making,
- the rehabilitation of the post-war state,
- the country's image-building in the international community,
- steps towards improving a bankrupt economy,
- changing the economic landscape of Pakistan in terms of economic planning, production and distribution,
- the problem of inefficient agricultural production along with the need for land reforms, and
- the internal security situation.

The aforementioned and other similar challenges have made this era, as well as the study of this period, significant in the political history of Pakistan.

Political parties and parliaments are the core institutions of a democratic political structure. Their significance for Pakistan is immense because the country itself is the product of a political and constitutional struggle. The working and growth of these institutions in Pakistan is a complex phenomenon, and this study will help to understand this complexity and shed light on some unexplored aspects of parliamentary politics in the country.

The nation has had three 'permanent' constitutions, namely the constitutions of 1956, 1962, and 1973; the first two were abrogated, while the third was suspended, and later significantly amended twenty-six times.[19] There have been two formal interim constitutions in 1947 and 1972, and for long periods, the country has been governed by 'constitutional' arrangements under martial law. However, Pakistan is still suffering from extra-constitutional steps.

In the study of the history and politics of Pakistan, institutional explanations have been deployed by a number of scholars. Lawrence Ziring[20] has linked the introduction of Pakistan's first martial law regime in 1958 with the institutional weakness resulting in part from the collapse of the Muslim League. Veena Kukreja[21] has similarly understood this period as one of general decay in political institutionalisation, resulting in a crisis of legitimacy. Maleeha Lodhi[22] analyses the army's 1977 intervention in similar terms of institutional weakness of the Pakistan Peoples Party (PPP).[23]

The weakness of institutions has created many problems, and often hindered the political development of Pakistan. Why are Pakistani institutions not strong? Why has the parliament remained incapable of being acknowledged within the country's political system, despite being the only representative body for the public?

A group of scholars believe that the Pakistani army is so powerful that it does not let any other institution (including the parliament) function smoothly or freely. Many prominent scholars of this school of thought, such as Hasan Askari Rizvi,[24] Mazhar Aziz,[25] Ayesha Siddiqa,[26] Shuja Nawaz,[27] Hussain Haqqani,[28] Ayesha Jalal,[29] and Hamza Ali Alavi,[30] have maintained that the institution of the army enjoys more power than other institutions.

Rizvi undertakes a comprehensive and documented study of the role of the military in Pakistan's society and politics with a view to explain why and how a professional military can acquire political disposition.[31]

Mazhar Aziz has studied the political structure under the umbrella of the Path Dependency theory. He has adopted the argument that the emergence of the military as the foremost decision-making entity creates its own set of precedents and institutions that enable the military to be, in effect, a parallel state, and continues to define the nature of governance within the polity. As a consequence, it is likely that the civilian governments in Pakistan will remain unstable and weak, given the scope of the military's capacity and influence.[32]

Ayesha Siddiqa has analysed the internal and external dynamics of the military's gradual power-building and the impact that it has on Pakistan's political and economic development.[33] She shows how the military has gradually gained control of Pakistan's political, social, and economic resources and how this power has transformed Pakistani society. Ayesha Siddiqa has tried to search for answers to questions of whether democracy has a future in Pakistan, where the armed forces have become an independent class, and why militaries become key players in a country's power politics; her answer is that the brass is protecting its gold.[34]

Shuja Nawaz has highlighted how the political circumstances caused military intervention in politics at different instances. He has argued that rapid development of the military halted the growth of the political system, and that leaders made no attempt to redress the power imbalance between the institutions of state and the army. He also observes that it is the power imbalance that converted the army into a power centre, and that politicians invited the army for the arbitration of their disputes, which exposed their weaknesses to the military.[35] To support his argument, he has quoted the appointment of two serving officers, Commander-in-Chief General Ayub Khan and Major General Iskandar

Mirza, as ministers, a direct violation of the constitution. This argument supported one of the hypotheses of this study as well.[36] Shuja's other argument is that the Americans did not wish to engage in the domestic political affairs of Pakistan but wanted to ensure political constancy for their alliance against communism. They decided to give their consent for imposing martial law by saying that they 'favour democracy but [there are] exceptions which can be justified for a limited period'.[37]

Hussain Haqqani has contended that Pakistan's state institutions, especially the military and intelligence services have been playing a leading role in building its national identity on the basis of religion. Explaining further, Haqqani has opined that, 'Islamist groups have been sponsored and supported by the state machinery at different times to influence domestic politics and support the Military's political dominance.'[38] Furthermore, Haqqani has built an interesting thesis that the alliance of the mosque and the military has been absolutely determined to overthrow civilian rule in Pakistan.[39]

Ayesha Jalal also focuses mainly on the first decade of Pakistan's history to show how politicians at the centre lost power, prestige, and authority to the military and bureaucracy. She argues that by the time Liaquat Ali Khan was assassinated in October 1951, the military had played an important, if not a dominating role in the formation of the policy for Pakistan. By April 1953, the 'bureaucratic-military axis had wrested the balance of power' from politicians and deposed them entirely in the coup of 1958.[40]

Writers of another group (including Frank Goodnow,[41] Ilhan Niaz,[42] Huma Naz,[43] Ali Ahmed,[44] Khalid B. Sayeed,[45] C. Bhambhari and M. Bhaskaran Nair,[46] Charles H. Kennedy,[47] and Aminullah Chaudhry[48]) while reviewing the early period of Pakistan's history, view that over-dependency on bureaucracy causes the weakness of other institutions of the state, including the parliament. According to Goodnow, the weakness of legislature or elected representatives, vis-à-vis the bureaucracy, which co-operated with the chief executive and was not barred, gave the Civil Service of Pakistan (CSP) full control over the government. Goodnow argues that a powerful bureaucracy may suppress institutions essential to economic development as well as to a democratic government.[49] In this context, Ilhan Niaz contends that from April 1953 to March 1969, Pakistan was governed by CSP officers, senior military officers, and elements within the judiciary. His main thesis is that in post-independence governance, the rulers have 'steadily regressed' into a pre-British form while exercising power. According to the author, in terms of performance, the period between 1947 and 1969 was 'probably the best' but 'prolonged authoritarian rule left a huge void in Pakistan's political leadership'.[50]

Khalid B. Sayeed, while observing the control of the institution of bureaucracy over the political system of Pakistan, commented:

> The Government of Pakistan might be described as a pyramid carved out of a single rock, and the civil servants had captured the apex of the pyramid. Below the apex are several layers of authority descending from the secretariat level to the base of the pyramid, the district administration.[51]

The ideas of the scholars who favoured the rule of masses, like Tariq Ali,[52] Badruddin Umar,[53] and Rasul Bakhsh Rais,[54] stress the role of the masses in the building of institutions. The gist of their views lead to the argument that parliament as an institution can be stronger if it is supported by the masses. Until and unless the masses are behind the decisions of the parliament and the people are satisfied with the working of this institution, the parliament cannot dictate the functions of other institutions. Without public support, the parliament even loses control of its functioning as well as its direction.

While considerable work is available on the general political history of Pakistan, and a plethora of writing has been produced on numerous aspects of Pakistani history, very few books have included any material or chapter on the institutionalisation of the parliament in Pakistan. Even those historians who have indirectly shed some light on the institution of parliament in Pakistan, have not gone far enough to appreciate the multiple aspects and dynamics of the institution in a historical perspective. The role and growth of legislatures in Pakistan has not been given sufficient space. Some writers have focused on the role of individuals in Pakistani politics, while others have highlighted the political history of Pakistan. Scholars have undoubtedly contributed a great deal to the political history of the country but have not focused keenly on the analysis of parliamentary history of Pakistan.

Even researchers who have focused on the Zulfikar Ali Bhutto era have not provided sufficient information on the role of Pakistan's first directly elected parliament. Most authors (such as Stanley Wolpert,[55] Anwar H. Syed,[56] Maulana Kausar Niazi,[57] Sheikh Muhammad Rashid,[58] Rafi Raza,[59] Salmaan Taseer,[60] Philip P. Jones,[61] and Shahid Javed Burki[62]) highlighted various aspects of the history of the Bhutto era but they did not discuss the parliament as an institution in detail. Z.A. Bhutto, who authored several books regarding his life and his contribution to the history of Pakistan, also neglected to mention the parliament's role in politics; in fact, the parliament is the most neglected subject in all of his works. Therefore, it is exceptionally significant to explore the parliament as an institution in Pakistan to understand its role in the history of the country.

Pakistani historians generally hold the military rulers, especially General Ziaul Haq, responsible for imposing martial law in the country without cogent reasons, and for overlooking the working of the institution of the parliament under the Bhutto period. These works provide an overall picture of the affairs in Pakistani state but miss the idiosyncratic study of the parliament. Finding historical background of Pakistani politics from these books, the present work sets the narrative that despite its lofty achievements, the opposition groups were often deliberately left out of parliamentary workings; such actions forced the opposition into a reactionary mode thus hurting the parliament's smooth working. The executive branch of government frequently bypassed the parliament. By and large, such actions weakened the parliament. Although other factors (like the role of the army and the existence of external powers) were important, it remains a fact that the weaknesses were inherent in the institution of the parliament during the Bhutto era, which consequently brought about its unfortunate and tragic demise.

The weakness of parliament could be understood only through its study as an institution. The concept of 'institution' has been used in multiple ways in different branches of knowledge, such as sociology and political science. 'An institution,' according to March and Olsen:

...is a relatively enduring collection of rules and organized practices, embedded in structures of meaning and resources that are relatively invariant in the face of a turnover of individuals, and relatively resilient to the idiosyncratic preferences of individuals and changing external circumstances.[63]

'Institutionalisation' refers to the development of a regularised system of policy-making. According to Kevin McGuire:

A political community develops routines, standard ways of doing things, by organisations endowed with resources and authority. Responses to regularly recurring problems are often institutionalized. Collective action comes to pass in the political community because standard procedures are established that provide political actors with appropriate incentives to take the action necessary to provide a public good or control an externality.[64]

Globally, valuable literature is available on the topic, which is very helpful in formulating arguments as well as the conceptual framework related to institution building, particularly the representative institutions. Drawing from political development literature, Polsby used the concept of institutionalisation to describe the process by which the American House of Representatives became more complex, autonomous, coherent, adaptive, and universal.[65] This theme of institutionalisation has since been pursued by Gehrlich,[66] Opello,[67] Hibbing,[68] Mezey,[69] Squire,[70] Patterson and Copeland,[71] and Norton[72] thereby providing the basic framework for this book.

The role of the political leadership in institutionalisation is another important theme, which is utilised by writers like Max Weber. His writings present the relationship between charisma on one hand, and the process of institution building in major fields of the social order, such as politics, law, economy, culture, and religion on the other. The concept of 'charisma' is therefore significantly important for understanding the processes of institution-building as Weber argues in his writings.[73] This argument provides a basis to examine the role of Pakistani leadership in institution-building, especially the role of Z.A. Bhutto in this context.

Institutionalisation (and its mechanisms) is one of the major preoccupations of modern social sciences. Samuel P. Huntington,[74]

Robert E. Goodin,[75] Max Weber,[76] Gabriel A. Almond,[77] Nelson W. Polsby,[78] and James Mahoney[79] have conducted some significant works of research, in this regard.

For the study of the first parliament of Pakistan, the level of institutionalisation of Pakistani political system could be defined by the adaptability, complexity, autonomy, and coherence of its organisations and procedures. If these criteria could be identified and measured in the Pakistani context, its political system can be compared in terms of these levels of institutionalisation, making it possible to measure increases and decreases in the institutionalisation of the particular organisations and procedures within its political system.[80]

Another tool for measuring the process of institutionalisation, according to Huntington, is the chronological factor, as political institutions are not created overnight. Political development is slow, particularly when compared to the relatively rapid pace of economic development.[81] An organisation's functions can be defined in many ways. Usually, an organisation is created to perform one particular function. However, when the previously desired function is no longer needed, the organisation faces a major crisis: it either finds a new function or settles to a lingering death. An organisation that has adapted itself to changes in its circumstances, and has survived one or more changes in its principal functions, is more highly institutionalised than one that has not.[82]

According to Norton, more institutionalised parliaments have a somewhat greater capacity to constrain governments than the relatively less institutionalised ones. At the heart of institutionalisation, is specialisation through committees.[83] According to Polsby, an organisation becomes institutionalised when it becomes differentiated from its environment, when it develops and channels career opportunities, develops a division of labour in which roles are specified, and becomes universalistic rather than particularistic in its methods of internal business.[84] The general idea is that as institutions move through time, they tend to adopt certain qualities and lose others. Specifically, the typical institution is thought to become more complex, autonomous, coherent, adaptive, universalistic, and less simple, subordinate, disunited, rigid, and particularistic.

It is significant to note that there is no acceptable general model of legislative change and study of the notion of institutionalisation. Polsby offers some works in this regard.[85] Some scholars like Cooper, Brady, Sisson, and Hibbing have criticised institutionalisation's general theoretical tenets. Still, the spate of studies[86] exploring institutionalisation attest to the continuing influence of Polsby's idea.[87]

The political context within which the legislatures exist—as well as their internal resource strength, and organisation—enormously affects their formation, development, and work. The fundamental relationship between the legislature and the executive are believed to be determined by the interplay of a number of social, economic, political, and intra-institutional factors. These are social factors like civil society, political history, culture, media, and interest groups; economic factors; political factors like the constitutional dimension and the party dimension; and finally intra-institutional factors like chambers and members.[88] Hence, the comparison between the parliament and the executive can be studied in light of these factors.

Examining a wide variety of organisations, different scholars, such as Mishler and Hildreth, Hibbing, Ragsdale, Theis, Keohane, Huntington, and Shepsle and Bonchek, have consistently sought specific indicators that reflect an underlying dimension of institutionalisation. Kevin T. McGuire has subsumed these indicators under three general headings: differentiation, durability, and autonomy.

A principal indicator of an institutionalised political organisation is differentiation from its environment, i.e., the establishment of clear boundary lines that mark its distinctiveness. In practical terms, its members should constitute a discrete group with a well-defined role in the political system. One common measure of such differentiation is the extent to which members are recruited from among the veterans within an organisation and thus, share a common understanding of their institution's goals.

Institutional growth can also be expressed in terms of durability—the ability to persist and to adapt to change. Resilience is the mark of a stable policy maker. If an organisation can maintain its role in the ebb and flow of politics, it serves as a gauge of its integration into the political system.

Therefore, a durable organisation would be able to pursue its goals even when confronted with changes.

An effective policy maker must also be autonomous, having 'some degree of independence in making its own decisions without dictation from outside actors'. Operationally, autonomy is indicated by the presence of procedures protecting the independence of the institution vis-à-vis other political actors and institutions.[89]

Polsby, on the other hand, utilises three elements of institutionalisation: the establishment of boundaries (autonomy), the growth of internal complexity, and the development of universalistic—as opposed to particularistic—decision-making rules.[90] This institutionalisation is evident in several ways:

1) Significant increase in membership continuity from session to session, and extended apprenticeship periods for leaders;
2) Increased autonomy and importance of committees, growth of specialised party leadership, and increase in aid and salaries for members;
3) Increased use of automatic means of handling affairs, such as the use of seniority in determining committee positions.[91]

One aspect of institutionalisation, according to Polsby, is the differentiation of an organisation from its environment. The establishment of boundaries in a political organisation usually refers to a channelling of career opportunities. In an undifferentiated organisation, entry to and exit from membership is easy and frequent. Leaders emerging rapidly as lateral entry from outside to positions of leadership is quite common, and persistence of leadership over time is rare. As any organisation institutionalises, it stabilises its membership; entry is more difficult, and turnover is less frequent. Its leadership professionalises and persists. Furthermore, the recruitment for leadership is more likely to occur from within, and the apprenticeship period lengthens. Thus, the organisation establishes and 'hardens' its outer boundaries.[92] In Pakistani context the common understanding of the parliamentarians through a study of their elections, the formation of parliament, and their mutual relationships could be studied.

As Polsby notes, when compared to the establishment of boundaries, 'simple operational indices of institutional complexity and universalistic automated decision-making are less easy to produce in neat and comparable time series.' Polsby is of the view that the obvious measure of internal complexity—the number of committees in the body—is misleading in that the raw number of committees may not reflect the true level of internal differentiation. The committees could be powerless, or they could be very powerful; they could have no staff, or they could be well-staffed; they could have set jurisdiction or variable jurisdiction; and they could have substantial or inconsequential oversight capabilities. In short, committees vary widely, and merely counting them may not be meaningful. This varied situation convinced Polsby to look for other indicators of internal complexity. He chose the growth in the autonomy and importance of committees, the growth of specialised agencies of party leadership, and the general increase in the provision of various emoluments and auxiliary aids to members in the form of office space, salaries, allowances, staff, and committee staff.[93]

Polsby's final indicator of internal complexity is 'the growth of resources assigned to internal management, measured in terms of personnel, facilities, and money'. The staff assistance constitutes an important part of these internal resources. By 'staff', Polsby means much more than simply personnel. He also comments briefly on the physical attributes of Congress and then presents the trend in yearly expenditures required to run the House of Representatives.[94]

The third and final feature of institutionalisation addressed by Polsby is concerned with the tendency of a body to adopt rules that are more automatic and less discretionary. These rules do not need to be written—informal norms may also qualify.[95] How the rules of parliament and the traditions were adopted by the parliament of Pakistan during its proceedings have been studied under this criteria.

This framework provides the most appropriate theoretical lens to coherently investigate and account for parliamentary institution building in Pakistan, as it facilitates a careful analysis of relevant events and institutional arrangements. Therefore, having borrowed concepts from Polsby and McGuire, this study will analyse the parliament of Pakistan under five different criteria: differentiation (common understanding of members of parliament), durability (pursuing goals in environmental change), autonomy (independence in making decisions and procedures while establishing boundaries), and growth of internal complexity and development of universalistic rules.

It is important to mention here the reason by which it became possible to shift the context for the application of these terms from America to Pakistan. McGuire and other writers mentioned above studied the institutions in the American context. The study of any institution whether the judiciary or the legislature, is possible under these models and terms due to the similarity of the basic ingredients of all institutions of the state. The parliament's functions and performance in Pakistan can be determined in the common characteristics of the institution existing globally because of the similarities in the functions and role of parliament of different countries. This is why the American model of study of parliament has been applied in writing the history of the parliament in Pakistan.

Chapter Two

The Parliament in Pakistan
A Brief Survey

THE COMPOSITION OF THE FIRST CONSTITUENT ASSEMBLY OF PAKISTAN

The constituent assembly of undivided India, established as a result of the 1946 elections, was divided into two parts—one for India and one for Pakistan. In addition to the power of framing a new constitution, these assemblies were allowed to exercise all the powers, which were formerly exercised by the central legislature. Prior to this, all territories were to be governed in accordance with the Government of India Act 1935. Until a new constitution was framed for each dominion, the existing constituent assemblies were temporarily considered dominion legislatures. The Indian Independence Act assigns the constituent assembly two separate functions: to act as the legislature under the interim constitution, and to frame a constitution for the country as a sovereign body.[1]

Thus, Pakistan inherited a parliament, comprising a constituent assembly, elected by the provincial legislatures. Muslim representatives were elected by the Muslim members of the provincial legislatures. In the first instance, Muslim representatives from the provinces North West Frontier Province (NWFP; now Khyber Pakhtunkhwa), Sindh, Punjab, and East Bengal (now Bangladesh) were elected by the members of the legislatures of the respective provinces in the ratios shown in Table 2.1:

Table 2.1
The Muslim Members of Constituent Assembly Elected by
Provincial Legislatures

Province	Members in Constituent Assembly	Members of the Provincial Legislature
NWFP	3	34
Sindh	3	36
Punjab	16	86
East Bengal	33	119

Source: Muneer Ahmad, *Legislatures in Pakistan 1947–1958* (Lahore: Punjab University, 1960), p. 8.

Similarly, five non-Muslim members were elected by the non-Muslim legislators of Punjab. The Hindu community elected one Hindu representative for Sindh while twenty-seven Hindu representatives were chosen by the Hindu members of the Bengal Legislative Assembly.[2] However, in Balochistan, where no legislature existed, there was dispute about the mode of representation. Viceroy Lord Mountbatten resolved that the members of the Shahi Jirga and non-official members of Quetta municipality should decide the future of the province.[3] the constituent assembly created four more seats for Bahawalpur, Khairpur, Balochistan, and the NWFP states, which were filled through the ruler's nomination. Furthermore, an addition of six members was made when the assembly accorded representation to the new population;[4] five members for Punjab and one for Sindh were elected by the provincial legislatures. Thus, further additions had to be made to accommodate representatives from the states which had acceded to Pakistan—the tribal areas, Balochistan, and the refugees from India.[5] After readjustment of the members, the strength of the assembly was accordingly raised from sixty-nine to seventy-nine.[6] Although the provinces were represented on a population basis, it was possible for a person from one province to be returned by the legislatures of other provinces. Territorially, the seats of the constituent assembly were divided as forty-four from East Bengal,[7] twenty-two from Punjab, five from Sindh, three from NWFP, one from Balochistan, one from Bahawalpur, one from Khairpur, and one from tribal areas of NWFP.[8]

In addition to the representatives from the states, two female members, namely Begum Shaista Ikramullah and Begum Jahan Ara Shahnawaz, were given additional seats. There were only two political parties in the constituent assembly: Pakistan Muslim League, comprising all the Muslim members with the exception of two, and the Congress Party, representing the non-Muslims of Pakistan. Pakistan Muslim League, the largest party in the parliament, had fifty-nine seats. Its members from East Bengal were drawn mostly from the middle class, while those from West Pakistan included several landlords.[9]

Though organised opposition did not exist in the parliament, there was some divergence of views within the Pakistan Muslim League.[10] The middle class in East Bengal and the feudal class in the western wing of Pakistan enjoyed a monopoly of representation. In this assembly, thirty-one lawyers, thirty-seven landlords, nine businessmen, and twelve from other professions[11] were elected as members. Among its original members the most important was Mohammad Ali Jinnah.[12]

Most of the leaders were migrants (*muhajirs*), and had little electoral support in the country. Liaquat Ali Khan himself fell into this category. He was from the United Provinces—a Muslim minority province that remained in India—and was nominated to represent a constituency from East Bengal in the constituent assembly.[13]

CONTRIBUTION AND ACHIEVEMENTS OF THE FIRST LEGISLATURE OF PAKISTAN

The first session of the Constituent Assembly of Pakistan, i.e. the first Parliament of Pakistan, was held on 10 August 1947 at the Sindh Assembly Building, Karachi. Jogendra Nath Mandal, a member of the minority community from East Bengal, was unanimously elected as temporary chairperson on the first day of the session. His name was proposed by Liaquat Ali Khan and was seconded by Khwaja Nazimuddin.[14] On the second day of the session, Mohammad Ali Jinnah, being the only nominated candidate, was proposed for presidency by seven members of the assembly, and was subsequently elected president of the constituent assembly.[15]

On 14 August 1947, the transfer of power from the British government to the new state of Pakistan took place. This was also the fourth day of the first session of the constituent assembly. Lord Mountbatten, the last viceroy of undivided India, delivered his farewell address to the assembly and welcomed Pakistan into the British Commonwealth.[16] On 15 August, Mohammad Ali Jinnah took the oath of office as the first governor general of Pakistan,[17] and spoke in his address on the principles of the state of Pakistan. He emphasised that the foremost task before the assembly was to frame a constitution for the new state of Pakistan.[18]

For nineteen months, after its first meeting held in August 1947, the constituent assembly transacted no constitutional work of any significance.[19] In order to carry out its foremost task, the assembly set up several committees and sub-committees in March 1949. The Basic Principles Committee was the most important one. Other important committees included the Committee of the Fundamental Rights of the Citizens, and the State Negotiating Committee, which dealt with the question of representation of those princely states, which acceded, to Pakistan and the tribal areas.[20]

On 7 March 1949, the Objectives Resolution, which later served as the *grundnorm* of Pakistan's constitutional life was introduced by its first prime minister, Liaquat Ali Khan, and adopted by the constituent assembly on 12 March 1949. On the same day, a Basic Principles Committee comprising twenty-four members was created by the assembly through a resolution. Its goal was to submit an outline of the basic principles on which the country's first constitution was to be based.[21] The chief ministers of East Bengal, Sindh, and NWFP, and Justice Abdur Rashid, were co-opted as members.[22]

The British government was privy to the internal workings of the Basic Principles Committee through the reports of Sir Robert Drayton, who had been hired as a constitutional advisor by the Government of Pakistan. He kept in close touch with the UK high commissioner in Karachi and apprised him of the developments taking place within the Basic Principles Committee.[23] The high commissioner suggested to the British officials that they respect Drayton's confidence since the utmost secrecy had to be observed in Pakistan regarding the discussions in the committee and Drayton's position would be very difficult if there were to be any leaks.[24] Drayton's inclusion as an advisor in the proceedings of the Basic Principles Committee, points to a critical weakness of the committee as an advisory body. It also exposed the incompetence of the membership of the constituent assembly in legislative procedure. Moreover, recurrent British interference based on Drayton's reports to the high commissioner, as well as Prime Minister Liaquat Ali Khan's frequent interference in the constitution-making process, pointed to the fact that the assembly was unable to exercise its freedom as an independent body, free of influence from foreign or local vested interests. Liaquat Ali also called himself the 'Prime Minister of the League' and not the 'country's Prime Minister', as chosen by the constituent assembly.[25]

The first constituent assembly of Pakistan was not able to win the support of the people whom it claimed to represent. When Prime Minister Liaquat Ali Khan presented the interim report of the Basic Principles Committee on 7 September 1950, the public reaction to this report, especially in East Bengal, was highly unfavourable. The main point of criticism was related to the quantum of representation in the proposed central legislature. East Bengal was not in favour of Urdu being retained as the national language.[26]

The working of the constituent assembly was influenced by factors external to the institution of the parliament. On Liaquat Ali Khan's proposal, on 21 November 1950, the constituent assembly agreed unanimously to postpone consideration of the interim report of the Basic Principles Committee with the proclaimed objective of 'enabling the people to offer concrete and definite suggestions', in conformity with the Objectives Resolution.[27] The direct involvement of the masses in constitution-making is not questioned when it is constitutionally approved by the parliament but the practice of the constituent assembly of Pakistan asking for suggestions marked the weakness of the assembly. This practice—neither a provision of any law or a tradition in India and Pakistan—ultimately prevented the smooth functioning of the assembly.

The working of the assembly was further affected after the assassination of Liaquat Ali Khan on 16 October 1951, when the regional conflicts between the two wings of the country came to the fore and presented a new and extraordinary dilemma in the framing of the constitution. With the elevation of leading bureaucrat Ghulam Mohammad to the office of the governor general, the clash between the bureaucracy and the politicians crystallised into a conflict between the governor general and the prime minister. The constituent assembly became a natural arena for the conflict of regional interests and personalities. It was in this supreme body that the struggle for the supremacy of politicians was lost.[28]

Therefore, the passage of the Basic Principles Committee's report through the assembly was unlikely to be smooth. It is worth mentioning here that several notes of dissent known to have been made were not included in the published report. Mian Iftikharuddin, leader of the Azad Pakistan Party,[29] walked out of the committee's final meeting when his dissenting note was not admitted. Several members of the committee (including the foreign, interior, and communications ministers) had earlier resigned from the committee while some of its members were absent from its final meeting.[30]

Prime Minister Khwaja Nazimuddin presented a revised Basic Principles Committee report incorporating some changes suggested by the general public and the Board of Talimat-i-Islamia to the assembly on 22 December 1952.[31] The report was not well received in West Pakistan, and was condemned by the Awami League. Consequently, discussion on the report was postponed in the assembly.[32]

Regarding East Bengal, some background information needs to be kept in mind. For example, in 1949, Khwaja Shahabuddin (federal interior minister, East Bengal; brother to Khwaja Nazimuddin), Ghulam Mohammad (finance minister), Chaudhri Khaliquzzman (president, PML), and Altaf Hussain (editor, *Dawn*), had engaged in a campaign against Liaquat Ali Khan.[33] Yunas Samad, in his article, exposed the political groupings in the assembly at that time and also shed light on a challenge the Bengali group had mounted to the prime minister—a rarity in politics of that time. This encounter was forced by Khwaja Shahabuddin who was backed by Bengal's chief minister, Nurul Amin, actively aided by Altaf Hussain, and supported by the dissident Punjabi politicians who were led by the Nawab of Mamdot.[34]

The differences between the Punjabi and the Bengali groups intensified after Liaquat's assassination in 1951. This was one of the factors which led to the dismissal of Prime Minister Khwaja Nazimuddin's government on 16 April 1953. The assembly was not summoned again for about five months after this dismissal. Governor General Ghulam Mohammad's new nominee, Mohammad Ali Bogra, was Pakistan's ambassador to the US at the time. His ready acceptance by the Muslim League's parliamentary group as its new leader led some in the assembly and the country to believe that his nomination was backed by external forces who were powerful enough to manipulate the workings of the house to suit their desires without prior consent or routine decisions of the parliament.

Moreover, according to the norms of a parliamentary system, the governor general cannot dismiss the prime minister as long as he enjoys the support of a majority in the assembly. Khwaja Nazimuddin had clearly demonstrated that he was backed by a majority by having his budget passed just a few days before his dismissal. Thus, by dismissing the prime minister without reference to the parliament, the governor general had flouted an established parliamentary norm in addition to highlighting the reduced importance of the parliament. According to Keith Callard, one of the damages of the governor general's action was that the role of the country's legislature—as the maker and sustainer of governments—was impugned. It is to be noted that six out of the eleven ministers of Nazimuddin's cabinet, including Chaudhry Mohammad Ali, had joined the new government.[35] This strongly suggests that the parliamentary norms were still not practised faithfully by even some of the senior members of a cabinet whose head had been summarily dismissed only a few days ago.[36]

After another eighteen months of the Bogra government, the task of constitution-making was still not complete. The aforementioned government had worked hard to prepare the final draft of the constitution before the close of 1954. He introduced an amendment, which came to be known as the 'Bogra Formula', relating to the representation of provinces in the legislature. However, just before the draft could be placed in the house for approval, the assembly was dissolved on 24 October 1954 by Governor General Ghulam Mohammad, and a state of emergency was declared in the country.[37] It seemed that the governor general was unhappy with the assembly because it had revoked sections 9, 10, 10(a), and 10(b) of the Government of India Act 1935, which gave the governor general extraordinary powers over the workings of the assembly.[38] The assembly had taken such a preventive measure to avoid a repeat of the dismissal of the Nazimuddin cabinet in April 1953. It could be described as an important step towards the growth of parliamentary democracy in Pakistan but the amendment was made in such haste that it was termed a 'constitutional coup'.

Following the curtailment of his powers by the assembly, the governor general felt threatened and decided to dissolve the assembly and announced an end to what he described as 'parliamentary bickering'.[39] This was yet another unconstitutional step taken by the governor general; in a parliamentary system, the sovereign authority of the constituent assembly is supposed to be invulnerable. Therefore, its dissolution led to legal proceedings against the governor general.

On 24 October 1954, the constituent assembly met and approved the final draft of the new constitution. However, the governor general was extremely unhappy with the progress being made by the assembly in drafting the new constitution with reduced powers for him. Lacking a provision for the dismissal of the assembly in the Act of 1935, on 27 October 1954, the governor general resorted to using the police, barring the entry of the members of the constituent assembly into its premises and signing the new constitution into law.[40]

As a result, the powers of the constituent assembly in contrast with those of the governor general came into question in the courts. The president[41] of the dissolved assembly, as well as its speaker, Maulvi Tamizuddin Khan, challenged the order of the governor general in the Sindh Chief Court on the grounds that no assent from the governor general was needed for legislation under subsection (1) of section 8 of the Indian Independence Act 1947 and Section 223(a) of the Government of India Act 1935.[42] The full bench of the Sindh Chief Court unanimously passed the verdict that the dissolution of the constituent assembly was illegal. Thereupon, the federation of Pakistan appealed to the federal court, on 21 March 1955. The federal court, with a majority of four to one, decided in favour of the government and rejected Maulvi Tamizuddin's petition. The federal court then reversed the judgment of the Sindh Chief Court on technical grounds.[43]

Although some historians consider the role of the assembly as an unproductive legislative body, some associated this trait to the overwhelming powers vested in the governor general. Even a cursory look at the composition of the assembly's membership would lead to an easy conclusion that with half of its members serving as full ministers, ministers of state, deputy ministers, provincial chief ministers, governors of provinces and ambassadors in foreign countries, the assembly could hardly have been expected to legislate honestly against its own privileges and powers. Moreover, nearly one-third of the ministers, between 1947 and 1954, were drawn from outside the assembly which clearly pointed to a severe shortage of talent in the assembly.[44] In addition, the assembly's members in general took little interest in legislative work and were more interested in enjoying the perks of their positions. Later on, sixteen ministers became ambassadors and governors while two of them, Ghulam Mohammad and Iskandar Mirza, rose to become governors general of the country. Another central minister, Ayub Khan, became the president.[45] They contend that the assembly was subservient to the will of the administration and unresponsive to the wishes of its people. It functioned as a subordinate branch of the government and not as the parliament of a free country. The assembly did not cultivate the electorate, and the members felt no urgency to consult their constituents.[46] The performance of the assembly was subpar, and during the seven long years of its existence, not only had it failed to produce a constitution, but the working of the assembly itself displayed signs of institutional weakness.[47] The parliament was supposed to resolve the controversies within the assembly and the country over the issues of the centre–province relationship, accurate representation in the federal legislature of all the provinces, religion's role in the government, the national language issue, and the relationship between the executive and the legislative branches. It clearly failed to resolve any of these major issues. In the absence of general elections, no fresh blood was infused into its membership.[48] The assembly's inefficient mood was evident from the very beginning. However, that was not the whole story. The assembly did pass several acts and had nearly completed the task of making the constitution in 1954. This meant that though the assembly had been inefficient on multiple occasions, it was not a complete failure. Its working sessions were few in number and extremely brief in duration. For seven years, the first constituent assembly met between 1947 and 1954, for an average of 51 sessions per annum, totalling 360 working days. The second constituent assembly met between 1955–6 for a total of ninety days.[49] Notwithstanding the challenging goals, which were supposed to be tackled by the proposed constitution, the constituent assembly moved ahead with the draft constitution, ably vetted by Sir Ivor Jennings.[50] It was announced by Mohammad Ali Bogra that the constitution was ready for publication and would go into effect on 25 December 1954—the birth anniversary of Quaid-i-Azam Mohammad Ali Jinnah.[51]

The legislative activity of the assembly were variegated despite continuous challenges, and extended beyond legislation to incorporate newer social trends in its law-making activities. Of the 283 bills adopted by the assembly, 130 pertained to commerce, industry, finance, insurance, banking, currency, and communications; 42 to matters of internal and external security; 17 to refugee rehabilitation, administration of evacuee property and citizenship rights; and 24 applied only to Karachi. Discussions on the original bills were often casual and the amending bills were generally rubber-stamped. However, the volume of amending legislation was disproportionately larger than elsewhere.[52] There were 111 private bills for which notices were given, but of these, only 28 were introduced in the house, and only 3 were actually passed. This was largely due to the lack of enthusiasm on the part of sponsors, and insufficient knowledge of the jurisdiction of the house, alongside the government's indifferent attitude.[53]

FORMATION OF THE SECOND CONSTITUENT ASSEMBLY (1955–8)

After the dissolution of the first constituent assembly, the governor general proposed to set up the constituent convention which would work in absence of the constituent assembly to frame a constitution. The members of the convention were to be nominated by the governor general himself. In response to his reference to the federal court, it was ruled that the governor general could only nominate the electorate and not the members of the constituent assembly.[54]

The new constituent assembly was formed under the Governor General's Order no. 12 of 1955, issued on 28 May 1955, and voting for the second constituent assembly took place on 21 June 1955, nearly eight months after the dissolution of the first assembly on the basis of the principle inter-wing parity. Only fourteen members from the previous assembly were re-elected.[55] The elected legislature met on 7 July 1955, and like its predecessor, the electoral college for this assembly also consisted of the provincial assemblies.[56] Also indirectly elected, the new assembly could not be said to have acquired a true representative capacity. It consisted of lawyers, landlords, industrialists, businessmen, religious scholars, teachers, trade unionists, tribal chiefs, and rulers of the princely states. The seats for this eighty-member parliament were equally divided in the eastern and western wings of the country. The seats for the western wing were further divided among its constituent units: twenty-one members were from Punjab, four from NWFP, five from Sindh, three from the Tribal Areas, two from Bahawalpur, and one each from Karachi, Khairpur, the Frontier States, Balochistan, and the Balochistan states, whereas, forty members were elected from East Bengal.[57]

Unlike the first constituent assembly, the Pakistan Muslim League lost its absolute majority in the second constituent assembly.[58] While it was still the largest party in the assembly with twenty-five members, it had neither an absolute nor even a simple majority.[59] Hence, no party enjoyed majority in the new house. The party position in the assembly was as follows:

Table 2.2
The Party Representation in the Second Constituent Assembly[60]

Muslim League	25
United Front	16
Awami League	12
Noon Group	3
Pakistan Congress	4
Scheduled Caste Federation	3
United Progressive Party	2
Independent Muslim	1
Others	6

This party position produced a strong opposition within the parliament. The representation of Bengali former dissidents in the assembly led to a consensus on the constitution, making promulgation of the constitution of 1956 possible. Meanwhile, floor crossing and conflict within the parliamentary parties became the order of the day. As many as eighty members of the assembly were defined as 'men of great wealth and affluence' as well as belonging to the humblest strata of society—men with high educational qualifications as well as semi-literates.[61]

Members of the constituent assembly belonged to nine different political parties, none of which had a clear majority, leaving no alternative but to form a coalition government. The first ministry which was formed in the assembly was a Muslim League–United Front coalition government with Chaudhry Mohammad Ali as the prime minister. One of the major decisions taken by this assembly was the establishment of the province of West Pakistan (One Unit).[62] An Act was passed by the assembly on 30 September 1955 to this effect, which received the assent of the governor general on 3 October 1955. The aim was to create parity in representation between the two wings (East Pakistan and West Pakistan). Earlier, the central government wanted to unify West Pakistan under the Emergency Powers Ordinance but the Supreme Court intervened, and informed the governor general that his powers did not allow him to amalgamate provinces and that this would have to be done by the constituent assembly.[63]

This parliament gave the country its first constitution.[64] Floor crossing was frequent in the assembly, and the issue of a joint or separate electorate was not resolved in this constitution. Moreover, the question of the centre-province relationship was also left unresolved. Unfortunately, bureaucratic and military involvement in politics also increased with time, due to which Pakistan's representative institution could not work properly, and the democratic traditions of the parliamentary system failed to establish firm roots.

The second constituent assembly, which served as the legislature in the interim period, was a diminutive body of eighty members, divided by regional and political loyalties. They were members without party discipline to hold them together and without the fear of accountability.

Most of the members of the assembly were driven by vested interests and ambition.[65]

The second constituent assembly had the advantage of profiting from the deliberations and workings of its predecessor. It successfully utilised the groundwork laid by the first constituent assembly, and had no need to appoint various committees and sub-committees like the former assembly did. Reports were already available for the second assembly to work. In fact, most of the 245 articles in the draft constitution reflected little change from those which had been rejected in October 1954.[66] It can be said that 60 per cent of the constitution was British, 30 per cent was Indian, and only 10 per cent was novel. In this regard, Sir Robert Drayton referred to the 10 per cent as the true constituent of a Muslim constitution.[67]

The parliament under the 1956 constitution proposed a unicameral parliament consisting of a president, national assembly, and 300 members, equally divided between East and West Pakistan. In addition to these 300 seats, five seats were to be reserved for women from each of the two wings for a period of ten years, bringing the total membership of the house to 310. Before the proposed parliament came into being, the second constituent assembly worked as an interim parliament. The assembly did not function as a legislature until it adopted the constitution on 29 February 1956. The national assembly, to which it converted, came into being on 23 March 1956.[68]

Several significant steps were taken by this parliament. In the 1956 constitution, the electorate issue was not decided and its solution was delegated to the provincial assemblies. Prime Minister Huseyn Shaheed Suhrawardy supported the joint electorate, and notwithstanding the few numbers of confident members in the assembly, he used his influence to get the joint electorate passed. The members of the Republican Party also lent their support to Prime Minister Suhrawardy. Thus, the issue of electorates was resolved, and the national assembly passed an amendment on 22 April 1957, enforcing joint electorates in Pakistan. However, the assembly was activated only at the time of the finalisation of the 1956 constitution, after which it relapsed to an average of forty-seven sessions per annum.[69]

In the absence of any law to control the political parties and the problem of floor crossing, political instability ensued perpetually. Politicians changed their loyalties overnight, so that no minister would stay in office for any reasonable length of time. Although the first general elections were scheduled in February 1959, due to the political problems stated above, President Iskandar Mirza abrogated the constitution, dissolved the national and provincial assemblies, banned all political parties, and postponed the general elections indefinitely. Prime Minister Malik Firoz Khan Noon and members of his cabinet were put under house arrest.[70]

On 8 October 1958, Iskandar Mirza and Ayub Khan imposed martial law. They feared that the anti-centre forces would capture political power and dismantle the constitutional structures used to keep the Punjabi group in power.[71] The main reason for the army's takeover was the bureaucracy's overriding urge to prevent Pakistan's first general election from taking place in February 1959.[72] In the words of Hamza Alavi:

> ...in Pakistan, the army and the bureaucracy had played a dominant and decisive role. The "seizure" of power in 1958 by Ayub Khan, in the name of the army was merely a dramatic movement in that continuing domination. The army came to the fore during crises, but the bureaucracy actively dominated the political scene then and in normal times.[73]

General Mohammad Ayub Khan, who was the commander-in-chief of the army, was appointed as chief martial law administrator.[74] In this way, the institution of the parliament was not allowed to function properly. The only way to eliminate the uncertainty of the situation was to hold general elections, but Iskandar Mirza and the prime ministers—H.S. Suhrawardy, I.I. Chundrigar, Malik Firoz Khan Noon, who rose to power between 1956 and 1958—delayed the elections for one reason or another. Consequently, by avoiding direct elections, the constituent assembly lost its legitimacy, and was unable to assert its role in the political system.

Control of the majority in the house was not secured through popular policies and programmes but rather by bestowing ministerial offices and pecuniary benefits to its members. Democratic traditions, which played an important role in the working of a parliamentary system, were rarely encouraged. Jinnah had set a democratic precedent by stepping down as president of the Muslim League when he was elected the governor general of Pakistan. The idea was to maintain neutrality of the governor general, and to allow the Muslim League to pursue its political activities, and function independently as a parliamentary party, without official interference. This practice would have served as a great restraint on the activities of the politicians but Liaquat Ali Khan, who was elected president of the Muslim League after amending the party's constitution on 8 October 1950, discontinued this practice.[75] This step retarded the growth of an autonomous party organisation and undermined democratic values. The weakness of the ruling political party weakened the parliament.

The Muslim League soon became a preserver of the landlord class and its members in the parliament were more interested in office than in party, and often crossed the floor.[76] The weakness of the Muslim League was that it encouraged the governor general to call Mohammad Ali Bogra, who was abroad at the time, and was not even a parliamentarian. He was to assume the leadership of party as well as premiership. Not only the Muslim League but the assembly too accepted this with open arms, which was entirely against the spirit of a parliamentary system of government. In reality, the essence of the parliamentary system is that the leader of the majority party is invited to form a government. Since the prime minister in some cases was not an elected representative,[77] he was not answerable to the party or the parliament. In such situations, he could neither enjoy the blessings of his people nor could he command support over the parliament.[78] During the first eleven years, Pakistan's constituent assemblies were installed and dismissed surreptitiously; the country had seven prime ministers in that interregnum, and that too, without a single general election in the country.[79] These practices hampered the development of the parliament, and brought about political instability, which ultimately led to the failure of the parliamentary system.

According to McGrath, neither the lack of education of Pakistanis, nor the alleged ill-discipline and corruption of politicians, was to blame for the demise of Pakistan's democracy. The responsibility lay with Iskandar Mirza, Ghulam Mohammad, and Justice Munir who provided a legal smokescreen for their authoritarian activities. The same personalities hijacked the parliament in different ways. These issues significantly hampered the smooth functioning of the parliament.[80]

Ayub Khan Era: The Parliament under the Presidential System

Ayub Khan's bias against the parliamentary system was well known. He had once categorically declared that the constitution commission, which was supposed to chalk out a new constitution for Pakistan, was 'not being appointed to tell us what we should do ... we are clear in our mind that we cannot adopt the parliamentary system'.[81] On 1 March 1962, the new constitution came into force. It differed fundamentally from the recommendations made by the constitution commission, which itself was not constituted through an act of parliament. At the time of its introduction, Justice Shahabuddin tried[82] to point this out but his statement was suppressed by the information department under instructions from Ayub Khan and Manzur Qadir.[83]

The 1962 constitution was formed without a parliamentary procedure,[84] and Ayub Khan introduced the constitution as 'his' system. The preamble of the document was closed with the words: 'Now, therefore, "I" Field Marshal Mohammad Ayub Khan…do hereby enact this constitution'.[85] The constitution envisaged a federal state with a presidential form of government. The legislatures, both at the centre and in the provinces, were unicameral. The national assembly at the centre was to function as a parliament for a term of five years.[86] The electoral system was said to be indirect, and the Basic Democrats for both wings were declared electoral colleges for electing the assemblies (on both federal and provincial levels), and the president.[87] The total membership of the national assembly was 156, of which 75 were to be elected from each province. Six seats were reserved for women—three from East Pakistan, and three from West Pakistan.[88] The general members were to be elected by the electorate consisting of 80,000 directly elected Basic Democrats, and six women were to be chosen by the members of the provincial assemblies who themselves were elected by the Basic Democrats of their respective provinces.[89] The creation of a unicameral legislature was a legacy of the pre-1958 period and was apparently implemented to avoid the complexities of the bicameral system, although the constitution commission had strongly recommended a second chamber.[90] The term of this parliament was fixed for five years, unless dissolved earlier. An earlier dissolution was possible through the second amendment in the constitution, which was approved in June 1964, when the term of the president as well as the assemblies was reduced from five to three years.[91]

There were 610 candidates for 156 seats, with members being elected indirectly by the electoral college of 80,000 Basic Democrats.[92] The elections were fought on an individual basis, since political parties were banned at that time, and under these circumstances the campaign failed to generate any enthusiasm or interest. The government sponsored meetings of the Basic Democrats during which the candidates expressed their views and met the electorates.[93] When the newly elected national assembly met in June 1962, party affiliations could not take any definite shape because political parties were still banned.

Elections for general seats were held on 28 April 1962, and elections for the special seats reserved for women were held on 29 May 1962. The rules for the conduct of the elections were laid down in the National and Provincial Assemblies (First Elections) Order.[94] The first session of the elected assembly that was to function as the third parliament of Pakistan was held on 8 June 1962 at Ayub Hall, Rawalpindi. On the same day, martial law was withdrawn after a period of forty-four months during which Pakistan had been governed without a parliament of any kind. Representative institutions were there only at the local government level, while all policy-making power as well as ultimate power remained in the hands of the military.[95]

Elected on a non-party basis, the national assembly was not properly organised for the discharge of its functions. The unanimous election of the speaker was a tribute to the personality of Maulvi Tamizuddin and his services to the cause of democracy. The majority was as heterogeneous as was the opposition, and both were composed of groups formed on the basis of personal and provincial loyalties. The leadership of the groups was more a matter of bargaining and convenience than standing and status in the public.[96]

There were no treasury or opposition benches but informal political groupings were formed.[97] Mohammad Ali Bogra formed his Democratic Group, with a claimed strength of forty-one members, extending support to the government. On the opposition, there was the Pakistan Peoples Party led by Mashiur Rahman, Farid Ahmed, and a number of well-known leaders. There was also an independent group led by Sardar Bahadur Khan, which had twenty-one members. The Pakistan Progressive Group was led by Mian Abdul Bari and Zahoor Elahi. Finally, five members apparently did not belong to any group but had confidential affiliations with some groups.[98]

Since the elections were held at a time when parties were banned, the groups that emerged in the national assembly were either factions led by certain leaders or formed on the basis of provincial loyalties. After the passing of the Political Parties Act 1962, these groups crystallised into the government group and the opposition group. The government group consisted of about seventy-eight members, with forty-six from the Convention Muslim League, and thirty-two from the Democratic Group and others. The opposition groups consisted of twenty-four people from the Pakistan Independent Group and thirty-six from the Pakistan Peoples Party. The remaining members were independent. It was significant that the bulk of the government support came from West Pakistan and a majority of the opposition members were from East Pakistan. The leader of the government coalition was from East Pakistan, while the opposition was led by a West Pakistani.[99]

The affiliation with the parties was not unalterable for the members of the assembly, and quite a large number of them crossed the floor in order to join the ruling party, Convention Muslim League, raising its membership in the house from nil to forty-six and finally to 106. These floor crossings violated the Political Parties Act, which the government itself had pushed through the assembly. And, being the biggest beneficiary of violations of this Act, the government turned a blind eye to all these illegal floor crossings. Being a stronger party, the treasury benches had no compunction in violating the law at will.[100]

The assembly contained a fairly high number of young and educated members whose average age was slightly below forty-six years. The predominance of lawyers from East Pakistan, and landlords from

West Pakistan showed a re-emergence of the same old pattern in the assembly's composition. Landlords, lawyers, and businessmen accounted for 136 of the total 156 members, and the remaining twenty members were teachers, doctors, retired government officials, and trade union leaders not belonging to the working class.[101] An interesting feature was that among the elected members of the national assembly, there was not a single representative from minority communities.[102]

This legislature was designed to perform a very different role from that of the previous assemblies. While it was deprived of control over the executive, the executive also did not have direct control on the legislation. The assembly was freed from the constitutional limitations on its power, and the validity of the laws it passed were not open to challenge in the courts. However, the legislative power was shared by the executive, as consent was given or denied under the president's discretion. The presidential veto was, in theory, liable to be overridden by a three-fourth majority. Prior consent of the president was necessary for introduction of an amendment to the Preventive Detention Act. Above all, its control on budget was restricted to the extent that a considerable portion of it, though debatable, was not open to vote. The approval of the budget was the assembly's most important function; however, in large parts, the budget was not open to vote, as the defeat of the government even on a votable item would have amounted to a vote of no confidence. The restriction did not prevent the opposition from criticising the policies of the government in every field of activity.[103]

The debates on foreign policy produced a much clearer definition of attitudes. The demand for opting out of agreements was almost unanimous from the opposition side. This discussion on the budget and the debate on foreign affairs did not produce any impact on government policies. The assembly, however, did succeed in enlarging the area of individual freedom, and removing some of the constitutional barriers to its institutional expression.[104]

The members were indifferent to their parliamentary responsibilities. Their participation in the discussion was no guarantee of their attendance in the house, due to which the house had to be adjourned on numerous occasions for want of a quorum, even at the commencement of a general discussion on the budget, and when other important issues were being discussed.

The national assembly closely resembled its predecessors in many respects. According to Tariq Ali, it was a 'pathetic and grotesque' body.[105] Some features resembled an old parliamentary regime. Treasury benches existed, and were occupied by ministers, parliamentary secretaries, and their supporters. Steamrollers were employed in majorities to push through official legislation. Privileges were used liberally by the opposition to criticise the government through speeches, question hour, and adjournment motions. Both sides also resorted to using non-parliamentary expressions, and protests, and walkouts were executed by the opposition. However, the assembly did contain a certain number of seasoned and experienced parliamentarians and some promising young members who were beginning to make their mark on its proceedings. Unfortunately, though, the mediocrities outnumbered the talented.[106]

THE SECOND ASSEMBLY UNDER AYUB KHAN

The second national assembly during Ayub's regime, and the fourth legislature of Pakistan, came into being in 1965. After much debate, the six opposition parties decided to contest the election. However, their squabbles over choosing candidates lost them much support, and on a number of seats, the candidates of several opposition parties contested against each other and even Pakistan Muslim League's candidates.[107]

The nominations for the national assembly were called for on 16 February 1965, withdrawals were allowed till 26 February, and elections were announced on 2 March 1965. Some 672 candidates (312 in East Pakistan and 360 in West Pakistan) filed nomination papers for 150 seats. Sixteen candidates in the west wing and two in the east wing ran unopposed. All (except one independent from West Pakistan) were Pakistan Muslim League nominees. After withdrawal, 419 candidates contested for the remaining 132 seats.

The Pakistan Muslim League contested 146 seats and the remaining four seats in the Tribal Areas, whose representatives were to be named by the (government-nominated) jirgas, could join any party after the elections.[108] The Combined Opposition Parties (COP) contested twenty-five seats in West Pakistan, while to contest for seventy-one seats in East Pakistan, it collaborated with the National Democratic Front (NDF).

Independent candidates totalled to 148 (with seventy-one from West Pakistan, and seventy-seven from East Pakistan).[109]

As compared to the presidential elections, the assembly elections were relatively uninteresting and insignificant for some obvious reasons. Ayub's victory in the presidential elections—against the aspirations of the people—had certainly affected the morale of the opposition parties. Also, the unicameral national assembly was neither powerful nor influential in the formulation of national policies, with all powers vested in the president.

The elections granted the Convention Muslim League the status of ruling party, due to its victory over 120 seats.[110] The opposition (COP and NDF) bagged sixteen seats, and independent candidates got fourteen seats.[111]

On 22 May 1965, the members of the national assembly met to co-opt six women, all supporters of the Convention Muslim League. The opposition was able to command only about 22 votes in the house of 156, compared to nearly 50 in the 1962 assembly.[112] The assembly was not a replica of the previous ones because of its election under the shadow of martial law. The composition of the assembly would have been very different had the elections preceded the presidential elections. Out of 150—excluding the six women's seats—forty-six were re-elected members; thirty-one out of forty-six were from West Pakistan, most of them being landlords and tribal chiefs with vested interest in their communities and region of influence. The class composition of the assembly remained almost unchanged. Like its predecessors, it was packed with landlords, lawyers, industrialists, businessmen, tribal chiefs, ruling families, and ex-servicemen.[113]

Previously, the government had had difficulty in marshalling 104 votes to achieve the two-thirds majority required for an amendment to the constitution. Contrary to that, the president could now amend it as he pleased, without approaching the members of the national assembly of other parties, in order to bargain, cajole, or threaten. President Ayub was more firmly established in power than ever before, while the members of the national assembly of all the parties were said to be dismayed at the reduction in their importance as individuals. But even if the voting figures were taken at face value, the Pakistan Muslim League's victory was not as overwhelming a display of public support as the party's new parliamentary strength might suggest. Its candidates obtained 57.5 per cent of the votes cast in West Pakistan (though this would be higher if its uncontested victories could be taken into account), and 48.6 per cent in East Pakistan.[114] Most members of the assembly, being conformists, were ready to oblige the executive with a vote, even if it was a vote against their own interests.[115]

The parliaments, from 1962 to March 1969, had made eight amendments in the constitution—except for the first amendment, which was done under popular pressure. The remaining were designed to safeguard and strengthen the position of the president.

1.	First Amendment—March 1963	Concerned the fundamental rights and Islamic aspects of the constitution.[116] The assembly carried out no amendment for enlarging its own powers, except one.[117]
2.	Second Amendment—8 July 1964	Made changes in the term of the president and the order of elections for the national and provincial assemblies.
3.	Third Amendment—June 1965	Added the Fifth Schedule to the constitution in which a number of offices or appointments were mentioned, and which did not disqualify a person from being elected as a member of the national and provincial assemblies.[118]
4.	Fourth Amendment—August 1965	Empowered the government to retire any person below 55 years of age who had completed 25 years of qualifying service or subject to rules, any person who had reached the age of 55.
5.	Fifth Amendment—November 1965	Empowered the president, during proclamation of an emergency, to suspend a number of fundamental rights.[119]
6.	Sixth Amendment—March 1966	An extension of the Fourth Amendment, and allowed a government servant to retire on completion of 25 years of service. The retirement age was fixed at 55 years. The requirement to consult the Public Service Commission could be dispensed with in specific cases.[120]

| 7. | Seventh Amendment— December 1966 | Amended the provisions relating to the ordinance-making powers of the president and the governors, and the ordinance-making power of the president during an emergency. |
| 8. | Eighth Amendment— December 1967 | Expanded the electoral college of basic democrats, as well as raising the number of seats in the national and provincial assemblies.[121] |

Notwithstanding the amendments in the constitution, a significant amount of legislation was done through ordinance making which was later rubber-stamped by the assemblies. The ordinances, framed by the law ministries of the central and provincial government, eventually became acts of legislature, without going through the requirements of successive readings of the bills, and without the benefit of meaningful discussion in the legislatures. When ordinances were placed before the assemblies, their approval without any amendment by the concerned legislature was deemed to be a matter of prestige for the government, and was hustled through the legislature with the help of brute majorities commanded by the government.[122]

The attendance during the sessions was fairly good, but the attention the members gave to what was happening inside the assembly was far from satisfactory. On several occasions, the assembly had to be adjourned for lack of quorum, and the opposition was found to complain that the members on the government's side were not willing to listen to their speeches. This happened even during the budget session. The absence of the ministers was not an unusual phenomenon.[123]

The leader of the house, Sabur Khan, was not a member of the house but a member of the presidential cabinet. The speaker of the house, Jabbar Khan, was the president's right-hand man who publicly announced that the president's leadership was indispensable for the country, not for just one or two terms but for the next twenty years.[124]

Even at a time when the movement for the restoration of parliamentary democracy was at its peak in 1969, Sabur Khan refused to discuss the political situation in the assembly on the pretext that law and order was a provincial subject, and that the provincial assemblies were the appropriate forum for its discussion. Of the forty-two adjournment motions, not even one was allowed to move and of the fourteen privilege motions, thirteen were disallowed. Only after persistent protests, stormy scenes, and ugly incidents did the government agree to a debate. It managed to prevent a thorough discussion by limiting its duration to only four hours shared by three speakers: two from the government's side and one representing the entire opposition.[125]

The assembly was not the true representative of the people of the country, and at the time of a crisis, nobody looked towards it for a solution. Moreover, with the disappearance of its creator, President Ayub, it died a death unhonoured and unwept.[126]

The number of seats for the two assemblies elected during the Ayub government remained the same. Two elections, in 1962 and 1965, were held for 150 general seats. However, the number of seats was increased in 1967. The Eighth Amendment of the 1962 constitution, passed in December 1967, provided for 218 seats of the national assembly to be distributed equally between the two wings of Pakistan.[127] This increase was to be enforced during the next elections, which were never held, as martial law was once again imposed in 1968, and an altogether new number of seats were designed in the Legal Framework Order 1970.

During Ayub Khan's regime, the national assembly was provided with all the legislative techniques (e.g. questions, resolutions, and adjournment motions) which are normally practiced in a parliamentary system of government. The first hour of every sitting was utilised for posting and answering questions. Every member of the national assembly was entitled to ask questions, subject to certain restrictions; the questions were usually addressed only to ministers or parliamentary secretaries, and not to private members. Since the privilege of asking questions may be abused by raising irrelevant, unnecessary, or vague questions, it was provided that a question addressed to a minister or a parliamentary secretary must relate to public affairs with which he was officially connected, or to a matter or administration for which he was responsible.[128] All questions raised on the floor of the house were expected to be clear and in precise language. However, an examination of questions put forward by members has revealed that vague and irrelevant questions were often asked; nonetheless the importance of the question hour could not be minimised. Question hour was undoubtedly the liveliest part of the legislative day it was an excellent opportunity for backbenchers to attain prominence. The main purpose of the questions was to influence the course of administration.

The legislature was saddled with an irremovable executive, which might be indirectly influenced but could not be made directly responsible for it. Most questions addressed the important departments of the government, and covered a variety of subjects, such as the armed and civil services (including recruitment, promotion, pension, salary, transfer, and other allied matters), political prisoners and political arrests, posts and telegraphs, radio and broadcasting, railways and communication, foreign affairs, insurance, banking, industries, agriculture, and regional disparities. Significantly, during the later years of Ayub's regime, more and more questions were posed about regional disparity and allied problems.

The privilege of asking questions was very popular, and the number of starred questions increased progressively from 1962 to 1969, which happened to be the clearest trend of this period. The number of questions posed in the assembly used to depend on several factors:

- the length of the session,
- the intensity of political feelings at the time (whenever there was a swing against the government in the country, more and more harassing questions were asked by members of the opposition),
- the volume of legislative and financial business before the assembly, and
- the incidence of natural calamities, such as floods and cyclones.[129]

The freedom to move resolutions was another important weapon which enabled members to pressurise the administration. The resolutions can be grouped under certain important subjects, including: education, health and welfare, posts and telegraphs, railways, police and custody matters, political grievances, jute prices, and constitutional issues. No resolution was binding to the government, as it was only a recommendation of the legislature, which the government could approve or disapprove.

Only on rare occasions did members receive an opportunity to discuss adjournment motions. As many as 678 such motions were received from 1962–9, but only 42 were actually admitted for discussion. As for the resolutions, they were either ruled out of order by the speaker, or withdrawn by the members. The discussions on adjournment motions were aimless and a waste of time.[130]

The legislature also had certain financial powers. Each year, the budget was presented to the national assembly by the finance minister on behalf of the president. However, under its rules, the national assembly had effective control over only a specific part of the budget that dealt with new expenditures. Recurrent expenditure did not require the sanction of the assembly, although demands for such grants could be discussed in the house. The 1962 constitution, in fact, divided the budget into portions that could or could not be voted upon. Such a practice was prevalent during the British period from 1921–47.[131]

When demands for grants were placed before the house, members were at liberty to move motions for reduction in the amount asked for. Such motions were usually moved only for the purpose of raising discussions. Most of the cuts proposed were for token amounts only, and only on rare occasions were such motions pressed to a division. Since the government always enjoyed a comfortable majority, it was futile for the opposition to press a motion to division, except to put the dissenting voices on record. The arrangement for placing only a portion of the total expenditure before the national assembly for approval can be criticised on several grounds. First, it gave an almost blank cheque to the bureaucracy, since the government did not require annual sanctions for recurrent expenditures, which constituted the lion's share of the annual budget. Secondly, without effective scrutiny on behalf of elected representatives, the system was prone to financial irregularities. The official argument was always strongly in favour of restricted financial powers for the national assembly. It was claimed that in a developing country like Pakistan, development projects require that funds be spent over a number of years. If the national assembly should refuse to sanction the required money in any year, the process of development would be hindered.[132]

The ministers were further helped in maintaining close liaisons with the legislators by parliamentary secretaries, who were members of the national assembly and were also appointed by the president. When ministers were absent, the parliamentary secretaries answered questions and served as spokespersons for the government inside the national assembly.[133]

If the government's weapons were coercion and patronage, the opposition resorted to their normal weapons of violent and pungent speeches denouncing government policy, adjournment motions, and a strenuous use of the question hour to extract information or embarrass the government. The government introduced 40 bills, of which 39 were passed; out of the 232 private members' bills, 35 were introduced, and only one was passed. Over 900 resolutions were offered by members, of which 696 were admitted, but hardly a score could be discussed, with only three having been adopted. There were 68 divisions. About 3,800 questions were offered, including over 300 short notice questions, and over 75 per cent of them were admitted and answered in the house.[134]

During Ayub's period, the assembly was neither powerful nor influential in the formulation of national policies. The assembly's control of the purse was limited; its sanction was only required for 'new expenditures' in the annual budget statement (which constituted a very small part). Presidential appointments and decisions, along with ministerial actions, were beyond its control. The procedure for circumventing the president's veto on bills passed by the assembly was extremely difficult and circuitous. Constitutional amendments called for a two-thirds majority with the presidential concurrence, and a three-fourths majority without such concurrence. In such a situation, the president still had the power to refer the matter to a referendum by the electoral college, or dissolve the assembly and seek re-election himself.[135]

The assembly proved to be a dysfunctional organ owing to its insufficient techniques of influence, its inadequate financial powers, and its control over party government. Many of its members from West Pakistan were young scions of upper class families—major non-political allies of the Ayub regime—while members from East Pakistan belonged to middle class professions, mainly lawyers, who were increasingly disturbed by the handicaps under which they had to work within the assembly. Even so, the national assembly was the only real national forum in which the views and grievances of Pakistan's various regions and interests could be expressed. Although, the executive was not responsible for the legislature, it was responsive to pressures exerted by it. However, the assembly, according to the government, still being inexperienced and immature, was in need of protection against its own inclination towards folly.[136]

To sum up, the effectiveness of the assembly was limited by several factors. Firstly, the system of indirect elections failed to inspire enough respect for the house as an important political institution, since it did not give the members a genuine feeling that they represented the people directly. Secondly, the national assembly's political status could not be enhanced in the absence of effective power. Thirdly, the overwhelming strength of the ruling party inside the national assembly induced pessimism among opposition members.

The preceding survey of the working of the National Assembly of Pakistan is not a story of success. A modern parliament sustains the executive and controls it. But the National Assembly of Pakistan did not play any part in this process because the executive was not responsible for it. The role of the national assembly in the political development of Pakistan under Ayub Khan was, therefore, twofold; it served as the all-Pakistan forum for the venting of grievances, and persistently tried to dilute the authoritarian character of the executive under the 1962 constitution.[137]

Ayub Khan pursued an uncompromising line by refusing to accommodate the demands of the opposition. His efforts to concentrate all power in the hands of a central oligarchy maximised the possibility of conflict, both, internally and externally.[138] The opposition parties launched a consistent campaign for the realisation of their demands, and during 1962–9, set up several alliances mainly for this purpose. The main thrust of these alliances, the National Democratic Front (1962), the Combined Opposition Parties (1965), and the Pakistan Democratic

Action Committee (1969), was to democratise the system of government provided in the 1962 constitution, and later on crystallised in the two constitutional demands: federal parliamentary form of government and direct election on the basis of adult franchise.

At the Round Table Conference in March 1969, Ayub Khan and the Democratic Action Committee came to an agreement on these demands, and the constitution was to be amended accordingly. However, before this could be done, the forces unleashed by the movement against Ayub Khan led to the imposition of another martial law.[139] Altaf Gauhar, federal secretary of information in Ayub's regime and one of his closest advisers, writes that Ayub felt isolated and looked to Yahya for help in the first week of November 1968, when agitation spread across the country like wildfire, in the wake of a single incident in which a student was killed during a clash between the police and a crowd of Bhutto supporters.[140]

By the end of 1968, the movement against Ayub Khan strengthened and the demand for restoration of a pure parliamentary system was raised by the opposition. Demonstrations and agitations engulfed the whole country; chaos reigned and the government was practically paralysed. As a compromise, Ayub Khan offered some political concessions to the opposition, i.e. not to seek re-election, restoration of the parliamentary system of government, and direct elections. However, the opposition was not prepared to accept anything less than his resignation and, albeit reluctantly, Ayub Khan decided to step down on 25 March 1969. Rather than following the procedure laid out in the 1962 constitution,[141] he handed over power to the army chief, General Agha Mohammad Yahya Khan.[142]

In the first decade of Pakistan's political history, two constituent assemblies were formed with seven governments and three heads of states. Unfortunately, this experiment faced a number of problems due to the powerful position of the military and civil bureaucracy. For most of the period, the country was under a bureaucratic-cum-parliamentary rule, or under military rule. Throughout the first phase of the parliamentary system, the continuous interference of bureaucracy in politics was observed. Finally, the parliamentary system was derailed with the imposition of martial law.

Pakistan's history from 1947 to 1958 is generally known as the parliamentary period. During this time, if the progress of democratic institutions (and especially of the parliament) is observed, the period cannot truly be called parliamentary, as democratic traditions, although not killed entirely, were definitely suppressed. That is why the institution of parliament could not take root in the body politics of Pakistan. The parliament delayed the formation of the constitution to such an extent that the undemocratic forces found an excuse to assail the very existence of democracy.

From 1958 to 1969, the country—as did the parliament—remained under the authoritarian rule of Ayub Khan. For the first four years of the Ayub regime, the institution of parliament did not exist at all and, for at least the last six years of the Ayub era, it could not assert itself as a free institution that may be called the pillar of a democratic state. Thus, before the birth of the 1970 assembly, the institution of parliament in Pakistan often distributed its authorities, sometimes in favour of the executive and sometimes to the head of the state. It could not survive as a well-established institution due to internal weaknesses. That is why the forces, which were not part of the parliament, continued to rule over the country without any claim from the parliament.

Chapter Three

Formation, Complexity, and Differentiation of Parliament

This chapter explores the formation of the first directly elected parliament of Pakistan on a 'one man, one vote' basis and the progress of internal complexity—physical attributes and internal formation of the institution—and the development of universal rules regarding the institution of parliament. The primary focus is on the historical and constitutional development from 1970 to 1977, when President Fazal Elahi Chaudhry dissolved the national assembly on the advice of Prime Minister Zulfikar Ali Bhutto. This chapter also deals with the economic, educational, political, and social backgrounds of the members of parliament to demonstrate the degree to which they are different[1] from one another.

Pakistan started with a parliamentary system, which was first debased by conflicting interests, then abolished by a *coup d'état* paving the way for a dictatorship in the guise of a presidential constitution. Since the proclamation of martial law in 1958, the people of Pakistan lived under such a regime, which acquired the legal veneer of a presidential constitution in 1962.[2]

THE NATIONAL ASSEMBLY

Formation

On 25 March 1969, the second martial law was imposed in Pakistan through means of which General Agha Mohammad Yahya Khan took over as chief martial law administrator. He also assumed the office of the president on 31 March 1969, and on the same day, issued a Provisional Constitution Order 1969 under which the government was to be run in accordance to the repealed 1962 constitution, subject to any regulation or order that might be made by the chief martial law administrator.[3] The Legal Framework Order envisaged the national assembly as a legislature comprising 313 members.[4] Allocation of general and women's seats[5] were as follows:

	General Seats	Women's Seats
East Pakistan	162	7
Punjab	82	3
Sindh	27	1
NWFP	18	1
Balochistan	4	1
Tribal Areas	7	–

Under Article 10 of the Electoral Rolls Order 1969, the voter age limit was set at 21 years on 1 October 1969,[6] and the election commission was formally constituted with Justice Abdus Sattar as chairman, and Justice A.M. Sayem and Malik Mohammad Akram as its two members.

From the Legal Framework Order, it was clear that the national assembly would not be a sovereign body. Its decisions were subject to the approval and authentication of the president, who also happened to be the chief martial law administrator. With respect to certain matters, the national assembly had no choice, even if its own views on concerned matters and views of the electorate differed from the provisions of the Legal Framework Order.[7] The national assembly, after being elected as a legislature, was to frame the constitution within a period of 120 days from the date of its first meeting, and its failure to do so would result in dissolution.[8]

G.W. Choudhury, who played a major role in framing the Legal Framework Order, left a valuable account of the discussions which took place in Yahya's inner circle before its announcement. According to him, this time limit was decided because of past experiences of constitution-making in Pakistan; it had taken two constituent assemblies nine years to frame a constitution—everyone wanted to prevent such a delay from recurring.[9] The political leaders agreed to the time limit, and it was further agreed that the majority group(s) responsible for producing a constitution would show the draft to the president before formally presenting it to the assembly.[10] The president was given the power to 'authenticate the constitution'.[11]

Describing the fundamental principles for the new constitution, the Legal Framework Order stated that the national assembly would be the first legislature of the federation for the full term if the legislature of the federation consisted of one house. In contrast, if the legislature of the federation consisted of two houses, it would be the first lower house of the legislature of the federation for the full term. Under the Legal Framework Order, the polling for the first general elections in Pakistan was to be held on 5 October 1970.[12] However, elections were delayed due to a catastrophic cyclone in East Pakistan, and were held on 7 December 1970.[13]

Parliamentary institutions in Pakistan have often performed what is called the 'exit function' of legislatures. Whenever the pressure for legitimacy rose, and restive elements of the public threatened to destabilise the system, elections for legislatures created an opportunity for them to stand up and be counted for the purpose of either government formation or oppositionist politics. In the concept of modern democracy, elections 'exit' the people from street protest and let them raise their 'voice', preventing them from 'disengagement' from a potentially extra-systematic activity. The 1970 elections were a direct result of the anti-Ayub movement that mobilised millions of industrial workers, students, peasants, and the public throughout the country,[14] thereby marking a clean break from the past and revolving around issues and not personalities. While there was considerable overlap in party programme, ideological and political forces clearly distinguished them. That issues and programmes were a determining factor in the success and failure of the parties is evident from the fact that parties had to give up the traditional methods of attracting voters and were forced to attract them on the basis of a platform. Furthermore, the nature and content of the issues involved in the elections were strikingly different from those in the past.[15] The anti-Ayub movement had also set the trends for incorporating public demands into party manifestos, and all major parties stressed welfare of the national economy, and suggested various reforms in social and political spheres.[16]

Elections were held on a 'one man, one vote' basis under the supervision of Justice Abdus Sattar as chief election commissioner, and were deemed partially fair. Yahya Khan did not directly interfere in the conduct of the elections, but several parties and groups were helped financially and otherwise, so that votes might be split and no single party (or even two parties) could obtain enough majority to form a stable government,[17] resulting in another case of a 'hung parliament'. In spite of all this, the elections were considered the fairest elections in the history of Pakistan. Yahya's advisors believed that it was essential to concede on the electoral front in order to contain the upheaval. They were confident that the bureaucracy, due to their long experience in such matters, would be able to manipulate the results satisfactorily.[18]

When nominations for election to the national assembly were received, no less than twenty-five different parties were represented. Candidates totalling 1,579 from all over Pakistan contested 300 national assembly seats, an average of five candidates for each constituency.[19] The election resulted in an overwhelming victory for Sheikh Mujibur Rahman's Awami League in East Pakistan—Mujib won two resounding victories in Dacca (now Dhaka). A large majority voted for Zulfikar Ali Bhutto's PPP in West Pakistan, achieving surprisingly strong support in Punjab and Sindh—Bhutto won five of the six seats he contested, including two in Punjab and three in Sindh, while losing only one seat in the NWFP to Mufti Mahmud by a small margin. The only other prominent candidate, Qayyum Khan, was the only one to contest from more than one seat, and won three out of three seats in the NWFP (see Table 3.1).[20]

Table 3.1
National Assembly Candidates and Results

Sr. No.	Name of Party	Symbol	East Pakistan	Punjab	Sind	NWFP	Balochistan	Tribal Areas	Total Candidates	Successful Candidates
1	AL	Boat	162	3	2	2	1	-	170	160
2	PPP	Sword	-	78	25	16	1	-	120	81
3	QML	Tiger	65	35	12	17	4	-	133	9
4	CML	Lantern	50	50	12	5	2	-	119	7
5	JUI(H)	Book	15	46	21	18	4	1	105	7
6	JUP	Key	-	41	8	1	-	-	50	7
7	NAP(W)	Hut	39	-	6	16	3	-	64	6
8	JIP	Scale	71	44	19	15	2	-	151	4
9	ML(con)	Bicycle	93	24	6	1	-	-	124	2
10	PDP	Umbrella	78	21	3	2	1	-	105	1
11	MJUI	Tree	49	3	-	2	-	-	54	-

		Symbol								
12	NAP(B)	Sheaf of Paddy	14	2	2	-	1	-	19	-
13	PNL	Plough	14	2	-	-	-	-	16	-
14	JGMD	Candle	5	-	1	-	-	-	6	-
15	SKMPPMM	Horse	-	1	5	-	-	-	6	-
16	IGD	Cow	5	-	-	-	-	-	5	-
17	KSP	Hooka	4	-	-	-	-	-	4	-
18	PNC	Pitcher	4	-	-	-	-	-	4	-
19	ML(Pak)	Spectacles	-	1	1	1	-	-	3	-
20	KT	Spade	-	2	-	-	-	-	2	-
21	MJAH	Rose	-	2	-	-	-	-	2	-
22	SUF	Stick	-	-	1	-	-	-	1	-
23	Independent		113	105	46	16	6	30	316	16
	Total		781	460	170	112	25	31	1579	300

Source: Iftikhar Ahmad, *Pakistan General Elections 1970* (Lahore: South Asian Institute Punjab University, 1976), 80.

Several seasoned politicians from West Pakistan managed to win under new party labels, i.e. the PPP. Out of 291 seats, the Awami League won 160,[21] and the PPP won 81 seats,[22] in short the Awami League and the PPP won 87 per cent of the seats. The results of the elections led to an observation in some newspapers that Pakistan's political development had acquired maturity.[23] Nine political parties entered the national assembly, and each of them had some popular following in certain regions of Pakistan, but none at the national level.[24] For the party position in the national assembly, *see* Table 3.2.

Table 3.2
Party Position in the National Assembly (1970 General Elections)

Party	Seats in National Assembly
Pakistan Democratic Party	1
Convention Muslim League	2
Jamaat-i-Islami	4
National Awami Party (Wali Group)	6
Council Muslim League	7
Jamiat Ulema-e-Pakistan	7
Jamiat Ulema-i-Islam (H)	7
Qayyum Muslim League	9
Pakistan Peoples Party	81
Awami League	160
Independent candidates	16

This election was applauded by most Pakistani and foreign observers and press alike as the most fair and impartial election; thus, making it the most successful one in Pakistan's history.[25] However, the results of the election were an utter disappointment for Yahya who was expecting a hung parliament. This was followed by a loss of the regime's political control. The overwhelming victory of the Awami League in East Pakistan greatly restricted the regime's ability to act as a broker, and the circumstances rapidly escalated out of control as the establishment soon found itself to be in the weakest position, relative to elected representatives, it had ever experienced before.[26] The 1970 elections transformed the nature of electoral politics in Pakistan, by virtue of being the first election that was dominated by mass politics rather than elite politics, by parties rather than by candidates, and by national issues rather than local issues.[27]

In the circumstances created by the results of this election, the danger of a confrontation between the country's eastern and western wings arose in the national assembly. Sheikh Mujib had won the election on a platform where the primary demand was maximum provincial autonomy. When, Yahya Khan summoned the national assembly to meet in Dacca on 3 March 1971, Z.A. Bhutto, who wanted consensus outside the assembly on the principles of the constitution first, announced that his party would not attend the session, and demanded its postponement. He also threatened a mass movement and called for a general strike on 2 March 1971, and reportedly said that if any member of his party attended the session, the party would liquidate them.[28] Bhutto felt threatened by the direct approaches being made by Sheikh Mujib and other politicians to the newly-elected members of PPP[29] to influence their viewpoint, which strongly favoured attending the national assembly's session proposed to begin on 3 March. Bhutto allegedly warned that he would 'break the legs' of any party member who dared to attend the first session of the assembly, scheduled to be held in Dacca. However, he later insisted that his remark had been meant metaphorically, and what he actually said was that if they went to Dacca to attend the national assembly meeting, they would have no political legs to stand on. All concerned members agreed to hand in their written 'resignations' to him in order to strengthen his bargaining position with Mujib and Yahya.[30] In response to this demand, Yahya Khan, on 1 March 1971, postponed the national assembly session.[31]

According to Rafi Raza, Yahya Khan proposed to Bhutto that he (Yahya) should remain president with Bhutto as prime minister. When Bhutto refused, Yahya Khan suggested that he should be allowed to continue as chief martial law administrator and army chief while Bhutto became president. But Bhutto desired full and effective control as president and chief martial law administrator.[32] This decision was attributed to Bhutto's lust for power, as is apparent from the evidence taken from Kamal Matinuddin and Matiur Rahman. Yahya's action of postponement of the assembly, and use of military might in East Pakistan were driven by Bhutto's megalomania.[33] From March to December 1971, Pakistan's political circumstances deteriorated with every passing day. The Pakistani government continuously underestimated the intensity of popular support for the Awami League. The establishment of a parallel government in East Pakistan, in the wake of the decision to postpone the calling of the national assembly in early March, came as a violent shock to the military authorities.[34] The internal crises as well as Indian aggression broke out in December 1971, and resulted in the separation of East Pakistan from West Pakistan and the formation of Bangladesh.

After the fall of Dacca in December 1971, Yahya Khan resigned and handed over power to Zulfikar Ali Bhutto, leader of the majority party. On 20 December 1971, Zulfikar Ali Bhutto took over as president of Pakistan as well as the civilian chief martial law administrator.[35] Sardar Shaukat Hayat Khan has recorded that desirous to continue martial law, Bhutto never wanted to summon the national assembly, and wanted only to restore the local bodies and provincial assemblies which were convened by 23 March 1972. The national assembly was not summoned,[36] and the country remained under martial law until 20 April 1972. Before that, on 14 April 1972, the remaining national assembly was called into session, and Bhutto received a unanimous vote of confidence and was elected as president of the national assembly. He announced that martial law would be lifted on 21 April instead of 14 August, as mentioned earlier, if the interim constitution was passed by 17 April 1972.[37]

In order to assemble the members of the national assembly, Bhutto issued a presidential order, National Assembly (Short Session) Order 1972.[38] It was under this order that the remaining members of the assembly, elected in December 1970,[39] attended the national assembly session with the power to adopt an interim constitution, to draft a permanent constitution, and prolong its own life. This assembly, with the following party composition, adopted the interim constitution of Pakistan in April 1972[40]:

Pakistan Peoples Party	81
Qayyum Muslim League	9
Council Muslim League	7
Jamiat Ulema-e-Pakistan	7
Jamiat Ulama-i-Islam (H)	7
National Awami Party (Wali Group)	6
Jamaat-i-Islami	4
Convention Muslim League	2
Pakistan Democratic Party	1
Independents	16

Although the PPP had bagged only 58 per cent votes, it replaced families which had been represented in legislative bodies since the 1921 election, including Qizilbash, Gilani, Noon, Shah Jiwana, Leghari, Hassan Mahmud (although both Mahmud and Leghari did manage getting elected to the provincial assembly). Some leaders survived, including Mumtaz Daultana and Shaukat Hayat of the Council Muslim League, but others like Air Marshal (retd) Asghar Khan and Nawabzada Nasrullah Khan failed to win. Following the election, Bhutto emerged successful with substantial victories in Punjab, which had seen the PPP candidates eliminate the traditional and politically stalwarts of the region, especially in Lahore and Multan.[41]

When the national assembly was first convened in 1972, there were four minority parties in the house: National Awami Party (NAP), Jamiat Ulema-e-Pakistan (JUP), Jamiat Ulema-e-Islam (JUI), and Muslim League. The Muslim League was eliminated by Qayyum's defection, the Jamiat Ulema-e-Islam and the Jamiat Ulema-e-Pakistan split, and hence, undermined by parliamentary members, started shifting to PPP. This scenario isolated only the National Awami Party in the assembly, and the Jamaat-i-Islami and Tehrik-i-Istiqlal outside the body to contest the power and policies of Bhutto and his party. The elimination of the NAP–JUI coalition government in Balochistan and the imprisonment of the National Awami Party Balochi leaders, however, made even the National Awami Party a less than potent force.[42]

The majority of the PPP and Bhutto's leadership produced close association amongst a majority of the members of the parliament. Another development was seen in the first two years of the life of this parliament when Bhutto succeeded in establishing an alliance with opposing political entities in the parliament. This made the parliament a very close association of members of different areas of Pakistan, belonging to different ideologies.

Bhutto's special knack of bringing people from varied political viewpoints round to his own, proved to be the glue which bound them together for a common cause. Bhutto, as chairman of his party, made all key decisions and losing those with independent views— whatever initiative it once had was curtailed. After Bhutto took power, a nationalization programme was implemented which stimulated the appetite of the leftists within the PPP.[43] Bhutto had consolidated his own party's position within the central and provincial legislatures, and broadened the party as well as the affiliation of the parliamentarians for creating differentiation. He achieved this through coalition, with the Muslim League factions headed by home minister, Abdul Qayyum Khan, former chief minister of the NWFP, and a long-time opponent of the opposition leader, Wali Khan.

The members exhibited strong relations when they agreed to change the parliament into a house without any opposition at the time of the formation of the constitution and at the time of the second amendment in the constitution. This ended when, after a period of uncertainty, the PPP replaced opposition ministries in Balochistan and the NWFP. This gave the party control over all levels of the government, including the newly formed senate. This consolidation of the majority party led to further fragmentation of minority parties.

The common understanding of members of the parliament (as far as the strong following of the leader of the lower house was concerned) was formidable enough that Bhutto attracted 108 votes in the national assembly for his candidacy as prime minister, although the PPP officially had only 81 seats out of 146 at the time. Opposition parties were disunited and vulnerable to governmental pressures. Parliamentary systems could survive, and the institution of parliament could have been stronger, due to the close affiliation of its members, with lopsided majorities for a prolonged period. However, the system was fragile, owing to the fact that the PPP lacked the organisational base to transform Pakistan into a functioning one-party state, effectively, and yet opposition parties lacked the stamina to withstand the pressure on them.[44]

Membership in the assembly marked that the old order had changed in Punjab, and that the politicisation of the countryside had progressed farther than expected, as many urban dwellers were ready to seek radical solutions to Pakistan's problems. The influence of major landowners was no longer a dominant factor in Punjabi politics, and the *biradri* (caste or sub-caste) of caste and tribal connections controlling the vote had broken down, for the time being at least. The PPP did well in the relatively prosperous areas of Lahore Division, Eastern Multan Division, and along the Grand Trunk Road as far as Rawalpindi, areas where industrial development had taken place and agriculturalists were moderately prosperous landowners.

Along the Indus River valley, traditional factors continued to operate as representatives of the fundamentalists and won many national and provincial seats. Bhutto's candidates were by no means all-young radicals. Even he drew upon landlords from the 'Punjab Chiefs' category, others of medium status, groups which were to prove resistant to the more socialist sections of his programmes. The PPP faced the inexperience of many of its legislators. In yielding two of his seats in the Punjab to retain one in Sindh, Bhutto chose more experienced politicians—such as Mahmud Ali Kasuri in Lahore—perhaps to offset this disadvantage. The Council Muslim League, led by Mumtaz Daultana, which some had expected to be the largest winner in Punjab, did achieve second place but with only seven seats. However, the seven, together with three other Muslim Leaguers from the other factions, were hailed as veteran political figures. In a period of constitutional negotiations, such political skill and experience became significant.[45]

Having a ruling majority in the assembly, the PPP and Bhutto's charismatic stature worked magic for the strength of differentiation of the parliament and for the interim constitution, which was passed with quick ease. The complexity of the rules was adapted as the interim constitution provided for a unicameral legislature, i.e. one house consisting of the national assembly as the federal legislature. The national assembly had a right to exercise the power to legislate on all subjects mentioned in the federal and concurrent legislative lists given under the fourth schedule.[46] Also, the national assembly could legislate for a province on the subjects enumerated in the provincial legislative list, during the president's proclamation of emergency. The president could withhold assent from any bill passed by the national assembly or return it to the assembly for reconsideration along with his recommended amendments. The national assembly, after reconsideration, could pass the bill once again without any amendment and the president was bound to give his assent, provided that the number of members voting for such a bill was not less than seventy-five. This meant an absolute majority of the assembly at that time.[47]

One factor, however, limited the complexity of rules with respect to the parliament: that despite the powers of legislation vested in the national assembly, the interim constitution had also vested powers in the president. Till 31 March 1973, president was powered to legislate as appeared necessary to him. Thus, the president was bestowed with sufficient power to amend the constitution.[48]

Both houses of the parliament also adopted the universal rules with the course of the proceedings. A member enquired from the speaker, Sahibzada Farooq Ali Khan, whether in the absence of quorum, a bill can be passed by the house. The speaker observed that if a lack of quorum was pointed out, the chairman had no alternative but to ring the quorum bells, and if the quorum was not complete then to adjourn the house. The speaker added, 'Even if you pass the Bill with four members; it cannot be questioned in any court of law on the grounds that the quorum was not there, unless lack of quorum had been pointed out.'[49]

Under the rules of parliamentary practice, an amendment to a privilege or an adjournment motion could not be made in the house. The speaker ruled that the proper procedure should have been for the member to first withdraw his original privilege motion and then table a revised motion. There was no rule by which a privilege motion could be replaced, and that replacement did not mean withdrawal of the original privilege motion.[50]

Another event during the proceedings of the assembly marked the differentiation of the institution of the parliament, as well as the formation of the universal rules for the sake of complexity. Rule 17 of the *Rules of Procedure and Conduct of Business in the National Assembly, 1973* provided that the secretary shall ensure a register to be kept, showing the attendance of each member during each sitting. However, the rule did not require members to sign the register. On 17 June 1974, an MNA informed the speaker of national assembly, Sahibzada Farooq Ali Khan that an attendance register had been kept in the lobbies, and the members had been requested to sign it in token of their attendance. On being informed that it had been done in accordance with the decision of the privileges committee, some members pointed out that the privileges committee had no jurisdiction or authority whatsoever to decide an issue unless it was approved by the house. The speaker upheld the objection and directed that the register be removed from the lobbies.[51]

One can observe how the complexity of the institution was established during the formulation of rules for the smooth functioning of the institution. The 1973 constitution provided for a bicameral system for the first time. The federal legislature was given the name of parliament and its two houses were to be known as the national assembly and the senate. The parliament was empowered to frame its own rules of procedure and conduct of business outline accordingly.[52] Parliamentary government and bicameralism related to federalism, was the provision in the constitution for an upper house of parliament, which was the senate.

The power of the senate was limited. As noted above, it would have the power to initiate legislation only on the subjects given in the second part of the federal and concurrent lists; it would only have temporary power to suspend, and not defeat bills, and would not take part in the votes of confidence. However, the senate was not subject to dissolution (half of the membership would retire every two years, the terms being set at four years), and could, in any changing political situation, be a bastion of the declining political party. The never-enacted constitutional draft of 1954, commended by Bhutto in his address to the national assembly on 14 April 1972, included a provision for an upper house, and there was little disagreement on this proposal made in 1972. The lower, popularly elected, house of the national assembly, was, as in most systems derived from the British example, to be the body with the greatest powers, both legislative and supportive of the prime minister and his cabinet. The existing national assembly would continue in office until 14 April 1977, unless dissolved sooner, a date five years after its first meeting. At the first election under the new constitution, its membership was to be expanded from its present 147 to 210 members, of whom 200 were to be elected from single member constituencies delimited according to population, and ten would be women elected indirectly by those who had been elected from territorial constituencies, voting separately by province.

The legislative powers of the national assembly were specified in two ways. Article 70 provided the body with the exclusive right to initiate legislation in the first part of the two legislative lists. Any bill passed by the national assembly was to be transmitted to the senate, which could act within ninety days to pass the bill, with or without amendment, or to reject it. The bill was to be presented for the president's assent and become law if the senate passed it or failed to respond within ninety days. In case of rejection or amendments by the senate, the national assembly could pass it again, accepting or rejecting any amendments seen fit. This would go to the president for assent, and would become law. Thus, the powers of the senate on Part I bills was limited to a ninety-day delay, with or without the suggestion for amendments. The bills under Part II might be introduced in either house. If the versions passed by the two houses were to differ, a joint session would be held. The result of that meeting was to be presented to the president for his assent. The second constitutional division of power between the two houses was contained in article 73. It stated that: 'notwithstanding anything contained in Article 70 or Article 71' (the two articles described in the preceding paragraph), 'a money bill shall originate in the National Assembly and after it had been passed by the assembly it shall, without being transmitted to the Senate, be presented to the President for assent.'[53] Thus, the senate had no powers with regard to money bills, whether they originate under Part I or II of the legislative lists. On the matter of presidential assent, the constitution leaves no room for presidential refusal or veto. Article 75 states clearly that the president 'shall assent' within seven days and if he does not do so 'he shall be deemed to have assented.'[54]

The complexity was attained through the formation of universal rules in 1975 when a privilege motion was moved regarding non-observance of article 54 of the constitution requiring the national assembly to sit for not less than 130 working days during a year. It was pointed out that the national assembly had its sittings on sixty-eight days during the current year, whereas it had to meet for sixty-two days more to comply with the above constitutional requirement. It was, therefore, maintained that with the balance of sixty-four days of the current year, it was not possible to meet the target. The minister for parliamentary affairs contended that the motion was premature because, out of the remaining sixty-four days of the year, the assembly could meet for sixty-two days to fulfil the constitutional obligation. The mover pointed out that the assembly was to sit up to 11 December 1975, according to the programme issued by its secretariat, and as such, sittings for sixty-two days were not practicable. Sahibzada Farooq Ali Khan (speaker of national assembly) observed that the programme was only tentative. Abdul Hafeez Pirzada argued that the previous year, the assembly had counted such days as its 'sitting days', which were utilized for sittings of special committees of the whole house. It was also stated that the government had several options to overcome the hurdle (if any) and that the opposition will be taken into confidence. The mover and some other members suggested that the motion may be kept pending. The speaker did not agree with this suggestion and ruled that the motion was premature. He, however, asked the mover to table a fresh motion, if necessary.[55]

The method of election for the national assembly, as described in the 1973 constitution, was not adopted anew for the national assembly, and the existing assembly continued to function as the first and lower house of the parliament. While taking decisions on the adjournment motions, the speaker often followed a well-established parliamentary practice: that an action taken by a lawfully constituted authority in due course of the administration of law could not constitute good grounds for an adjournment motion.[56] For instance, the speaker observed over an adjournment motion that it could not hold an inquiry in an election dispute; the remedy for any irregularity or illegality of an election was to be done by filing an election petition with the chief election commissioner.[57]

Professional Background of the Parliamentarians

The members of the national assembly, before being elected, belonged to different professions. However, two major professions, agriculture and law, dominated the assembly. This similarity of professions amongst a large majority of the members of the parliament also brought homogeneity in the assembly, which helped establish the distinctive status of the parliament. Forty-four per cent of the members were agriculturists while 23 per cent were legal practitioners—they accounted for 67 per cent of the total strength of the assembly. Moreover, the business-class constituted 10 per cent, and the clergymen 7 per cent of the total number of the house. The minority formed the remaining 17 per cent of the assembly. In addition, former bureaucrats and civil servants constituted a small 2 per cent of the assembly, while those from the military formed the remaining one per cent.[58]

Kamal Azfar's analysis of the composition of the national assembly of Pakistan disclosed another similarity among the members, which created a close link among the parliamentarians in respect of their common interest: 80 per cent of the members had landholdings of over 100 acres.[59]

The significant presence of agriculturists marked the agrarian strata of the society, which the lower house of the parliament represented. The presence of law professionals, however, was a blessing in disguise. The need of the hour was the formation of the constitution for Pakistan, and the presence of legal experts on the second position made the task easier for the government.

However, due to the dominant presence of landowning members, the assembly could not take any revolutionary steps with reference to land reforms. Perhaps, Bhutto had also observed this fact, which made him arrange for the introduction of major reforms outside of the assembly and before the imposition of the constitution.

The professional outlook also left a deep mark on the position of the assembly. Proportionally, a lower representation of clergy and business community could frustrate these two important elements of society. Though ten clergymen and the fifteen business experts could be more active than many of the agriculturists, work done by the whole parliament in the interest of these two classes was of significant proportion. Even then, the interesting absence of secular educationists in the assembly and the activism of religious members created assimilation among the parliamentarians largely. Virtually no educational expert of high rank was present in the assembly. While in comparison with education, the representation of the medical profession (4 per cent) was greater, along with a presence of one per cent of engineers as well.

Gender

There have been two to six women representatives in almost all assemblies since the creation of Pakistan. The only exception was the constituent assembly from 1955 to 1958, which had no women representation. There were two women members in the first constituent assembly (1947–54), Begum Jahan Ara Shahnawaz and Begum Shaista Ikramullah. Moreover, in both the assemblies elected during Ayub's regime, there were six female members. The assembly under discussion also had six women members, like its predecessors, all of whom were elected against the reserved seats for women, as no woman member had been elected through the general seats.[60]

Due to several reasons—either the party had not given any of the tickets to women, or the women were not interested in electoral politics or a general lack of support for women in the agriculturist society—the presence of women elected in general elections was nil. It could be maintained that women were not entering the assembly through the channel of popular vote. Regardless, the female members participated in the assembly debates actively. One female member, Dr Mrs Ashraf Abbasi, was elected deputy speaker of the national assembly. She was the first female in Pakistan elected for this office. Female members served in different parliamentary committees. For instance, Begum Nasim Jahan, Dr Mrs Ashraf Abbasi, and Mrs Jennifer Jehanzeba Qazi Musa served in the Constitution Committee that drafted the 1973 constitution.[61]

Educational Qualification

The assembly primarily consisted of educated people with one PhD (Dr Mubashir Hasan). Only twelve members had rather average or unknown educational qualifications. Members below matriculation level were about fifteen. Eighty members of the assembly were graduates or had studied till higher level. Also, there were ten religious scholars who had obtained degrees of Fazil/Alim, or were educated in religious seminaries. The group of thirty-three law graduates served as the dominant educational presence within the assembly. Therefore, it was naturally expected that a sufficient number of these educated parliamentarians could create close relationships to enhance the differentiation of the assembly.

Thus, the first elected bicameral legislature in Pakistan was formed and regularised. The formation of the parliament served as a precedent for future parliaments in Pakistan. The formation and workings of the national assembly and senate between 1971 and 1977 initiated a new set of traditions, which were followed later on by succeeding elected parliaments. The composition of this assembly reflected that members of the first parliament were mature, educated, and skilful. These people served as the torchbearers of a legacy in the constitutional and political history of the parliament.

Age Group

The assembly consisted of eighty-two people of the age group between 30 and 54 years. The highest number of members belonged to the age group 45 and 49 years. Fifty-one members ranged between 25 and 44 years. Only one member was above 70 and one was less than 25 years old.

THE SENATE

Formation

The formation of the senate, created for the first time in Pakistan's parliamentary history and also known as the second or the upper house of the parliament, was born at least one year after the start of the national assembly that had formed the 1973 constitution.[62] The senate was virtually the offspring of the national assembly that adopted the constitution in the light of which the senate came into existence.[63]

In the 1973 constitution, indirect election to the senate was adopted. The members of the provincial assemblies were to elect ten members from each of the four provinces, the members of the national assembly were to elect three members from the Federally Administered Tribal Areas (FATA), and then all the members of the national assembly were to elect a single member for the federal capital. The idea underlying indirect election was twofold: the strength of the political parties in the provincial assemblies would be reflected in the senate, and the second house was to present and safeguard the interests of the provinces. Necessary legal provisions for election to the senate were enacted under the Senate Election Order (P.O. No. 9, 1973). For election to the senate (from the federal capital) provisions were enacted under the Senate Election Order (P.O. No. 12, 1973). For the purpose of election to the Senate from FATA, the Senate Election Order (P.O. No. 9, 1973) was applied.[64]

In 1973, the first elections to the senate were held in the Punjab on 4 July, in Sindh on 6 July, in Balochistan on 8 July, in FATA on 9 July, and in the NWFP on 10 July. The party position of the forty-five senators elected in July 1973[65] was as follows:

PPP	29
NAP	8
Independent	3
JUI	2
UDF	2
PML	1

PPP claimed that it had emerged as the majority party in all four provinces in the senate elections but it did not represent the NWFP or Balochistan provinces. According to *Dawn*, the senate election did 'not testify to the emergence of the PPP as the dominant political force in the Western provinces.'[66]

The term of the first group consisting of five members from each province (two members from FATA and one member from the federal capital) was two years,[67] while the term of the second group (five members from each province, one member from FATA, and one member from the federal capital) was four years. Under clause (d) of article 272 of the constitution, the term of office of persons elected or chosen to succeed the members of the senate at the expiration of their respective terms is four years, while that of a person elected or chosen to fill a casual vacancy is the unexpired term of the member whose vacancy he has filled. The two-year term of twenty-three out of forty-five members expired in July 1975, and elections to fill these vacancies were held in July 1975. The party position[68] in the senate after these elections was as follows:

PPP	31
NAP	8
PML–Combined	1
JUP	1
UDF	1
Independent Group (FATA)	3

The constitution provided that as soon as the first general election for the national assembly is held, four additional members from each province and two additional members from the FATA would be elected to make up the permanent strength of the senate, which is 63 so as to correspond to the national assembly (of 216 members) which was elected to succeed the first assembly. In addition, elections to fill the vacancies of nine more senators, who had resigned because they were elected to the national assembly or a provincial assembly had to be held. All of the newly elected senators were divided into two groups as mentioned above. The term of the additional members was determined in the same manner as of those who were elected before.

The first meeting of the senate, elected in July 1973, was held in the national assembly hall on 6 August 1973. The gathering saw the election of the senate's chairman and deputy chairman. Whereas, the first regular session of the senate, for transaction of normal business, was held from 4 to 15 September 1973.

The constitution provides that a house may make rules for regulating its procedure and the transaction of its business, and until the rules are made, the procedure and conduct of business is to be regulated by the rules of procedure made by the president.[69] On 13 December 1974, the senate appointed a special committee to frame fresh rules. It had completed its work, but before it could submit its report, the senate was dissolved as a consequence of martial law.

In accordance with article 272 of the constitution, eighteen additional members: four from each of the four provinces and two from the FATA were to be elected. On 23 April 1977, the members of provincial assemblies elected on 10 March 1977, in turn elected the senators to make up the full strength of the senate. All political parties, except the PPP, boycotted the elections to the provincial assemblies, thus the senators elected by the new provincial assemblies belonged exclusively to the PPP. The party affiliation of the sixty-three members after the elections to the senate held in April 1977[70] was as follows:

PPP	47
NAP	8
PML–Combined	2
UDF	1
Independent	5

WORKING RELATIONSHIP BETWEEN THE TWO HOUSES

Under the 1973 constitution, the federal legislature was bicameral, with the lower house elected on the basis of population and the upper house elected by the provincial assemblies with each assembly electing an equal number (tribal areas elect fewer, and the federal capital is represented by two members selected by the president). The powers of the president were restricted and real authority resided with the prime minister, who was accountable to the assembly. This helped avoid the deformation of parliamentary and presidential practice of earlier constitutions.

In opting for a parliamentary form of government post-1947, Pakistan had opted to do away with the 'viceregal' system of the British period. However, the new constitution had somehow allowed for the remote possibility of deviating from a bicameral and parliamentary form of government and a return to the viceregal system based on Bhutto's predilection for the latter. The senate, protector of the provinces, had almost no real power.

The role of the senate as a federal institution under the 1973 constitution was important. In the matter of legislation, the participation of both houses of the parliament was essential, but in some respects, the national assembly enjoyed a distinctly superior position.[71]

Under the constitutional obligation, the two houses of parliament were required to meet in a joint sitting for election under article 41(3), and removal under article 47(8) of the president of Pakistan. This was to resolve disputes between the two houses in regard to legislation under article 71, to issue directions to the Council of Common Interests in a particular matter to take action as the parliament may deem just and proper under article 154(4), and to resolve disputes between the federal and provincial governments in regard to such directions under article 154(5).[72]

If bills relating to matters in Part II of the Federal Legislative List or the Concurrent Legislative List were rejected or not passed within ninety days by the second house, it was referred to a joint sitting where it would be passed by the majority of the total membership of the two houses.[73]

On 15 April 1976, Abdul Hafeez Pirzada, the minister for law and parliamentary affairs, in pursuance of article 234 of the constitution, moved a resolution regarding enactment of law by the parliament to regulate cooperative banking in Balochistan. Raising a point of order, a member took objection to the moving of the resolution, saying that under the constitution, the senate is not competent to pass resolutions mentioned in the constitution. According to his interpretation, the power to pass constitutional resolutions was vested in the parliament during its joint sitting, and not by the senate in a separate meeting. In support of his argument, he referred to articles 47 and 234, which clearly provided that such resolutions shall be passed by the parliament in a joint sitting. On enquiry by the chairman, the member said that the constitutional words 'parliament in joint sitting' have been used with reference to resolutions mentioned in articles 47, 154, and 232 of the constitution. The chairman observed that wherever in the constitution the phrase 'joint sitting' is used, it refers to joint sitting of both houses of the parliament. The minister for law and parliamentary affairs stated that under article 50 of the constitution, the parliament consists of two houses known as the national assembly and the senate. Both houses constitute the parliament. Thus, an 'instant' resolution could be moved in and passed by the national assembly or the senate separately. When both houses pass it, it is treated as having been passed by the parliament.[74]

The chairman observed that if the parliament in joint sitting, only meant the parliament, then the words 'in joint sitting' were redundant. The word 'parliament' and the phrase 'parliament in joint sitting' conveyed different meanings. Referring to paragraph (b) of clause 1 of article 234 of the constitution, he added, the president may, by proclamation, declare that the power of the provincial assembly shall be exercisable by, or under the authority of, the parliament. The resolution, which the law minister sought to move was one which should have been passed by the provincial assembly. However, since the assembly is suspended as a result of the proclamation, the parliament was acting on behalf of the provincial assembly. Thus, this was a resolution, which the parliament could debate and pass. As for the question of what constitutes the parliament, it refers to the two houses, but not necessarily in a joint sitting. Whenever the parliament, in joint sitting, is required to debate an issue or take a decision, it is specifically mentioned in the constitution. However, in the case of this resolution there are no such limitation. The parliament, i.e. the two houses sitting separately are therefore, competent to pass this resolution. Hence, concluding his observations, the chairman ruled: 'My ruling on the objection raised by Khawaja Mohammad Safdar is that the Law Minister is quite competent to move the resolution, and this House is fully competent to entertain, discuss and pass or reject it. That disposes of the objection.'[75]

If a matter had been discussed in the national assembly, it could not be discussed in the senate during the next six months.[76] However, if the motion was ruled out of order by the speaker, and thus a matter was not discussed in the national assembly, it was not barred to be discussed in the senate on the grounds that the speaker had ruled it out. On 1 April 1974, Khawaja Mohammad Safdar sought to move an adjournment motion in the senate to discuss the failure of the federal government to get the Kashmir issue included in the agenda of the Islamic Summit Conference held in Lahore. Opposing the motion, the minister of state for defence and foreign affairs stated that an identical adjournment motion moved in the national assembly had been ruled out of order by the speaker of the national assembly. Agreeing with the mover of the motion, the chairman held that the motion was not barred by reason of the fact that an almost identical motion had been ruled out of order by the speaker.[77]

On 10 December 1975, when clause 125 of the Divorce (Amendment) Bill was taken up in a joint sitting, it was pointed out that this was a new clause added by the senate to the bill passed earlier by the national assembly. The speaker observed that for a new clause, leave of the house was necessary.[78]

Article 154 contained a novel federal provision under which the parliament, in a joint sitting, may issue directions to the Council of Common Interests, which formulates and regulates policy in relation to matters in Part II of the Federal List and the Concurrent List. Proclamations of emergency under article 232, breakdown of constitutional machinery (article 234), and declaration of financial emergency (article 235) must be laid within thirty days before a joint sitting, which must approve such proclamation by a resolution.[79]

Professor Ghafoor Ahmad, a Jamaat-i-Islami MNA, brought to the notice of the national assembly that the white paper issued by the Government of Balochistan had been discussed in the senate and suggested that it should be taken up in a joint sitting of both the houses. However, a member expressed the apprehension that the matter once discussed in the senate may not be reopened in the assembly. Speaker, Sahibzada Farooq Ali Khan, further added:

> I made it clear and, so far as I recollect, I said, that this is a new experiment in our country and, for the first time, both the Houses are there. Our aim should be that we should work in cooperation with each other and a discussion in one House, although there is a rule to this effect, should not shut or bar a discussion in the other. If need be, we can again discuss it.[80]

It seemed highly unlikely that the senate would exert, in practice, any real check on the executive or on the national assembly, as its powers were very limited and it was totally dominated by the PPP. The latter would have thirty members out of the house of forty-five. In addition, it would be able to count on the votes of the three representatives of the Tribal Areas and that of Haji Abdul Halim of the National Awami Party.[81] Therefore, they would be able to outvote the opposition three to one, and thwart any attempts on the part of the senate to 'play an effective role in articulating regional demands' or to give 'substance to the concept of provincial autonomy'. Moreover, as the *Pakistan Times* rightly observed, there would be a 'few tall figures' in the senate. Aziz Ahmed, J.A. Rahim, and Rafi Raza would stand head and shoulder above the others, and dominate the debates of such a small gathering almost at will.[82]

In the duration between August 1973 and May 1977, thirteen joint sittings were held. The first sitting was for the election of the president, while six sittings were devoted to the approval and extension of the proclamations of emergency. In addition, one sitting each was summoned for debate on foreign policy, for address by the prime minister of Sri Lanka, and for reference to hundredth birth anniversary of Quaid-i-Azam Mohammad Ali Jinnah. Moreover, two sittings were devoted to legislative work. At the joint sitting held in June 1976, the annual budget of Balochistan was passed. Finally, the last sitting, held on 14 May 1977, was summoned for adoption of a resolution expressing confidence in the prime minister.[83]

PARLIAMENTARY COMMITTEES

The national assembly session, which started 14 August 1972, and was adjourned *sine die* on Sunday, 24 September 1972, had the primary goal of enacting various bills. These had previously been promulgated only as presidential ordinances. The more important bills to have been dealt with were:

1. Amendments to Industrial Legislation
2. Amendments to Criminal Law
3. Development of Industries
4. National Book Foundation
5. Foreign Exchange
6. Transfer of evacuated land to squatters (*Katchi Abadi* Bill)

7. State Bank Amendment Bill
8. Drugs (Generic Names Bill)[84]

Machinery was set up early in the session in the form of seventeen standing committees (on information, law, interior, procedure and privileges, education, etc.) to study the subjects for legislation and report to the house. The house got through most of this legislative work smoothly and quickly, with little obstruction from the opposition.[85] It remained the practice of the national assembly that the names of the members chosen for the select committee should be supplied beforehand.[86]

The discussion above has demonstrated that the parliament succeeded in attaining differentiation and complexity through the formation of universal rules. It is easy to conclude that the parliament contributed significantly during this interval. However, why was the parliament ultimately terminated, and the whole parliamentary system derailed in 1977 when martial law was enforced? In the beginning, through the formulation of universal rules, a differentiation was successfully created between the government and the opposition. However, later on, the non-compliance of some rules and attempts to create unnecessary discord between the government and the opposition wasted all earlier gains.

Members of the national assembly belonging to the opposition who raised their voice against the undemocratic actions of the central government were manhandled on the floor of the house and thrown out of the premises. Moreover, the Federal Security Force was habitual of humiliating and terrorizing the opposition party leaders and workers.[87]

An adjournment motion, relating to the alleged firing by the Federal Security Force in Lahore, on the orders of Abdul Hafeez Pirzada, federal law minister on 15 October 1975 came up before the national assembly. However, Pirzada denied the allegations in a vicious manner and resorted to scathing poisonous attacks. The mover tried to intervene but the speaker of the national assembly observed that personal remarks should be avoided; otherwise, the concerned minister had the right to make a statement. Abdul Hafeez Pirzada, thereafter, made a statement denying the allegations and stated that the Federal Security Force was kept in reserve but never used. He further contended that he was in

Rawalpindi at that time, deeming allegations against him as false. The speaker, relying on the statement of the minister, ruled the motion out of order.[88]

The creation of rivalries, even between his subordinates, gave Bhutto a sense of security. As his confidante, Rafi Raza admitted that, 'By nature, suspicious, he sought to have 'dirt' available against his ministers and leading party members, and in early 1976, assigned to his intelligence chiefs the task of preparing secret dossiers about them, to be used against them in case of need.'[89]

The NAP–JUI government in Balochistan was dismissed illegally and unethically, and in spite of sending Baloch leaders to jail, the federal government had not been able to form a majority government there. People were shot like rabid dogs, the army had blockaded sizeable populations, the air force had been used to strafe people, Iranian ammunition was being used against the locals, and thousands of political workers had been jailed.[90] Mazari shared that on 25 June, he came to know that over 900 people had been slain by armed forces in the Marri tribal area. Newspapers mentioned the use of the Pakistan Air Force in the aerial bombing of helpless civilians.[91]

OPPOSITION AND THE PROCESS OF LEGISLATION

The opposition, which is the very essence of any parliament, was part of the legal apparatus of the governing machinery. The government and opposition, both being important partners in national progress and integral parts of the democratic process, must have respect for one another.[92] The opposition was expected to be responsible and to place national interests above the interests of their parties. While there could be differences on principles and programme, it was the foremost function of the opposition to always keep the government on its toes, and strive to improve its performance through constructive criticism and accountability.[93] However, several actions on the government's part created serious breach and rift between the government and the opposition.

In a parliamentary form of government, the opposition is considered as an alternative to the government. The presence of the opposition marks the complexity of the institution as well as its strength. However, from 1973 to 1977 under the preventive laws, from the powers flowing from the continued state of emergency and the Defence of Pakistan Rules, political leaders began to be detained extensively and were met with physical violence, indignity, and even torture. The heavy hand of authority which fell on their humble followers can be easily imagined.[94]

Within the national assembly, sometimes such a condition was created that some opposition members had to say that:

> If the House proceeded in this way, it is obvious that no business could be transacted here with dignity and decorum. If the majority party preceded in this way and if an attempt was made to create noise like this in this august House.[95]

This state of affairs would lead to an assembly where the presence of an opposition was not tolerated. Every member was called a sovereign member of the sovereign house.[96]

It may, at first, be remarked that the policy adopted to deal with the opposition was not related either to any resistance within Bhutto's own party or to a threat from the parties in opposition. Dissent within the party had been silenced or won over by the weight of executive authority or patronage. Most members of the assembly, belonging to the ruling party, owed their election to Bhutto's personal appeal, and wielded little influence in their own right. As for the opposition in the assembly, it comprised of splinter groups, the fate of which followed the fable of the lamb that lay with the lion. The president of the Council Muslim League, Mian Mumtaz Daultana, accepted an ambassadorial appointment in the UK, and resigned from his membership of the assembly. His exit dealt a heavy blow to the Council Muslim League, though some of his party members continued to take a stand against the government.[97]

It was not in Bhutto's nature to encourage opposition, and his three years in power had left the political opposition in disarray. The Muslim League scarcely existed, except in the NWFP where its Qayyum faction formed part of the coalition government. The Jamaat-i-Islami was well organized and could still exert pressure on religious questions. Its student wing, the Jamiat-i-Talaba, was dominant in most universities as a rightist party, but with little representation in assemblies. Due to the absence of a dynamic leader, the Jamaat could not cause Bhutto any serious worries.[98]

At the first national assembly session in 1972, being the most experienced man in parliamentary affairs, Sardar Shaukat Hayat Khan was elected as an official spokesperson for the opposition, a post, which he retained till 1973. It was only after this that Wali Khan agreed to become the leader of the opposition at the request of Chaudhry Zahoor Elahi.[99] In the national assembly session from 14 August 1972 to 24 September 1972, the leader of the opposition, Sardar Shaukat Hayat, was often on his feet in defence of his concept of the democratic process. He stood out as one of the more honest and conscientious politicians in the assembly. However, the most vocal man against the PPP government was the large, truculent and rather muddleheaded young MNA from Kasur, Ahmad Raza Kasuri. As one of the founding members of the PPP, he had (up till then) led a stormy political career. Earlier that year, he was shot and wounded in a factional PPP fight in Kasur. He had always been one of the left-wingers of the party, and was mostly at odds with the hierarchy.[100]

On 31 January 1975, Ahmad Raza Kasuri was suspended from the assembly for the rest of the current session for 'disregarding the authority of the Chair'. This was not surprising as a running battle had gone on between the speaker and Kasuri during most of the assembly session, largely due to the latter's propensity for constant interruption, not in any constructive way, but usually a frantic railing at the chairman. [101]

The government failed to implement an accord reached by the government with the opposition on 6 February 1975, resulting in a deadlock and abstention of the members of the opposition from attending the assembly. Sardar Shaukat Hayat moved an adjournment motion to discuss this alleged failure of the government. The speaker ruled out the motion on the grounds of it being based on the opinion of a member, namely, Mufti Mahmud.[102]

The opposition boycotted the assembly proceedings on the account of an incident, which took place on 14 November 1975. Some of them had tabled privilege motions and adjournment motions, which were pending before the house. On 17 November 1975, when the said motion was to be taken up, the speaker found the movers absent. Thereupon, he observed:

> I have not received any intimation from the honorable members who had moved adjournment or privilege motions to keep them pending or postpone them for a day or two, but still I will wait for a day for all these motions which were filed before 15 November 1975, and were being heard or remained pending, or it was declared that they would be taken up the next day. But I will call out those privilege motions which were filed after 15 November, because there is no justification, at all, to keep them pending.[103]

As a temporary measure, following approval of the Fourth Amendment, the opposition in the national assembly decided to renew their boycott.[104] The UDF's boycott of the national assembly continued, though its member had each been attending for a few minutes every few weeks, in order to satisfy the constitutional requirement for their presence.[105]

Possibly, the government was a little less worried that the opposition—or rather the UDF—would use the incident of barring Ahmad Raza Kasuri from the assembly session in February 1975 as a trigger to activate a former threat of boycotting the parliament altogether. In any case, the government was ready to meet the opposition in private talks over the past two days to discuss the latter's grievances. Consequently, the opposition, on 6 February 1975, returned to the chamber, and their spokesperson, Professor Ghafoor Ahmad, read out a statement containing 'Points of Understanding' between the government and the opposition. This was, subsequently, endorsed by the education minister, Abdul Hafeez Pirzada. The opposition appeared to achieve, at least, a promise of better treatment in the future. However, according to the British ambassador, these truces between the government and opposition were usually short-lived.[106]

At the time of the boycott of the opposition, the UK high commissioner taxed an opposition MNA with what appeared to be a boycott in support of a bad cause. The MNA replied that the boycott was not in support of Kasuri, but rather a mark of protest against what the opposition saw as an impartial attitude on the part of the speaker.[107]

The boycott of the opposition, while demonstrating the fault of the government, also showed the incompetence of the opposition that had lost the differentiation of the institution of the parliament. The national assembly started its budget session on 26 May 1975. However, its proceedings thus far had been somewhat farcical because only one member of the opposition had been attending on a regular basis.[108] Sardar Shaukat Hayat, an active member of the opposition, stated on 25 May that, 'By prolonging the boycott, opposition may be delivering a catastrophic blow to the democratic process.'[109] Bhutto appealed to the UDF to return to the assembly and end the boycott, but was soundly rebuffed for his pains. Speaking in the assembly on 26 May 1975, Bhutto pungently attacked the whole concept behind the boycott; the opposition, he said, now stood, 'condemned before the people of Pakistan for not doing their duty by democracy, their respective constituents and the country ... I pay tributes to the people for not demanding their resignations.'[110]

In response to this, the opposition came to the assembly on 27 May 1975 with the aim of stating their case in public once more. However, this tactic failed miserably as a result of the inept manner in which their spokesperson, Mufti Mahmud had drafted his chosen weapon of attack—a privilege motion seeking to debate Bhutto's speech of the previous day. After much argument, shouting, and confusion, the speaker ruled the motion out of order, at which point the opposition once more marched out in its entirety.[111]

Bhutto made his contribution to the budget debate on 23 June 1975, and commented in passing that a way had to be found to bring the opposition back to the assembly. The manner of their return, however, was, 'not for the government to suggest; it is for them to suggest it. We are prepared to consider any feasible proposal for their return, if they want to do their duty.'[112]

All reasonably objective observers agreed that the tactic of the UDF were surpassing in incompetence and inflexibility even by their abysmal standards. The opposition leaders left themselves wide open to attack, enabling the government to pose as the voice of democracy and sweet reasoning, making the opposition members look stubborn and foolish.[113] As the *Pakistan Times* referred to their contention with the government, they fled from reason and discussion, and left their opponents masters of the field. *Dawn* spoke of unreason and obduracy, and attacked the UDF for abdicating from its responsibilities, for being so stupid as to stay away from 'the one forum where the freedom to express views and opinions and to criticize the government is virtually unlimited.'[114] Hassan Akhtar, a journalist of liberal outlook, wrote in the *Morning News* of the general feeling that 'the opposition has lost its bearings. It lacks political finesse and the parliamentary maturity to play the role it is expected to play.'[115]

Having withdrawn to lick its wounds, the opposition parties planned to hold a convention in Lahore between 14 and 15 June 1975, attended also by Air Marshal (retd) Asghar Khan of the Tehrik-i-Istiqlal. They had to consider among other things the implied threat in Pirzada's observation to the press at the end of May, that according to the constitution (article 64), the national assembly 'may declare the seat of a member vacant if, without leave of the House, he remains absent for forty consecutive days of its sittings.'[116]

The Fourth Amendment Bill (1975) was put forward for consideration of the national assembly on 14 November. The opposition members, who had ended their eight-month boycott of the assembly proceedings a few days ago, started discussion on the bill. The government wanted to get the bill passed hurriedly, but the treasury benches did not take the debate seriously. One member, Malik Hamid Yasin, interrupted the proceedings with rude remarks against Maulana Abdul Mustafa Al-Azhari during his speech that initiated the debate on said bill. After the speeches of some members, the opposition maintained that the bill should not be passed in a hurry, and the house should be adjourned before Friday evening as it should be a holiday and the debate on the bill should be resumed on Monday.[117]

On the presentation of the amendment bills, the explanations requested by members were not provided. On 24 November 1975, Ahmad Raza Kasuri pointed out that the concerned minister explained the aims and objects of the constitution (in particular, its Fourth Amendment) concisely without going into its details. This led to vagueness during discussions both inside and outside the assembly. The speaker responded that, 'the practice is that the minister makes only a very brief speech at the time of consideration. In other countries, there is debate outside the House, as well as inside the House.'[118]

During their meeting in November 1975, the opposition agreed to resign its assembly seats, 'at an opportune moment'. Though the parties present at the meeting (holding few or no assembly seats) were enthusiastic about the prospect of resignation, those with more seats at stake were correspondingly less keen. Behind the opposition's decision (if it can be called that), there was a view that the Fourth Amendment represented a basic change in that constitution; and since the constitution was agreed to unanimously before its promulgation in August 1973, the opposition considered that amendments of a fundamental nature should also be agreed upon unanimously.[119] They also considered that the assemblies had lost their utility, and that the discharge of their duties as elected representatives had been made impossible. Mufti Mahmud, leader of the opposition, stated that further dialogue with the government was useless, and that the opposition was now determined to launch a mass movement against the government. Yet, another meeting of all opposition parties was to take place in Lahore on 3 December 1975 to decide their future course of action.[120]

The Balochistan operation was the foremost issue that widened the rift between the government and opposition, within as well as outside the parliament. The action committee of UDF, formed for highlighting government atrocities, considered that the actions taken by the federal government in Balochistan were unconstitutional and unlawful. The opposition deemed that in compliance with such orders the Pakistan Army and Air Force were indiscriminately shelling, strafing, and killing innocent inhabitants, which included women and children. Their properties were being destroyed and their livestock looted. Concentration camps were established where the innocent and patriotic people of Balochistan were being kept and maltreated. Their women were dishonoured and innocent children tortured.[121] In the views of opposition, implementation of such orders of the federal government by the Pakistan Army and Air Force was damaging the unity of the country, and led to further disintegration. Thus, a reign of terror prevailed in the whole province merely because the people of Balochistan did not vote for the PPP in the last general elections.[122]

On 8 February, Hayat Mohammad Sherpao, the PPP senior minister of NWFP, was killed in a bomb explosion at Peshawar University. There were many conspiracy theories about perpetrators of his assassination. One theory was that it had been carried out on the direct orders of Sherpao's own leader—Bhutto. It was a known fact that before his death, Sherpao had become very disenchanted with the leader whom he had once worshipped. Bhutto had noticed Sherpao's growing popularity and had come to resent it and had begun politically side-lining him at every available opportunity. Even one of their close PPP colleagues commented:

> A few months before his death, Sherpao seriously considered leaving the party altogether. He only changed his mind on the persuasion of myself and other friends from the Frontier.... Of all those around Bhutto, Sherpao's personal devotion had been the greatest and his subsequent disillusionment was, consequently, the most profound.[123]

The death of Sherpao provided Bhutto with an excuse to clamp down on Wali Khan and his NAP. It was eerily reminiscent of the dismissal of the Balochistan government on trumped up charges of being responsible for the arms and ammunition found in the Iraq Embassy two years earlier in February 1973. On the day following Sherpao's assassination, Wali Khan, along with national and provincial leaders of NAP, were either under detention or being urgently sought out by authorities. The next day it was announced that NAP had been banned, and all its assets confiscated. The First Amendment to the 1973 constitution allowed the federal government to ban political parties formed or those 'operating in a manner prejudicial to the sovereignty of Pakistan'.[124]

The opposition government in Balochistan and NWFP were openly discriminated against, and their leaders frequently criticised for being unpatriotic. Finally, on 12 February 1974, the Government of Balochistan was dismissed on charges of having incited the people of that province to rebel against the federation. The power of declaring any political party illegal was used to ban the NAP, by now the only effective opposition to the PPP. This was a step taken toward Bhutto's unstated (but obvious) objective of turning Pakistan into a one-party state.[125]

Acting under the Political Parties Act 1962, which had been amended by an ordinance in October 1974, the government banned the NAP and forfeited its funds and property throughout the country. In addition, it arrested its leaders or placed them under house arrest, which included Wali Khan of the NAP, the leader of the opposition in the national assembly.[126] No public outcry on the matter was reported in Peshawar.[127] This action of the government created unbridgeable rifts between the government and the opposition.

USE OF RULES BY THE SPEAKER OF THE ASSEMBLY OR CHAIRMAN OF THE SENATE

As far as complexity on the basis of universal rules is concerned, the following instances show how the government and the speaker or chairman of the senate misused rules or created such rules which were injurious to mutual confidence and trust among the parliamentarians, or injurious to the trust of the masses. On 12 November 1975, a member gave notice of a privilege motion. He observed that the federal government had failed to put the recommendations of the National Finance Commission regarding the distribution of revenues between the federation and the provinces before the senate. He alleged that this failure of the government had amounted to the breach of the privilege of the senate.

The minister of state for parliamentary affairs opposed the motion with reference to article 160(5) of the constitution which stated that the report of the National Finance Commission, together with an explanatory memorandum, was included in the orders of the day. It was, therefore, evident that no time was lost in laying before the house the recommendations of the commission. It was not practically possible to present the report in the last session of the senate, as some action had to be taken and the document had to be printed, which was a time-consuming process, he added.

The mover suggested that the motion may be referred to the Committee on Rules of Procedure and Privileges. The committee would look into the causes of delay due to printing or any other reason.

The senate chairman, Habib Ullah Khan, asked the mover to state his grievances clearly, as recommendations of the commission had already been laid before the house. Clause (5) of article 160 did not specify the time during which such recommendations were required to be laid before both houses. If that was the intention, the time limit would have been specified, as had been done in clause (4) of article 160 of the constitution which reads, 'As soon as may be, after receiving the recommendations of the National Finance Commission, the President shall by Order specify....' But the expression 'as soon as may be' had not been used in clause (5) of the article.

The mover, in response to a query from the chairman, said that in the absence of any time limit prescribed in the constitution, the government should prepare this document in a judicially reasonable time. After some discussion, Habib Ullah Khan deferred consideration of the motion till the next day at the request of the minister of state for parliamentary affairs.

On 13 November 1977, discussion on the admissibility was resumed. The minister for finance, planning and economic affairs opposing the motion observed that article 160 (5) of the constitution provided that the report of the commission should be laid before the two houses of the parliament. This provision of the constitution had been complied with. However, firstly, the constitution did not specify the time during which the report was required to be laid before the two houses of parliament. Secondly, he remarked that the decisions taken by the government on the recommendations of the National Finance Commission were mentioned in the last budget speech of the finance minister in the national assembly, and were discussed in detail on the floor of the assembly during that session. Since these decisions had been made public, there was no bar to these being discussed by the members of the senate. Therefore, he argued, no breach of privilege of the senate or its members was involved.

The chairman observed that the senate had a right to discuss a document when it was laid on the table of the house. The mover, in disagreement with the view of the minister of finance, said that although no time limit was prescribed; a reasonable time limit should be fixed. He added that when the decisions were mentioned in the last budget speech, these should have been laid before the senate in July or even in August when the sessions of the senate were held. According to him, this breach of privilege was committed during last July and August.

The minister of state for parliamentary affairs inquired of the mover as to why he did not table this motion in last July? The mover responded that it was a case of continuous offences, and was, therefore, of recent occurrence, and the condition of taking up this matter at the 'earliest opportunity' was not relevant here. The chairman, disagreeing with the view of the mover, remarked that the question of the earliest opportunity was material and the 'opportunity' was not continuous. He announced his written ruling.

Khawaja Mohammad Safdar gave notice of the following motion:

> The National Finance Commission has sent its recommendations with regard to the distribution of Revenues between the Federation and the Provinces a long time ago, and the Federal Government was bound under Article 160 (5) of the Constitution to lay those recommendations together with an explanatory memorandum as to the action taken thereon before the Senate. The Federal Government has failed to discharge its constitutional obligation, and the Senate has been denied its right and privilege to bring the recommendations of the National Finance Commission as well as the action taken by the Federal Government thereon under discussion. This has lowered the prestige of the Senate and the privileges of this august House have been badly violated.

The subject matter of the motion concerned the federal government under article 160 (5) of the constitution, and the recommendations were to be laid before the senate under rule 135 of the *Rules of Procedure and Conduct of Business in the Senate 1973*. According to sub-rule (ii) rule 59 of the *Rules of Procedure*, the question of breach of privilege shall be raised at the earliest opportunity. In this case, as the motion reads, the recommendations of the National Finance Commission were sent to the federal government long ago. In view of the aforementioned circumstances:

> I need not go into the details, so far as the merits of the case are concerned, and I rule the privilege motion out of order only on this ground that the earliest opportunity was not availed of by Khawaja Mohammad Safdar.[128]

Again, on 12 April 1976, four adjournment motions related to the increase in gas prices, cement, oil, power tariff, PIA and railway fares and freights were moved, but were deferred till Friday, 16 April, on the suggestion of the finance minister. He said that the same adjournment motions had also been moved in the national assembly and a date for discussion there had already been fixed. The leader of the house in the senate had made a proposal that they should wait till the discussion took place in the national assembly. The finance minister explained that the subject matter of the adjournment motions and the subject matter of the motion under rule 187 were, more or less, the same because once they started discussing the increase in prices of certain items, naturally they would have to discuss all such matters. That would save a lot of time if they undertook them together as these were related matters.

The chairman observed that there was another way out of the dilemma in which they found themselves. Let this motion be amended, instead of saying 'consumer goods' one could say 'prices of articles and fare'. It would cover all the adjournment motions as well as this motion because consumer goods would not include, obviously, the 'increase in the PIA and railway fare and other such things.' It could be amended and read like this: 'Khawaja Safdar to move that the situation arising out of spiralling prices of the consumer goods and other articles and fares'. If the house agreed, it could be amended to cover all the adjournment motions as well as this motion. Both sides of the house agreed to this proposal. The chairman, again, observed that when its turn came, any gentleman could move an amendment and the house might agree to it. It may be the 16th, as suggested by the finance minister. Then this motion would become a substantive motion and it would cover all the adjournment motions. The members approved the suggestion. Thereupon, the chairman observed that the motion under rule 187, in the name of Khawaja Mohammad Safdar, set down for today as item No. 4 in the *Orders of the Day* would be amended in such a way as to cover all the adjournment motions pertaining to the increase in prices of consumer goods and other articles and fares, and the 16th would be fixed for its discussion. No such adjournment motions were moved in view of the agreement and accord was reached between the two sides of the house.[129]

Another example of the misuse of rules by the custodian of the house was observed on 16 April 1974, when a member asked a starred question regarding the number of various industries in each province. The minister for labour and works responded that the information to the extent available had been placed on the table of the house on 1 April 1974, in response to starred question No. 37 asked by the member on 9 February 1974. The member was not satisfied and said that his was a starred question for an oral verbal answer. He failed to understand why the information in response had been placed on the table of the house. The chairman remarked that what seemed to have happened was that, as the reply was not ready on the day on which the question was set down for answer; it was said in response that the required information was being collected and would be placed on the table of the house in due course. Later, the aforementioned case was carried out. The minister then said that the procedure, actually, was that when an answer is laid on the table of the house in the circumstances mentioned by the chairman, it is up to the member to look into the answer and put in supplementary questions. He, therefore, suggested that the member might go through the answer and put supplementary questions if he so desired. The member reiterated his view that the answer should have been given verbally because it was a starred question. The answer was cleverly avoided, he added. Chairman Habib Ullah Khan observed:

> That would not be done. The entire answer, the entire information the member wanted has been laid on the Table of the House which means that it is not being concealed from anybody. It is now a public document. Everyone can have look at it. You can have a look at it and if you want to put any supplementary questions, I can defer it to some other date.[130]

Thereafter, the question was deferred to a later date.

To conclude, the study of the formation and composition of the parliament from 1971 to 1977 reveals that universal rules were utilised for its foundation. From time to time, such rules and regulations were also adapted by the parliament itself, which brought about complexity within the institution. In the composition of the parliament, the members had such close affiliation that it came to achieve a greater degree of differentiation as well. In this regard, education and party affiliation of the members and the leadership of Z.A. Bhutto exerted a positive influence. However, escape from implementation of the rules, which were adapted by the parliament lost the complexity, which was achieved during the course of establishing its foundation and workings. On the other hand, due to rash use of brute force against the opposition by the government, the opposition's ineptness and the government's mishandling of the opposition, it could not continue the standards of differentiation in the parliament, which it previously reflected. As a consequence, it failed to cope with the conditions, and could not maintain its existence, shattering all the persons of political intelligence and maturity of the parliament.

Chapter Four

Sovereignty of Parliament as a Constituent Assembly

This chapter analyses the process of the making of the 1973 constitution. The two years of the working of the constituent assembly have been discussed to examine its sovereignty in the assembly. The sovereignty of any institution is defined as the power of an institution in making its decisions independently, without any external influence. It is through the sovereignty of an institution that it influences other organs of the state to function in a desired manner. The assembly in its initial period, from 1971–3, remained active and proved to be the most significant institution of the state of Pakistan, while it tried to recover from the trauma of 1971.

The early phase of Z.A. Bhutto's governing era was also the initial period of the national assembly, which was elected in 1970. The national assembly,[1] then known as the parliament of Pakistan, consisted of a single house, and enjoyed substantial sovereignty, both legally and politically. It was able to take innovative action in the sphere of public policy and institution building. Mohammad Waseem rightly noted about the aforementioned period that the PPP government at the time remained to be the sole example of a clearly supreme parliament over non-elected institutions, both *de facto* and *de jure*, throughout the political history of Pakistan.[2]

The assembly, in its initial days, was a constituent assembly and enjoyed the mandate to produce a new constitution for the post-1971 Pakistan. Hamid Khan believes that the members elected from West Pakistan could not act and form a constituent assembly of their own. It would have been appropriate to hold fresh elections in West Pakistan for a constituent assembly on the basis of altered constitutional and political realities. Similarly, Hamid Khan is of the opinion that new elections should have been called immediately after December 1971, and a truncated assembly should not have been rejuvenated for the role of the constituent assembly.[3] However, despite this constitutional lacuna, the assembly was given a status to complete the prestigious task of making a constitution for the state. Whereas, in the former East Pakistan (now Bangladesh), fresh elections were held soon after December 1971, and a constituent assembly was elected under new political circumstances.[4] Bhutto deemed it politically expedient after the separation of East Pakistan to rely on the assembly. In the case of new elections, his role in the East Pakistan crisis would certainly have been questioned, and he was by no means certain that his party would attain the same strength in the national assembly again.[5] Moreover, political parties in the opposition did not demand a re-election, perhaps because they were not sure of themselves after the drubbing they had received from the PPP in the general elections of December 1970. They were demoralized and, thus, contented themselves by the seats they had obtained.[6] Hence, in this situation, the assembly attained unanimous prominence over all the institutions of the political system and the parliament's powers were increased. It was evident from the fact that in the period post-1970, under the leadership of Z.A. Bhutto, elected public officials began to establish their supremacy over non-elected public officials.[7]

Moreover, the government was giving significance to the assembly. The trauma of the defeat in East Pakistan made it possible for the politicians of West Pakistan to agree to a new constitution.[8] In order to make that possible, reliance on the parliament was essential. For the same reason, the government initially announced that there would be no interim constitution. The reason for avoiding the hassle of an interim constitution, according to law minister, Mian Mahmud Ali Kasuri, was that, 'it would amount to giving a constitution by one man. The country had had a very unpleasant experience of a one-man constitution, and therefore, it would not be proper to repeat it.'[9]

However, continuation of martial law was not acceptable to the opposition parties. Wali Khan, president of NAP, criticized Bhutto for continuing martial law, and opposed the plan for a 'phased democracy'.[10] On 6 February 1972, Wali Khan gave the ultimatum to lift martial law or lose the cooperation of NAP. He even threatened to launch a mass movement for the restoration of democracy.[11] The demand was soon reinforced by other political parties. Consequently, Bhutto had to promise to announce a schedule to lift martial law and return to democracy 'for all times to come' once certain basic reforms had been introduced.[12]

In order to overcome political tensions and appease the opposition whose impatience about the martial law was heightening, the PPP opened the door to negotiations with the NAP and the JUI on 4 March 1972 to reach a feasible settlement.[13] These parties not only had substantial representation in the assembly but were also the majority parties in the provincial assemblies of NWFP and Balochistan.

THE TRIPARTITE ACCORD FOR THE CONSTITUTION[14]

Under the terms of settlement, the assembly was given primary importance. There was a unanimous opinion about the role of national assembly as a constitution-making body; the practice of forming a commission for the approval of the interim constitution was not followed. However, both opposition parties disagreed with the dates for the convening of the assembly. The PPP proposed that a short session of the national assembly should be convened on 21 April 1972, for a period not exceeding three days. The NAP–JUI, on the contrary, proposed that the national assembly session be convened on 23 March 1972. It was settled that the invite should be issued on 23 March 1972, and the national assembly session should convene on 14 April 1972, for a period not exceeding three days. During this time, matters like the basic interim constitution, confidence on the government, and approval for the continuation of martial law would be voted upon.

The PPP proposed that, the national assembly should meet for the purpose of endorsing an interim constitution based on both the Government of India Act 1935, and the Independence Act 1947, with consequential amendments or the 1962 constitution with consequential amendments. The NAP–JUI proposed that the interim constitution should be passed on the basis of the Government of India Act 1935, and the Independence Act 1947, with consequential amendments. The aforementioned proposal was accepted by all parties. Furthermore, it was agreed upon, that there should be a debate held, not exceeding three days, during which only the party leaders or their nominees would speak. For this purpose, the parties would be the PPP, the PML (Qayyum Group), JUI, the NAP, the JUP, the PML (Council), the JI, the PML (Convention), a representative from the independent MNAs of the tribal areas, and a representative of the remaining independent MNAs.[15]

Thus, the mechanism through which the business of the assembly would be conducted during the approval of the interim constitution were settled amongst the political parties. The basis of the interim constitution was settled by the political parties of the assembly. All of them were given an opportunity for participating in debate over the interim constitution. The government, or any other committee/commission formed by the government, was not given a mandate to function as a directing or decision-making body, regarding the selection of the basic document of the interim constitution.

Again, the national assembly was given prominence to legitimize the continuity of the government. Accepting the right of the assembly to pass a vote of confidence for the majority party, it was settled that there would be a vote of confidence in the government and approval for the continuation of martial law until 14 August 1972. NAP–JUI had proposed that martial law be continued until 7 June 1972. However, the proposal of the PPP was accepted. The party had proposed continuing martial law till 14 August 1972.

The parties of the parliament then devised a procedure for the making of a permanent draft constitution. Again, the national assembly was relied upon without any reservations, and both sides accepted the hegemony of the institution of the parliament. No one suggested negating the right of the parliament to make the constitution. The PPP proposed that the national assembly, on being convened for a short session, should appoint a committee of the house to draft a constitution to be presented on 1 August 1972. The NAP–JUI proposed that the draft constitution be presented by 1 July 1972 and that the national assembly should reconvene on 7 July 1972. It was settled that the report of the Constitution Committee should be submitted by 1 August 1972, and that the national assembly reconvene on 14 August 1972.

The role of the assembly and the modalities for its smooth functions were also devised with the consent of the government and opposition parties. The PPP proposed that when the national assembly was reconvened on 14 August 1972, it should act only as a constitution-making body to ensure the early framing of the constitution. However, the NAP–JUI proposed that it should also act as a legislative body after 14 August 1972. Both the proposals were accepted simultaneously, until the new constitution came into force.

PPP cleverly succeeded to preserve the powers to declare a state of emergency, making Bhutto successful in retaining his extra-parliamentary powers.[16] However, notwithstanding the acceptance of the presidential power for continuity of the emergency, the parliamentary style of the formation of government was adopted. It was decided that the government, both at the centre and in the provinces, would be formed on the basis of a parliamentary majority.

The composition of the assembly would not be changed until the constitution was framed. The assembly was to function smoothly in order to form the constitution. It was agreed that until the new constitution came into force, any person elected as a member of more than one assembly would be permitted to retain his seat in both the houses. Similarly, the president, the vice-president, governors, ministers and advisors, both at the centre and in provinces, would retain their seats in their respective assemblies. [17]

Bhutto got all that he wanted through this agreement, and the two opposition parties were no match for him at the negotiating table.[18] However, the hegemony of the parliament was accepted by both the parties involved. The parliament rose equivocally as a highly powerful institution whose role as a constitution-making body as well as a government-legitimizing institution was accepted by Bhutto despite his power.

Wali Khan, the opposition leader in the assembly, in his interview on 8 March 1972, as well as in a public statement made before lawyers in Peshawar and Charsadda on 11 and 16 March 1972, and before a NAP working committee on 6 March 1972, expressed his unequivocal faith in the Tripartite Agreement, especially about the lifting of martial law by 14 August 1972.[19] The Balochistan NAP chief, Mir Ghaus Bakhsh Bizenjo, also made a similar comment in an interview given at Rawalpindi on 8 March 1972.[20] Thus, the parliament was accepted as a legitimate, powerful institution by the opposition as well.

THE INTERIM CONSTITUTION 1972

In 1972, martial law was still in force, and the three main reasons for its continuance were: to establish civilian supremacy over the Bonapartism of the generals, to affect PPP's socio-economic reforms, and the extreme difficulty of summoning the national assembly to get any constitutional scheme ratified on short notice.

Under the cover of martial law, the National Assembly (Short Session) Order was promulgated on 23 March 1972 to call a session of the national assembly.[21] The session lasted three days, and the first meeting took place on the 14 April 1972. It was the first meeting of the directly elected national assembly in which all the elected members of the assembly took oath. The national assembly was to be the one provided for in the Legal Framework Order 1970. The business of the assembly was restricted to:

- a vote of confidence by the president of Pakistan
- continuance of martial law until 14 August 1972
- framing of the interim constitution of Pakistan
- appointment of a committee of the assembly to prepare a draft of the permanent constitution of Pakistan no later than 1 August 1972, for submission to the national assembly.

The maximum number who could attend the meeting was 146; the quorum of the meeting of the national assembly was fixed at 40.[22]

The national assembly promptly played the role that was assigned to it in the political setup. It introduced an interim constitution on 14 April 1972, and adopted it on 20 April 1972, putting an end to martial law the following day.

Meanwhile, another development took place in the Supreme Court of Pakistan. On 20 April 1972, the court, while giving judgment in the

Asma Jilani vs the Government of Punjab case, declared that General Yahya Khan had usurped powers and that his action was not justified by the revolutionary legality doctrine, consequently labelling his martial law illegal.[23] Asma Jilani's case paved the way to strengthen democracy, and Bhutto was compelled to formulate the constitution.[24]

During the three days of debating, twenty-seven amendments were proposed by the minister of law and parliamentary affairs, Mian Mahmud Ali Kasuri, for the interim constitution and, subsequently, all these were collectively passed by the assembly, along with the primary resolution of the adoption of the interim constitution.[25]

The interim constitution was passed as a result of Bhutto's tactics, and as a result he decided to lift the martial law early on 21 April 1972.[26] Such a dramatic announcement took the opposition members by surprise and they had no alternative but to endorse the interim constitution. This declaration completely pulled the rug from beneath the feet of the opposition.[27] Many of them expressed their helplessness because they could neither accept the interim constitution as is, nor could they tolerate the continuation of martial law. Eventually, the interim constitution was passed, un-amended, and martial law was lifted on 21 April 1972. At this announcement, Shaukat Hayat Khan on behalf of the opposition said:

> The acceptances of this Constitution which I say is half fish and half fowl, on the other side, we are given a choice of the martial law, we have to perforce accept this Constitution rather than the martial law and we have, therefore, decided to abstain from voting on the Resolution [regarding the Interim Constitution].[28]

The interim constitution was a 112-page document divided into twelve parts (288 articles), and seven schedules. The president was empowered with huge discretionary powers relating to the executive, judiciary, and legislative branches of government. Bhutto combined the offices of the head of state and head of government, while there was no provision for dual authority. The courts were barred from challenging the interim constitution.[29]

The constitution, being federal and presidential in nature, was based primarily upon the abrogated 1962 constitution, with certain important changes made to it.[30] Some of its features were of historical importance, and illustrated certain ideas, which commanded a wide measure of general assent. It was as if the state was to exercise its powers through the chosen representatives of the people.[31] Baxter was of the opinion that under the terms of this document, Bhutto as president was granted broad powers, reminiscent of the powers granted to the viceroys under the British Raj, while the national assembly was left weak and ineffective.[32] Practically, the national assembly seemed stronger, especially in respect to the making of the constitution. It provided for a unicameral legislature—a house consisting of the national assembly as the federal legislature. The national assembly had the power to legislate on all subjects mentioned in the federal and concurrent legislative lists given under the fourth schedule.[33]

The parliamentarians also took active part in the formation of an interim constitution. A number of objections to the draft of the interim constitution were put forward, not only by the opposition parties but also by some members of the government.[34] The opposition parties demanded a parliamentary form of government, but the draft of the interim constitution presented to them had provided for a presidential system. The NAP, led by Abdul Wali Khan, characterized the draft as placing Bhutto on the status and powers of the governor general of India, the viceroy of India, the American president, and everything else. Mir Ghaus Bakhsh Bizenjo, another opposition leader, criticized the anti-federal character of the interim constitution as it failed to equitably distribute resources between the centre and the provinces. He also demanded that the ministers be made accountable to the legislature and not to the president alone.[35]

During the same session, Bhutto was elected as president of the national assembly with 104 votes, whereas, his opponent, Sardar Sherbaz Khan Mazari obtained only 38 votes. The national assembly unanimously adopted a resolution reposing confidence in Bhutto as the president.[36] Thus, the parliament's prominence appeared in legitimizing the government of Z.A. Bhutto. He was in dire need of the support of the national assembly, which he received from different parties.[37]

After adopting the interim constitution, the government and the opposition moved further. On the resolution by Ghulam Mustafa Jatoi, the minister for political affairs, the national assembly established a

24-member Constitution Committee[38] under the chairmanship of law minister, Mian Mahmud Ali Kasuri.[39] A glance at the names of the members of the committee would clarify that the committee was a true representative of the assembly, as almost all parties in the assembly were given representation in that committee. However, the committee faced discord and violent controversies over major constitutional issues such as choosing between presidential or parliamentary form of government, the division of power between the centre and the provinces, the distribution of powers to the head of the government, and the Islamic provisions in the constitution.[40]

The Constitution Committee met for the first time on 22 April 1972, where there was an agreement on the generalities; difficulties in respect to particular issues were considered in the second session commencing 18 May 1972. Statements and discussions in the committee, without a draft document, proved pointless. The committee asked Kasuri to submit a draft by the end of June 1972. In the absence of a specific direction or a basic agreement, no draft could be prepared, due to which the committee was unable to meet the deadline. The delay was ascribed to serious differences between the ruling PPP and the NAP over the form and extent of federalism in the country and to the debate concerning the 1972 Simla Agreement in the national assembly. When the assembly met on 14 August 1972, it unanimously extended the time for submitting the draft constitution until 31 December 1972.[41] On the floor of the house, the law minister committed that they should not have to come back to this assembly again for further extension.[42] The powers of the president in pursuance of the declaration of emergency continued until the emergency was lifted.

MEETING OF PARLIAMENTARY PARTY LEADERS

Approval of the constitution in the parliament could only be possible after an agreement between political parties. Many major issues of the constitution were settled in the deal that came out after negotiations. Bhutto called a meeting of all parliamentary party leaders on 17 October 1972, in which, after a long discussion, they produced what is commonly known as the 20 October Constitutional Accord, which formed the basis

of the 1973 constitution. The accord was signed and applauded by all
the parties present in the national assembly.[43] The accord was hurriedly
dictated by Rafi Raza, with Mubashir Hasan filling in certain financial
aspects, in order to confirm points of agreement in writing before any of
the participants had any second thoughts.[44] There were ten signatories
and forty-four articles in the accord, which covered the most ticklish
and fundamental issues.[45]

Bhutto was delighted with the outcome, observing nothing ominous
since participants' group photographs indicated that nothing could go
wrong again. The accord was drafted and agreed upon more smoothly
than was anticipated. In a brief public statement, Bhutto thanked
all representatives of the parties who participated in the discussions.
He recognized their role by saying that they had made significant
contributions, and that without their contribution, a satisfactory
compromise would not have been possible, and that each one of them
had played a part.[46]

The parliament gained autonomy with this compromise, as
the opposition as well as the government parties, which had some
representation in the parliament agreed to the points of the draft
constitution, which later led to smooth decisions within the party. This
was possibly the first (and certainly the last) time Bhutto expressed such
gratitude to the opposition.[47] The task of the Constitution Committee
was considerably simplified with this accord.

REPORT OF THE CONSTITUTION COMMITTEE

Despite lingering disagreements and differences, the committee was
able to place the draft constitution before the national assembly on
31 December 1972, together with the objections and dissenting notes
of five out of the twenty-five members. The report of the Constitution
Committee was presented by the law minister, Abdul Hafeez Pirzada.

Several committee members appended notes of dissent to the report,
even on matters settled earlier during the 20 October accord. Primarily,
they were in respect to the Political Parties Act, fundamental rights
concerning property, the dissolution of assemblies, separation of the
judiciary from the executive, Islamic provisions, and an independent

election commission.[48] Five of the original members of the committee resigned gradually, four of them (Dr Mubashir Hasan, Mustafa Khar, Meraj Khalid, and Mumtaz Ali Bhutto) because of other governmental responsibilities, while Ghaus Bakhsh Bizenjo resigned because his party, the NAP, had not whole-heartedly supported his signature on the constitutional accord. They were replaced by five other MNAs: Malik Mohammad Jafar, Chaudhry Jahangir Ali, Chaudhri Barkatullah, Malik Sikander Khan, and Mrs Jennifer Jehanzeba Qazi Musa.[49]

The draft constitution comprised 278 articles and six schedules. The committee held forty-eight sittings, stretching over a period of thirty-eight working days and 175 working hours. The average attendance throughout the sittings was eighteen out of twenty-five members.[50]

In its deliberation, the committee made every endeavour to arrive at a consensus, and differences of opinions were resolved as far as possible in an atmosphere of free and open debate.[51] In preparing the draft of the permanent constitution for Pakistan, the members of the committee took full cognizance of the realities and objective conditions of Pakistan. They kept their pledge with God and Man in proposing a basic law for Pakistan 'which would not only help create a progressive and egalitarian society but would also provide effective deterrence against exploitation of all forms.' The basic law, if accepted and adopted by the national assembly, would open all possible avenues of progress and prosperity.[52]

During deliberations, the law minister said that the committee was particularly conscious of the unfortunate constitution-making history of Pakistan and past failures of the process. He stated that the highest consideration before the committee were the people of Pakistan. He emphasized that the focus was on establishing the power of the citizens and giving them the right to elect their representatives, thus having an important say in the matters of the nation. [53]

However, the committee's report, which prefaced the draft bill, contained a number of 'Notes of Dissent' from which it reneged on their previous commitment in the accord. The bone of contention was the degree of power in the hands of the prime minister/chief minister by virtue of the articles governing no-confidence motions (99 and 136). Under article 99, a resolution for a vote of no-confidence against the prime minister could be moved.[54]

Although the Constitution Committee's report was signed by all the members (except Daultana), a number of 'Notes of Dissent' were attached to it.[55] After Pirzada's presentation, Wali Khan requested the government to facilitate a national debate on the draft through media.[56] According to Maulana Noorani and Prof. Ghafoor Ahmad, 'the provision of article 230 (3) will make the advice of the Islamic Council ineffective, therefore, article 230 (3) be deleted.'

PPP, however, did not honour the accord fully during the functioning of the assembly. On 22 January 1973, Sardar Shaukat Hayat (the opposition spokesperson in the national assembly) gave the first of several promised radio and television broadcast appearances by opposition leaders on the constitutional crisis. He accused the PPP of violating some provisions of the constitutional accord, and suggested six points[57] that he felt should be implemented at once.[58] Shaukat Hayat pointed out that the constitutional accord had been a package deal and that by altering some of its provisions, the PPP had struck at the spirit and foundation of the accord.[59]

DISMISSAL OF THE NAP–JUI GOVERNMENT IN BALOCHISTAN

Difficulties in the assembly heightened in February 1973 due to the dismissal of the NAP–JUI government in Balochistan, the change of NAP governors in the two provinces, and the resignation of the NAP–JUI government in the NWFP. Bhutto's attitude towards the opposition brought unity in their ranks and they jointly presented a list of proposed amendments to the constitution bill on 17 March 1973. The relations further deteriorated following the bloody disruption of the opposition's public meeting at Liaquat Bagh, Rawalpindi on 23 March 1973. They had already boycotted the assembly proceedings, and the following day, published their eleven-point demand.[60]

THE FRAMING OF THE CONSTITUTION

The task of the framing of the constitution, which the parliamentarians completed within the assembly or by coming to a compromise outside the assembly, was not an easy one. It was expected that after the separation of its eastern wing, 'new' Pakistan should have no exceptional difficulties or problems in framing a constitution. However, unlike Bangladesh, Pakistan's constitution making in 1972–3 was a complicated task and was marked by several acute clashes between the government and the opposition parties, both in and out the assembly.[61]

The old and complicated issues faced by constitution makers in Pakistan were revived: the relationship between the state and religion, i.e. controversy over the details of an 'Islamic constitution', distribution of power between the centre and the provinces, and the kind of executive suitable for Pakistan. All these old issues generated extensive and heated debates in the country even after its dismemberment, at a time when unity in the truncated Pakistan was vital for its survival. The controversy over an 'Islamic State'—with its prolonged record[62]—took a dramatic turn when the 'secular oriented' Bengalis were no longer present in the assembly. The orthodox elements in the western wing of the country, though defeated in the general elections of 1970, joined together to put up a brave fight to preserve cherished Islamic values and traditions.[63]

The constitution bill was finally introduced in the national assembly by the law minister on 2 February 1973, where it was debated on 17 February. By that time, the national assembly, acting as the constituent assembly, began a clause-by-clause examination of the new permanent constitution. Therefore, the house reconvened to debate on the draft constitution after thirty-three days of the introduction of the report. It was for the first time in the history of Pakistan that a formal bill was being introduced to provide for a permanent constitution for the country; for the first time, this constitution was to be framed by a representative assembly.[64]

The opposition, who had boycotted the legislative proceedings due to the government's unethical act in the form of the removal of the Balochistan government, or banning of the NAP, returned for the constitutional session, when many clauses were contested. The opposition (with about forty votes) could not gather enough PPP rebels to present any real challenge to the government in terms of votes. However, they did not allow themselves to be trampled by the PPP majority either.[65]

The opposition, by now, realized that they could not continue the boycott of the assembly session any longer. This way, the government could do anything to further its own agenda, and frame the constitution without including opposition in the process, thus taking credit for the making of the constitution. Despite having serious reservations, the opposition preferred to participate in the constitution-making process instead of remaining outside it. This automatically increased the status of the parliament, and also made the task easier.

The assembly formed the constitution autonomously, and it was almost a unanimous function of the assembly that a constitution with the consent of both government and opposition came into existence. After the approval of the constitution, the role of the assembly as an institution diminished because a rubber stamp was Bhutto's ally, and he amended the constitution according to his whims and caprices.[66]

The majority party, the law minister said, was wide open for compromise on all points except the measure of provincial autonomy and the division of power between the federal and provincial governments. During the debate, the government made a number of concessions to the opposition's views, for example, by dropping the clause providing that a motion of no-confidence against the government could only be passed by a two-thirds majority. Even so, the bill seemed certain of a rough journey until approved; all the opposition parties, ranging from the profoundly radical NAP to groups on the far right, banded together in the UDF and suggested some 1600 amendments. They seemed determined to obstruct the bill until it was modified to meet its large majority and to force the bill through the national assembly by sheer might of voting power; this was not President Bhutto's intention.

Prior to the introduction of the draft constitution as a bill on 2 February 1973, the opposition parties in the assembly resolved that they would resist all efforts to pass an un-Islamic, undemocratic, non-parliamentary, and non-federal constitution, and that if their legitimate amendments were not accepted, they would have no choice except to go back to the masses. However, when the national assembly initiated debate on the constitutional bill on 17 February, the ruling PPP seemed willing to seek the co-operation of opposition parliamentary groups 'in rectifying whatever mistakes might have crept into the draft'.[67]

There were certain problems in the functions of the parliament. The debate over the constitution continued in its usual desultory fashion even after 17 February 1973. This first reading produced a crop of very lengthy, repetitive, and often irrelevant speeches from both sides of the house—the PPP extolling, the opposition denigrating the draft constitution, and little being done to prepare the way for some sort of constructive consensus or compromise.[68] Nevertheless, the activity of constitution-making continued. The debate on the draft in the assembly sustained spasmodically from February to April of 1973, during which time the opposition parties formed, for greater leverage, the UDF.[69]

Formation of United Democratic Front (UDF)

The major opposition parties gathered together in Islamabad on 2 March 1973 to form an alliance. The aim of the alliance was to restore democracy, combat dictatorship, and to devise a plan for a truly Islamic and parliamentary constitution.[70] After Sheikh Mohammad Rashid's amendment for a socialist basis of economy was passed on 13 March 1973, opposition parties formed a formal alliance called the UDF. Pir Syed Shah Mardan of Pagara Sharif was appointed its president and Maulana Shah Ahmad Noorani became the chairman of the coordinating committee.

By March, the assembly had proceeded to a second clause-by-clause reading of the bill. Meanwhile, the UDF drafted a charter of demands and handed them over to Prime Minister Bhutto on 16 March. The demands were related to the independence of the judiciary, the election commission, fundamental rights, and powers of the chief executive. After getting no response from Bhutto, they decided to organize a public meeting in Rawalpindi to explain its position. As a result of this action, the government accused the opposition of threatening the assembly of boycott after their attempt to slow down its proceedings.[71]

On 23 March 1973, PPP workers aided by the Punjab police opened fire on a public gathering of UDF in Liaquat Bagh, Rawalpindi, killing and injuring several.[72] After this tragic incident, the UDF boycotted the session of the national assembly.[73] The UDF, being unable to stop the approval of articles by normal methods, walked out of the assembly and said that they would not return until their demands were taken into consideration. They demanded amendments to the bill based on their eleven-point agenda. The main difference of opinion was on the provisions relating to fundamental rights, the powers of the prime minister, the courts and the senate, the continuation of the state of emergency, and conducting fresh elections.[74] Thus, most of the matters were discussed outside the parliament. The UDF eventually reduced their demands after the passage of the constitution act, to the one demand that a caretaker government should be installed, and assurance that the elections should be held within six months.[75]

The second reading of the draft constitution got off to a bad start on 9 March 1973 with two walk-outs by the opposition, and the whole session taken up with just one article—article 2—which stated that that Islam would be the state religion. However, before debate on article 2 began, there was an hour-long argument over the decision to leave discussion of the preamble and article 1 towards the end of the debate. The question of whether to postpone discussion on article 1 was put to vote, and carried by eighty-nine votes to nineteen. Due to this, the opposition walked out. While they were out (for about five minutes), the house proceeded to article 2 and rapidly dispensed with nine of the opposition's twelve amendments. The opposition returned and protested bitterly at this inconsiderate treatment of their amendments, but to no avail. Their three remaining amendments, which sought to bring all laws into conformity with the injunctions of the Quran and Sunnah, were also rejected after considerable discussion, all by large government majorities. This episode produced the sight of the avowedly secular NAP backing the demands of the right-wing religious parties to the hilt.[76]

The opposition's response to these reverses was to issue a press statement the next day claiming that the constitution, which the government was 'bulldozing through the House', would destroy any remaining chances of national integrity. It castigated the government for its refusal, both to define the territories of Pakistan and to make the declaration of Islam really effective.[77]

The process in approval of article 2(a) on 13 March 1973, marked the collective work done by the parliament. The government proposed and passed a new article, laying down that Islamic Socialism, which reflected the concepts of *Musawat-e-Mohammadi* (equality as preached by the Prophet [PBUH]) would be the basis of the nation's economy.

Sheikh Rashid, the minister for food, first proposed that socialism should be the basis of the economy. The addition of the word 'Islamic' was later proposed by a PPP backbencher. Kausar Niazi, the minister for information, sensed that a large number of PPP MNAs were unsatisfied and thus introduced the *Musawat-e-Mohammadi* phrase. The new article 2(a) was passed with a significant majority.[78]

When the opposition continued their boycott on the constituent assembly, on 30 March 1973, Bhutto announced that he would make every possible adjustment to achieve consensus over the constitution. However, he also added that 'consensus was desirable but not essential'.[79] On 1 April, UDF allowed its members to meet Bhutto and reduce their differences.[80]

On 2 April 1973, Bhutto made an unconditional final offer to the opposition for negotiations to end the boycott. At this, some members belonging to opposition parties met with Bhutto.[81] On 4 April 1973, Bhutto offered a further concession related to the dissolution of the assembly, centre-province relations, and stability on the condition that the opposition return by 7 April and remain in the house until the adoption of the constitution. He threatened to pass the constitution without the opposition if they did not comply; the government had the support of 110 of 146 members.[82]

The opposition turned down Bhutto's offer and decided to continue the boycott.[83] Abdul Hafeez Pirzada told the national assembly that despite the decision of the opposition to continue the boycott, the government would amend the constitution in light of the concessions made by Bhutto.[84] The opposition continued bargaining till the last moment. However, it made a dramatic return a few minutes before the final adoption of the constitution, and it was unanimously adopted.[85] It is important to mention that the boycott of the UDF was not very effective as many opposition members, including Maulana Ghulam Ghaus Hazarvi and Maulana Abdul Hakeem, did not take part in the boycott, and continued their efforts to Islamize the constitution with their amendments.

Articles 3 and 4 were passed again with an overwhelming majority; but the opposition was said to have tabled 300 amendments on the first 40 articles. However, the government appeared confident, and it seemed unlikely that they would allow the opposition's harassment to prevent the adoption of the constitution within the scheduled time.[86]

The achievement of the government, and particularly of Bhutto's and Abdul Hafeez Pirzada's (minister for law and parliamentary affairs) of getting the new constitution drawn up and accepted by representatives of all political parties first and then almost unanimously by the assembly, all in less than a year, was indeed a considerable one.[87]

The support of the opposition in strengthening the parliament and for its help in the parliament's smooth functioning cannot be ignored in spite of the government acting without taking the parliament into full confidence. A presidential ordinance of 8 March 1973 amended the interim constitution so that the central and provincial ministers who were not MNAs were able to retain their posts until 14 August 1973, instead of 21 April 1973 (as was originally stated in articles 63 and 104 of the interim constitution). This meant that central ministers, J.A. Rahim and H.M.K. Sherpao, had received an extension of four months in their role.[88]

On 8 March 1973, Mumtaz Daultana (MNA and Pakistan's ambassador to the UK) appealed to all political parties, including his own, to facilitate the approval and adoption of the draft constitution at an early date. According to him, the draft was more Islamic than the '1956 Constitution as it had declared Islam as the state religion' and 'is more stringent in its Islamic clauses.'[89]

The constitution represented a consensus on four matters: the role of Islam in politics, the sharing of power between the federal government, the federal provinces, and the division of responsibility between the president and the prime minister.[90]

The formation of the constitution may be called one of the most brilliant successes of the parliament, despite disputes and controversies. On 24 July 1973, during his visit to UK, Bhutto said that Pakistan had established institutions of government which assured the stabilization of its political life. The federal constitution developed with the nation's unanimous support solved the problem of the autonomy of the constituent units and safeguarded national solidarity. Bhutto also shared that Pakistan had staged an economic recovery much more rapidly and confidently than that of any nation ravaged by war. [91]

At that time, the representative institution was comparatively strong. Bhutto obtained a mandate from the parliament just before leaving for his UK tour to accord a *de jure* recognition to Bangladesh at an appropriate time.[92] Despite being a strong chief executive of the country, Bhutto decided not to decide on his own and preferred to get the backing of the parliament as it was the representative institution. This shows the legitimate worth of the representative institution, although in practice it was not as strong.

Bhutto's desire for the adoption of the constitution by the parliament unanimously increased the possibilities of the strength of the parliament. However, there was one member of the assembly, a *maulana* (Muslim religious scholar), who wanted money in lieu of his vote. The amount was settled, and Bhutto, in describing the situation to Mubashir Hasan, said that when the fellow came to the President House to collect the money, Bhutto threw the stack of notes on the floor in front of him. The man was moving on all fours on the carpet, picking a bundle from here and there.[93]

The activities in the corridors of the assembly, during the constitution-making days and on the day of the adoption of the constitution, marked that the parliament was the primary institution of the state. Every member of the assembly became significant when the ruling party directed members to include the opposition and bring an end to the boycott.

The third reading of the constitution bill began on 9 April 1973, in the absence of the opposition. The federal minister of law and parliamentary affairs made an appeal to the opposition as a last attempt to reach a settlement with the majority party. As a result of discussions which took place outside the assembly, the UDF leaders agreed to meet President Bhutto. Once again, with a characteristic *coup de theatre*, Bhutto pulled a rabbit from his hat. It was apparent on 9 April 1973 that activities were underway to bring the opposition back into the assembly for the adoption of the constitution. Negotiations continued on the morning of 10 April 1973, in the national assembly lobbies, when at first Pirzada, and then Bhutto himself met the opposition leaders. These meetings proved to be a turning point; the president agreed to accept all of the UDF's eleven points if the opposition returned to the assembly. The compromise necessitated the amendment of seven articles which had already been adopted. Meanwhile, in the assembly, which had met at 10 a.m., members were marking time with inconsequential speeches. At about 1 p.m., Pirzada announced that the opposition had called off its boycott, and at 1:20 p.m., the opposition members entered the chamber.[94]

The amendments suggested by the opposition were included, and the constitution was made into a document on which a consensus existed. Pirzada moved the seven amendments which, ostensibly, had led to the opposition's return. Following this, Pirzada and Bhutto made their speeches, and finally adopted the constitutional bill without a dissenting vote, though not unanimously.[95] In the house of 144 members, the constitution was approved by 125 of the 128 voters.[96] The members who abstained from the voting included Shah Ahmad Noorani, Mian Mahmud Ali Kasuri, and Ahmad Raza Kasuri.[97] On that occasion, the law minister moved a motion that, 'this Assembly resolves that steps be taken to enable Members of the Constituent Assembly to sign the Constitution of the Islamic Republic of Pakistan for the purpose of it being deposited in the National Museum.'[98]

In his speech, Bhutto said that one lesson of politics he had learnt was that one should avoid the 'points of no return'. To this end, he had kept the door open for the opposition, right up until 11:30 a.m. that morning, when he had agreed to have discussions with opposition leaders.[99] He denied the opposition's claim that he wished to be a dictator and pointed out that the final verdict on this would lie with the people. On the constitution-making issue, he said that the opposition's argument that all federating units must individually agree to the constitution did not hold good in the case of units within a state. Since the opposition too had conceded to provide Pakistan with a constitution which was unanimously agreed upon, Bhutto requested them to let go of this demand. He was not prepared to commit to lifting the emergency regulation. He reminded them that there would be time to consider such an option after the POWs returned. After the adoption of the bill, the house was adjourned *sine die*. There were emotional scenes as members from both sides, including Wali Khan and Pirzada, embraced each other.[100]

It seemed strange that the opposition had been lured back by these seemingly insignificant amendments. Possibly, the opposition had realized that Bhutto had manoeuvred public opinion against them, and were content with the amendments as a face-saving device. Bhutto may have promised them more in private. Ghafoor Ahmad, the leader of Jamaat-i-Islami, for instance, said that the government had promised to cease its attacks on the opposition leaders in the news. He also claimed that there could have been some understanding with the NAP–JUI about the administrations in NWFP and Balochistan. [101]

It was clear that President Bhutto would be able to pass the constitution with the support of the large majority which he commanded in the national assembly, but it was uncertain whether or not he would be able to gain the opposition parties' approval. They had contested nearly every clause of the constitution in its passage through the assembly until they decided to boycott the proceedings altogether just over three weeks ago.[102] They maintained this boycott right up to the last minute. But the amendments which were introduced as a result of the talks between the opposition and the government satisfied enough of their demands to enable them to return to the assembly and take part in the nearly unanimous vote in favour of the constitution.

Afterwards, the ceremony of signing the historical document of the constitution took place. In that ceremony, 137 members signed the original document of the constitution. Eight members of the assembly who did not take part in the voting also put their signatures on the approval of the constitution. This fact proved that there were fewer controversies in its approval. Eight members refrained from signing the document.[103]

The PPP felt miraculously lucky to get unanimous authentication of the constitution. It was the fifth to be drafted, the third to be adopted with no opposing vote, and gained the support of all but three members of the opposition group.[104]

Opposition leaders explained why they cooperated with the government in the constitution-making process, despite being treated unfavourably. Dr Abdul Hayee Baloch shared that the quality of the constitution owes itself to the participation of the opposition. If the opposition did not contribute positively or play a vibrant role in the formulation of the constitution, it would remain a controversial document.[105]

The UDF issued a statement that bore the details of the constitutional amendments proposed by the opposition. These suggestions were made public; they were not adopted by the assembly. On that occasion, the opposition declared that they signed the constitution to save the country from possible civil war.[106]

Two days later, on 12 April 1973, the constitution was authenticated by the president. Bhutto was keen on the constitution carrying broad political consensus; his concern for a stable executive was also conceded. Through this constitution, Bhutto was made powerful, and a vote of no-confidence against the prime minister was virtually made impossible for ten years in view of the conditions which were required to be satisfied before it could be moved.[107]

The elected representatives of the people solved the difficult and sensitive issues regarding the autonomy of the provinces, and the conflict on whether a presidential or parliamentary system of governance should emerge. It also reflected on the sense of responsibility that the parliamentary opposition in the national assembly showed in solving the intractable problem of framing a constitution for Pakistan. The opposition, therefore, accepted many of Bhutto's proposals including the powers assumed by the federal government that were not normally associated with a parliamentary democracy.[108]

The adoption of the new constitution became an occasion for nationwide celebration; 12 and 13 April were observed as public holidays; Pakistani missions abroad also remained closed while office workers throughout the country received two days of paid holidays. Over the course of the national celebration, President Bhutto visited Lahore and Karachi and laid a wreath on the mausoleums of Allama Iqbal and Quaid-i-Azam Mohammad Ali Jinnah. [109]

This most impressive work on the part of the assembly made Bhutto express pride and take credit for it as if it were his own personal achievement. Bhutto's biographer, Stanley Wolpert, pens down this achievement in the following words, 'Zulfi fondly hoped that his most impressive political achievement to date would long outlive his own tenure in high office, ten more years seeming to him at this time perhaps all that remained for his enjoyment.'[110]

Bhutto's claim was not without substance. However, the endorsement of Bhutto's claim does not lessen the status of the achievement of the parliament. It, in fact, strengthens the view that Bhutto empowered the assembly in order to frame and adopt the constitution. The support of the parliament made it possible for Bhutto to take credit for what the assembly did.

The 1973 constitution was adopted along with the compromises by all the political parties in the national assembly. Undoubtedly, no constitutional document could be described as perfect. It was a product of compromises amongst various political parties and other forces present within the constitution-making body.[111]

The constitution passed by the parliament received applause from across the country. Almost all the newspapers were full of praise over this brilliant venture of the elected representatives of Pakistan. On 11 April 1973, all English and Urdu newspapers published stories about the adoption of the constitution by the national assembly as a result of a 'dramatic last-minute consensus'. Highlights included welcome statements by opposition leaders such as Wali Khan of NAP and others who agreed to end their boycott of the assembly after the ruling party had agreed to incorporate more of their amendments to the constitution.[112]

Although pro-opposition and independent *Nawa-i-Waqt* criticized some of the clauses of the constitution, it still praised the adoption and did not deny the superiority the parliament gained with its adoption. The leader of *Nawa-i-Waqt* said some of the clauses of the constitution smacked of despotism. It spoke of mass arrests of political opponents, and took strong exception to the weeklong celebrations and the two holidays 'at a time when more work was the need of the hour'.[113]

Bhutto's treatment of the opposition in the last stage of the adoption of the constitution was also admired by some of the newspapers. *Jang* and *Taameer*, editorially congratulated the people of Pakistan on the 'auspicious occasion' and prayed for the stability and prosperity of the country. Both praised the consensus on the constitution. *Jang* said a constitution must be regarded as a sacrosanct guide to the conduct of national affairs. It praised Bhutto's foresightedness, with particular reference to the way in which he had kept the doors open for reconciliation with the opposition.[114] The opposition's treatment of the government and their common efforts to take credit for the venture raised the standard of the parliament to new heights.

The adoption of the constitution was considered to be a success on the part of the government and other political forces in the country. Like *Jang*, *Taameer* expressed positive views, 'The whole world has seen that a staggering, stumbling Pakistan has managed to come to stay after having faced heavy odds'.[115]

Jamhoor, a pro-opposition paper, while objecting to the celebrations, also accepted the fact that the approval of the constitution was a great success for the ruling party. However, the paper also strongly praised the opposition in glowing terms for helping incorporate important amendments in the constitution.[116] Praise for the ruling party from a pro-opposition paper marked a collective admiration for the work of the parliament.

Another independent newspaper, *The Sun*, praised the parliament in unequivocal terms. The headline 'O Joy' expressed the satisfaction and pleasure that the paper experienced at the time of the adoption of the constitution. The satisfaction over the performance of the parliament was described with the following words:

For us, it's a matter of no ordinary satisfaction that the elected representatives have honoured their mandate...no doubt there will be problems and transitory difficulties. But, they who have succeeded in giving the country the Constitution can be counted upon to work on it and also to improve it.... As for Mr Bhutto, it is a personal triumph.[117]

Pakistani vice-president, Nurul Amin (who belonged to the former East Pakistan), admired the constitution's capacity to curb separatism. He pointed out that the adoption of the constitution had lessened the chances of the division of the country in more parts. He did not endorse those people who boycotted the session of the assembly when it was adopting the constitution.[118]

Some newspapers welcomed the venture of the national assembly, especially as a productive development since the setback of 1971. Under the title 'Welcome to Sunshine', the *New Times* described the adoption of the constitution as the dawning of a new epoch in the history of Pakistan, 'We had virtually lost our soul, and now, thank God, we have regained it.'[119]

On 14 August 1973, the constitution came into effect.[120] Bhutto stepped down to become prime minister and the speaker of the national assembly, and Fazal Elahi Chaudhry was elected president of Pakistan. In this way, Pakistan gave up the presidential system introduced by Ayub Khan, and reverted to the parliamentary tradition upon which the entire sub-continent had been educated by the British.[121]

In enacting the constitution, the national assembly reverted to the blend of federal and parliamentary government that existed in the 1956 constitution.[122] In many respects, the adoption of the new constitution marks a turning point in the history of Pakistan. For the first time, a constitution was created by the elected representatives of the people, closely in touch with public opinion. It was based on a consensus, and provided for an adult franchise as the basis of its election, and set up a federation consisting of all the provinces.[123] It is claimed that the 1973 constitution resolved all long-standing issues in Pakistan, especially those between the provinces and the centre; this proved to be chimerical.[124]

As far as the sovereignty of the assembly during the aforementioned period is concerned, it is easy to conclude that the assembly proved to be a sovereign body at least between 1971 and 1977—the fateful years of the life of Pakistan. The assembly conceded to most of the members' desires. Even the aspirations of the opposition were respected to a large extent. The assembly was a success in real terms, as it determined the fate of all of the institutions of the state of Pakistan. It was the assembly that gave constitutional recognition to all the institutions of the state, including the executive branch, the army, the judiciary. Even the state itself derived its sovereignty from the sovereignty of the assembly, when the latter framed and adopted the constitution. The assembly, while determining the role of other institutions, also determined its own role as well as that of future legislatures of Pakistan.

Chapter Five

Parliament's Durability
Efficiency on National Issues (1973–7)

A common practice in most countries governed under democratic and parliamentary systems is that the contents of the bill on any issue are made known to the press, so that all sections of society are informed. Discussions follow within the basic organizations, industrial and agricultural undertakings, professional and trade organizations of all kinds, people's councils, social, scientific and economic institutions, and local and regional administrations. Opinions are gathered, and suggestions, amendments and perhaps counter-proposals are drawn up, which are then forwarded to the parliament, and in particular to their appropriate committees. These committees examine them, and may, if necessary, formally take them into consideration. Thus, a countrywide discussion takes place which introduces, to some degree, a new form of direct democracy.[1] In this way, the durability and the debate of the parliament become of high value due to the inclusion of the masses and their feedback.

In Pakistan, however, amendments have been passed suddenly and without any discussion in the press, or even within the parliament. Most of the time, major changes received little attention from the press before the bill was safely passed. The government was seemingly engaged in a large-scale campaign to justify that amendment,[2] while in actuality, it wanted to control its political opponents.[3] The government's narrative stated that the amendments in no way affected the three basic pillars of the constitution: provincial autonomy, independence of state institutions, and parliamentary democracy. The government also asserted that the controversial elements in the amendments merely clarified the powers of the judiciary and the executive. These justifications would have been more useful had the matter been made public before the assembly actually considered the amendment.[4]

The parliament could not take up the issue of the jurisdiction of the superior court having been curtailed in the Fourth Amendment (November 1975) because the bill was rushed through the parliament. This was despite the outcry of the opposition members[5] who were physically thrown out of the national assembly by Federal Security Force personnel in civilian clothes at the time the Amendment Act was being passed.[6] The amendments in the constitution were passed the same day that they were suggested to the assembly. The rules of the assembly authorized the speaker to adjourn the proceedings at the beginning of the discussions. However, these powers were never used at the behest and demand of the opposition. Mahmud Ali Kasuri, the first law minister, could not understand what havoc would arise if a discussion on any bill was adjourned for a few days for its proper consideration.[7] The bill was also passed in the senate on 17 November 1975 during its thirteenth session.

PROCLAMATION OF EMERGENCY

Before the establishment of the first ever directly-elected parliament, Yahya Khan had imposed martial law in the country on 25 March 1969.[8] During the phase of the martial law, he also placed the country under emergency on 23 November 1971 when Indian forces attacked the eastern wing of the country.[9] The parliament had inherited the proclamation of emergency, which was not a new experience. Under the proclamation of emergency, fundamental rights, though available on paper, were practically non-existent.[10] Unfortunately, the emergency had been invoked without due approval of any parliament.

The constitution was inaugurated, but the uninterrupted state of emergency continued. Through an ordinance, the government continued to curb access to fundamental rights that the constitution guaranteed.[11] In order to extend the period of emergency, the 1973 constitution required a reference to be made in a joint sitting of the parliament every six months. Under the constitution, the period of emergency could be six months at the most, and that also by the resolution of a joint sitting of the two houses of parliament.[12]

The parliament, for the first time, addressed the said issue during its joint sitting on 5 and 6 September 1973. That was the first special joint session of the parliament after the establishment of the senate, following the enforcement of the 1973 constitution. On the issue of an extension of emergency proclamation, the opposition boycotted the parliament session on the grounds that using extension as a tool, the government intended to humiliate the institution of parliament, and render it ineffective. The opposition alleged that an individual was running the country, whereas the assembly was present just to endorse his decisions.[13]

Discussion over the resolution for the continuation in force of the proclamation of emergency took place again during a joint session on 4 March 1974, when the parliament extended the state of emergency for a further six months.[14] The law minister advocated the extension of emergency on the grounds that the circumstances in the country were the same as they were in September 1973, when emergency was extended. He believed that the enforcement of the Simla Agreement required the continuation of the emergency state.[15] However, as many as nineteen parliamentarians expressed views against the extension[16] on the grounds that there was no cause for the extension of emergency, and that the government's objective was only to deprive the people of their fundamental rights. While the treasury resolution for the extension of the emergency period was approved, all amendments suggested by the opposition were rejected. The opposition resorted to a walk out in protest.[17]

Bhutto, the chief executive, was interested in retaining the proclamation as long as possible. Therefore, through the Third Amendment, the 1973 constitution was amended to empower the government to continue the state of emergency for an indefinite period, unless revoked by an adverse vote in the parliament.[18]

The parliament, in the changing circumstances, did not maintain its power of review of the proclamation of emergency, and voluntarily surrendered the compulsion on the government's part to present the proclamation every six months before the parliament. Malik Meraj

Khalid, the chairman of the select committee, in regards to the constitution's Third Amendment Bill, while presenting it in assembly, referred to the bill as 'democratic'. He pointed out the precedent of India where a state of emergency only ended when both houses of the Indian parliament ended it through means of a solution. Most important, in the context of the parliament, was a statement made by Meraj Khalid, in which he stated that 'we have provided the safeguards in the constitution which are altogether unnecessary; that we have to take approval of the parliament after every six months.'[19] When the bill was presented, the opposition had already boycotted the proceedings of the assembly due to protests on the political circumstances of the country.[20] Again, the report of the select committee was presented verbally, after the suspension of rules, as the written report was not yet ready.[21]

The opposition also seemed to be uninterested in the discussion over the bill in the select committee, indicating that the bill was 'not really a matter of controversy, and therefore, they did not consider it necessary' to participate in deliberations which were then conducted by six treasury members out of a total of ten members of the select committee.[22] However, Rao Khurshid Ali Khan, a PPP member from Sahiwal, opposed the bill in the house. He asserted that the solution suggested in the amendment was fatal for the country. The process of the amendment, in his view, was limited to some people only, and public opinion was not given any importance at all. Rao Khurshid pointed out that such an important amendment bill was included in the agenda on the very same day of its presentation in the assembly. Objection was also raised on the appointment of a member of the senate to the select committee. In his opinion, the amendment needed a considerably long debate in the house because of its importance.[23] However, Abdul Hafeez Pirzada refuted Rao Khurshid, and said that the elected parliament reflected the opinion of the people.[24]

Only three speeches were delivered on the amendment during the debate in the national assembly. The government was usurping rights of the parliament to review the emergency after every six months on the grounds, as Abdul Hafeez Pirzada mentioned, that they disrupt the functioning of the parliament for a joint meeting at the end of the year in order to fulfil constitutional obligations.[25] The bill was passed with a majority of hundred votes in favour and one against. No debate over the bill was conducted. It appeared that the national assembly was just a rubber stamp that was used for the approval of any amendment made in the constitution. The leader of the house, Zulfikar Ali Bhutto, in his speech, stressed on the need for the opposition's debate on the amendment,[26] but he did not mention that the responsibility of the government in regards to such an important role of amending the constitution would be delayed by one or two days, in order to get significant feedback and consensus from the opposition as well as from the treasury benches.

The Third Amendment Bill was passed on 12 February 1975 in the national assembly, and on the very same day, in the ninth session of the senate. Although, through this amendment, the parliament was awarded the right to revoke emergency even a day after its imposition with 50.1 per cent votes,[27] yet, the presentation of such a resolution, and obtaining the specified majority was more difficult for the parliament as compared to the obligatory presentation and review of the issue by the government. If the amendment was not placed, the state of emergency would come under review of the parliament every six months, as it was a constitutional obligation. The PPP government used the instrument of emergency throughout the period. Hence, the constitution was amended time and again to empower the government to continue the emergency indefinitely.

THE QADIANI ISSUE

The first directly elected national assembly was confronted with the question of the religious status of the Qadianis (or Ahmadis) soon after it passed the constitution in 1973. It was the second most important issue that the assembly had to deal with after the framing of the constitution. The decision of the parliament regarding this matter was passed through the Second Amendment to the constitution. After the dismemberment of Pakistan, the Qadiani question dominated the political scenario in mid-1974, and paved the way for the Second Amendment Bill.[28] The issue would reflect the strength of the parliament in terms of its institutional durability.[29] The parliament, as an institution, ultimately asserted its role despite the fact that the executive and the government were apparently not in favour of the parliament.

On 22 May 1974, at least 170 students of Nishtar Medical College (Multan) passed through Rabwah, the sacred and central city of the Qadianis. The latter alleged that these students raised slogans containing hate-speech at the Rabwah railway station.[30] Upon the students return on 29 May 1974, the compartment of the Chenab Express carrying them was attacked at Rabwah Railway Station. Allegedly, Qadianis detached the compartment from the train, and the student passengers were taken out and mercilessly beaten and harassed by armed hooligans, badly wounding many of them and depriving them of their valuables. This caused countrywide unrest forcing the issue to be discussed and resolved in the parliament.[31]

On 30 May 1974, the leader of the opposition in the Punjab assembly, Allama Rehmatullah Arshad, speaking on the incident, demanded an immediate investigation and urged the government to declare Qadianis a non-Muslim minority, and to remove them from all key posts.[32] The following day, Mufti Mahmud, Chaudhry Zahoor Elahi, and Sahibzada Safi Ullah moved adjournment motions in the national assembly to discuss the incident.[33] Abdul Hafeez Pirzada (law minister) opposed the motion as being an issue of a provincial nature. However, Chaudhry Zahoor Elahi, Prof. Ghafoor Ahmad, and Maulana Ghulam Ghaus Hazarvi spoke in its favour, but the motion was ruled out with a statement by Prime Minister Bhutto, stating that a court of inquiry would be appointed to look into the matter.[34]

Initially, the government and the speaker did not let the parliament discuss the issue on various pretexts. The parliament appeared to be somewhat less important compared to the institution of the judiciary and the provincial government. Moreover, rules of the parliament also barred discussions to be held on the issue. In fact, for the time being, the government succeeded to side-line the parliament on the issue. However, a number of members of the national assembly tabled a number of adjournment motions relating to the incidents which were taken up together. Though the motion to suspend rule 84—which was the bar to take up the motion before the disposal of the adjournment motion received earlier[35]—was put forward to the house and passed unanimously, the law minister raised preliminary legal objections in the text of the motion. The arguments advanced were that, under the constitution, maintenance of law and order was the exclusive responsibility of the provincial government, and that a judge of the High Court had been appointed to probe into the matter.[36] Hence, the motion was hit by rule 40 (f) and (n). The law minister insisted on waiting to see developments.

The opposition MNAs, Chaudhry Zahoor Elahi, Prof. Ghafoor Ahmad, Maulana Ghulam Ghaus Hazarvi, and Mufti Mahmud were successfully able to prove that the federal government was competent enough to tackle the situation. They argued that since the occurrence had taken place at a location which had attracted the provisions of the Railways Act, and that discussions in the provincial assembly could not bar discussions in the national assembly, the appointment of a provincial judge to probe the matter should not be taken as a hurdle to discussing the matter in the national assembly. They also contended that discussions would be useful in order to look into the basic problems of the issue, and to figure out a solution.[37]

Responding to arguments of the opposition, the prime minister stated that the adjournment motion was not the solution to the immediate problem. He said that the government was worried about it and the solidarity of the country was at stake. However, he believed that the situation should not be ignited, and that the citizens should not be allowed to kill each other. Moreover, he suggested that common sense demands that the matter should be taken up for discussion, either on-camera or on a party basis in the house, or whatever feasible method was devised. Therefore, instead of debate in the parliament, he supported an impartial inquiry by a judge of the High Court. He managed to convince the parliament to wait until the report of the tribunal was finalized.[38]

On 3 June 1974, the speaker allowed the matter to be discussed in the house after confirming the competency of the house to discuss it. However, the law minster again urged to let judicial inquiry be completed before the matter was discussed in the house. The prime minister realized that the issue was a serious one, but in his view, an adjournment motion on the subject was pointless as it was not an immediate problem.[39] He asked the JUI and JI that if the question of the Ahmadis as a minority was so serious, why they had not raised it at the time of framing of the constitution, or why they signed the constitution at all. He reminded the opposition that if they had objected to the category of minorities at the time of framing the constitution, they should have walked out because they had objected vehemently on other matters up to the last minute. [40]

Bhutto further argued that the issue had already been resolved in the question of oath-taking in which belief in the finality of the prophethood of Prophet Muhammad (PBUH) was clearly stated. He insisted that if the opposition still felt that there was scope to discuss it then they would do that but at a more appropriate time.[41] Finally, on 4 June 1974, the speaker ruled out any possibility of debate on the Qadianis issue by stating that the minorities had already been defined.[42] He ruled out all adjournment motions as out of order on the grounds that legal objections raised by the law minister remained unanswered, and stated that law and order was a provincial subject. Furthermore, since the matter at hand was a judicial matter, the determination of the status of any community required an amendment in the constitution which already had defined minorities. [43]

Bhutto did not want to resolve the matter through the assembly because he was more concerned about the nuclear testing that India was conducting around the same time. He asked his special assistant, Rafi Raza,[44] to meet with chief minister of Punjab, Hanif Ramay, to sort out the matter. According to Raza, Ramay was a mild person and an intellectual. Hence, both of them discussed the matter and suggested to Bhutto to take some administrative measures.[45]

The government was not willing to discuss the Qadiani issue in any case even if a group of parliamentarians, the majority of the electoral college, and public opinion was skewed against the Ahmadis. Meanwhile, the Rabwah incident had sparked demonstrations and protests throughout the country. On 14 June, a strike was observed on the call of the Majlis-i-Amal against the Qadianis.[46] According to Naeem-ud-Din, general secretary, Ahmadiyya Movement in Islam (Huddersfield, UK), about 500 houses and 600 shops of Ahmadis were looted and burnt, killing several members of the community.[47] Within two weeks, riots spread to the NWFP, costing a hundred lives. Only after it became clear that the riots which broke out in Punjab were serious, Bhutto referred the problem to the national assembly.[48]

Later on, developments outside the parliament forced Bhutto to address the nation through radio and television on 13 June, and to promise to place the matter before the national assembly after the ongoing budget session and have a resolution passed on the status of the Qadianis. The matter, he said, could be referred to the Supreme Court or the Council of Islamic Ideology.[49]

There were some important factors which may have led him to change his previous decision of not solving matters through the assembly. Firstly, he was disturbed by the reports that the Qadianis were changing their allegiance from PPP to Air Marshal (retd) Asghar Khan.[50] Secondly, at a foreign level, Zafarullah Khan started to appeal to international institutions and foreign offices to exert pressure on Pakistan for the safety of the Qadianis. Also, international media, especially of India and Britain, started to assert statements by Mirza Nasir and Zafarullah Khan, and described the situation as PPP-sponsored.[51] Zafarullah Khan also invited the international press to directly investigate the allegations. Hence, Zafarullah Khan and the Ahmadiyya chief made the issue more controversial by involving foreign media and agencies in their support.[52] On 10 June, three petitioners pleaded to call and examine Mirza Nasir as a witness after his interview with the Associated Press of America; but the court did not pass any orders to subpoena him.[53] In reaction, Mirza Nasir Ahmad termed this inquiry an 'aggression' engineered by Bhutto to crush their community.[54]

Bhutto sensed the workings of a foreign conspiracy in the anti-Ahmadiyya movement. He spoke about these problems in his address to the nation on 13 June 1974. He talked about international involvement in this issue, as well as the Indian atomic explosion, the Afghanistan President Sardar Dawood's visit to Moscow, and Wali Khan's presence in Kabul as a chief guest.[55] Under the above-mentioned circumstances, and extensive discussions with the chief minister of Punjab, the chief of army staff, and the ulema, Bhutto decided that the matter should be taken to the national assembly.[56] Moreover, on 9 June 1974, some eighteen political and religious parties held a conference, and established Muttahida Majlis-e-Amal for Tahaffuz-i-Khatm-i-Nabuwwat; Maulana Yusuf Binori was elected as its president and Mahmud Rizvi as its secretary general. Abdur Sattar Niazi, vice-president of Majlis-e-Amal, demanded the declaration of Ahmadis as non-Muslim and Rabwah an open city in addition to the removal of Qadianis from key posts along with the arrests of Mirza Nasir Ahmad and the culprits of the Rabwah incident by 13 June. Otherwise, he said, they would observe a strike on 14 June 1974.[57]

On 30 June 1974, Maulana Shah Ahmad Noorani passed a resolution in the assembly, signed by twenty-two members from both the government and opposition benches.[58] Bhutto was unhappy and disturbed with this resolution passed by the ulema, which declared Qadianis as non-Muslims. Despite Bhutto's disapproval, many members from PPP favoured the resolution due to their conviction that evidence against the Qadianis was irrefutable. Soon after this, Bhutto himself turned in favour of the resolution because, as Shah Ahmad Noorani observed, he became aware of certain intrigues of the Qadianis.[59]

The issue gained momentum with time. It was officially announced in Islamabad on 5 July 1974 that the prime minister's visit to the Soviet Union, scheduled to take place in the same month, had been postponed until October 1974. His representatives reasoned that there were more pressing issues to deal with in the national assembly. The sensitivity of the issue demanded attention, causing Bhutto to postpone all his visits in light of the countrywide chaos that ensued.

On 30 June, the national assembly, with the government's consent, previously engaged in the budget debate, turned its attention towards the Qadiani issue.[60] A resolution of motion was submitted by the law minister to determine the status of persons who did not believe in the finality of the prophethood of Prophet Muhammad (PBUH).[61] The house formed itself into a special committee to consider and make recommendations for the determination of the status of Qadianis and put the issue to rest.[62] From 30 June to 7 September 1974, the special committee, comprising the whole house, considered the matter on-camera.[63] The house adopted the procedure unanimously[64] and summoned many theological experts, including Sunni and Ahmadi scholars.[65] The house invited suggestions, motions, and resolutions from the members. The house also decided to set up a steering committee that would formulate a procedure for the special committee of the whole house, and would also assist the special committee in resolving the issue. The steering committee represented almost all parties in the house.[66]

The resolution, submitted by Hafeez Pirzada, regarding the determination of the status of the aforementioned individuals was carried unanimously. Also, another resolution from the opposition was moved which was also referred to the special committee of the house. From 30 June 1974, the committee of the house considered this matter. The sittings that took place during this period all took place on-camera. Also, it was decided that a steering committee would be formed to formulate the procedure for the special committee of the house. The steering committee consisted of some members from the PPP and the PML (Qayyum Group). There were also members from the opposition parties, with JUI represented by Mufti Mahmud and Maulana Ghulam Ghaus Hazarvi.[67] Additionally, there were representatives from the Council Muslim League, NAP, JI, Convention Muslim League, JUP, and Independents.

During this entire period of three months, a consensus and unity in the assembly was reached. Although there were some procedural and substantive difficulties, members were unanimous in the deliberation inside the committee, which also continued to work between the opposition parties and the prime minister (i.e. the leader of the house). During the final phase, representatives of the parties joined in the discussions and an informal concurrence was sought, as far as possible, of all the viewpoints represented in the house. Afterwards, a formal resolution was moved before the special committee; there were seven signatories, but informally, Maulana Ghulam Ghaus Hazarvi was also consulted who supported the viewpoint of the committee.[68]

During the sittings, the assembly examined witnesses who volunteered to appear before it. The assembly considered papers, and finally proposals were brought before the special committee, which were unanimously approved in the form of a recommendation. The committee recommended that:

The Special Committee of the Whole House, assisted by its Steering Committee and Sub-Committee, having considered the resolutions before it or referred to it by the National Assembly, and after perusal of the documents and examination of the witnesses, including the heads of Sadar Anjuman-i-Ahmadia, Rabwah, and Anjuman-i-Ahmadia Ishaat-i-Islam Lahore, respectively, unanimously made the following recommendations to the National Assembly:

(i) That in Article 106 (3) a reference be inserted to persons of the Qadiani Group and the Lahori Group (who call themselves 'Ahmadis');

(ii) That a non-Muslim may be defined in a new clause in Article 260.

That in the constitution of the Islamic Republic of Pakistan in Article 106, in clause (3), after the word 'communities', the words and brackets 'and persons of the Qadiani Group or the Lahori Group (who call themselves 'Ahmadis') shall be inserted; in the constitution, in Article 260, after clause (2), the following new clause shall be added, namely:

(3) A person who does not believe in the absolute and unqualified finality of the Prophethood of Muhammad (peace be upon him) the last of the Prophets, or claims to be a prophet, in any sense of the word, or of any description whatsoever, after Muhammad (peace be upon him), or recognizes such a claimant as a prophet or a religious reformer, is not a Muslim for the purposes of the constitution or law.[69]

Apart from these constitutional amendments, there were some recommendations with regard to legislative or procedural measures. These were:

That an explanation be added to the already existing Section 295 A of the Pakistan Penal Code to the effect that:

'A Muslim who professes, practices or propagates against the concept of the finality of the Prophethood of Muhammad (Peace be upon him) as set out in clause (3) of Article 260 of the Constitution, shall be punishable under this section.'[70]

It was also recommended that consequential legislative and procedural amendments might be made in relevant laws such as the National Registration Act 1973 and the Electoral Rolls Rules 1974.

The national assembly unanimously adopted the recommendations of the special committee of the whole house on the question of status in Islam of persons who do not believe in the finality of the prophethood. The Constitution (Amendment) Bill sought to amend the constitution of the Islamic Republic of Pakistan, which would allow the state to declare any person who does not believe in the absolute and unqualified finality of the Prophethood of Muhammad (PBUH) to be a non-Muslim.

The law minister reported that during the entire period, the house found consensus and unity. Although the assembly had some difficulty which was procedural and substantive, the parliamentarians were unanimous in the deliberation inside the committee. On 7 September, the law minister put recommendations before the house which were adopted as the Second Constitutional Amendment Bill 1974.[71] Finally, the special committee recommended to the national assembly that non-believers in the finality of the Prophethood of Muhammad (PBUH) were outside the fold of Islam.[72] The text of the proposed amendment was supported by Abdul Hafeez Pirzada, Mufti Mahmud, Maulana Hazarvi, Maulana Shah Ahmad Noorani, Professor Ghafoor Ahmad, Ghulam Farooq, Chaudhry Zahoor Elahi, and Sardar Maula Bakhsh Soomro.[73] Before the finalization of the decision of the special committee, a team of opposition in the national assembly consisting of Mufti Mahmud, Prof. Ghafoor Ahmad, Maulana Shah Ahmad Noorani, Chaudhry Zahoor Elahi, Ghulam Farooq, and Maula Bakhsh Soomro, had intense discussions with Bhutto and a government team consisting of Abdul Hafeez Pirzada, Maulana Kausar Niazi, and Yahya Bakhtiar (attorney general).[74] Thirty-one senators and 130 MNAs voted for the bill with none against it (the opposition's demands had been accepted). Voting in both the houses was a free one, with no party whips seen in action[75]

However, the unanimous adoption of the Constitution (Second) Amendment Bill 1974 did not give birth to a political détente, as both the PPP government and the opposition claimed it as their achievement. Thus, after this brief holiday of reconciliation, the pre-second amendment confrontational posture was resumed by PPP and the opposition.[76] This was considered a landmark victory for both the opposition and Bhutto who solved the ninety-year-old issue. Hanif Ramay, commenting on it, said that by resolving the religious issue, the national assembly had established a fundamental point that the institution of the national assembly was competent for *ijtihad* (logical reasoning to find a legal solution).[77]

If the situation had not been out of control, Bhutto would have neither decided to declare Qadianis as Ahmadis nor would the matter have been brought to the national assembly for a decision. In fact, Bhutto was not enthusiastic about rigid Islamic provisions in the constitution.[78] His acceptance of the assembly's decision was to save face and ward off foreign pressure. When the parliament wanted to initiate discussions on the issue, he did not let it do so, but when he found the parliament as an appropriate platform that could save him from the criticism from the secular groups within PPP, secular foreign powers and the Qadianis, he felt it expedient to call upon the parliament.

The MNAs sat in the house, first in the budget session and then in a secret session, for almost four months. The secret session was a rare experiment in a democratic process. The house sat for ten to fifteen hours, and on one particular day, it sat for sixteen hours through continuous cross examinations and speeches.[79]

The national assembly's resolution also recommended among other things, (1) that the following explanation should be added to section 295 (a) of the Pakistan Penal Code: 'a Muslim who professes, practices or propagates against the concept of the finality of the prophethood of Muhammad (peace be upon him) shall be punished under this section' (which allowed up to two years imprisonment); and (2) 'that the life, liberty, property, honour and fundamental rights of all citizens of Pakistan, irrespective of the communities to which they belong, shall be fully protected and safeguarded'.[80]

A majority of Muslims in Pakistan had long been in favour of the Ahmadi sect to be declared a non-Muslim community. There were approximately three to four million Ahmadis in Pakistan, and a disproportionately large number of them had been in positions of influence. The problem Bhutto faced during his election campaign in 1970 was that the Ahmadis had extended monetary and organizational support to him, but when he came to power, he sacked the chiefs of the three armed services and appointed two reputed Ahmadis as heads of the air force and the navy. With Ahmadis in command of at least two of the five army corps under the orthodox Tikka Khan, they seemed to be reaping their rewards.[81] Thus, Bhutto was not against the Ahmadis. There were other factors which led Bhutto to take steps for the declaration of the Ahmadis as non-Muslims through the constitutional amendment made by the parliament.

Through patience and artful tact, Bhutto managed to defuse the situation, and the Ahmadis were finally declared a non-Muslim minority in Pakistan, but without explicit prejudice to the positions or careers of individual Ahmadis.[82] Bhutto's position, through this decision, could get the support of all the Muslims in Pakistan, and for the time being, at least, was strengthened. It was possible that he could call elections to cash in on this.[83]

Instead of taking the risk of confronting the religious agitators, Bhutto decided to concede to their demands. This decision was followed by the formation of the ministry of religious affairs. According to left-wing members of the PPP, Maulana Kausar Niazi, the new minister for religious affairs and an erudite former member of JI, was believed to have close ties with security agencies.[84]

Bhutto said that he did not want to make a political capital, and that it was a unanimous decision of the entire house. Also, he said that the government had had elaborate discussions with all members of the house, representing all shades of opinions and all parties of the national assembly. Hence, the decision was a national decision. He remarked that he would not want any individual to take any credit for it. He opined that the decision had raised the status of the parliament and further expressed the necessity of a parliament for good governance. Bhutto further stated that the decision taken by the parliament was difficult and it could not have been made without democratic institutions and authority.[85]

Being a purely religious issue, it was not appropriate for Bhutto's government or for Bhutto, as an individual, to make a pronouncement on 13 June on this matter. Bhutto said that many had grievances about the issue and had asked him why he would not pronounce a decision there and then—a decision that the vast majority of the Muslims wanted—and that if he did this it would be a great credit to his government, and to him as an individual. There was an overwhelming stress on the fact that he would be losing the opportunity of a lifetime if he did not seize upon that moment to make a popular announcement.[86] He responded that the issue was very complicated and sensitive. It was a problem that had caused distress to the Muslims of the sub-continent for ninety years. Therefore, after restoration of democracy, he deemed the national assembly the highest forum in the land, and believed that the appropriate forum for the settlement of this dispute would be the national assembly and that he would like to leave this issue to the conscience of the members of the assembly and to the conscience of the members of his own party.[87]

Bhutto stated that he had let the members of his party decide by themselves. He mentioned that on many previous occasions, he had advised and instructed members of the PPP, but that in this particular matter, with the exception of one general meeting, he had given his members the liberty to make the decision without any influence.

Bhutto made himself aloof from the function of the assembly on the Qadiani issue by saying that it would not be his achievement. It would not be the achievement of the government. He stressed time and again that:

> It will be Pakistan's achievement. It will be the achievement of the people of Pakistan in which all of us will share. I want to give the whole House the credit for this decision. I know that this decision could not have been taken unanimously without adjustment and accommodation, and without the spirit of understanding shown by the whole House and by all parties represented in this House. We had this kind of spirit and understanding when we framed the constitution.[88]

On another occasion, Bhutto mentioned that it was important for the national assembly to meet in secret session because if the national assembly had not met in secret, all the truths would not have been revealed, and that the people would not have spoken as freely and as candidly as they did.[89]

Therefore, it can be concluded that the decision of the Qadiani issue was very difficult for Bhutto, even for PPP. Also, the decision could not be made by the judiciary alone, as there was need for legislation. Hence, it was only the parliament that could have taken a decision on this issue. Although, initially, Bhutto was not ready to put the matter before the parliament, some events and the pressure from religious scholars did not leave him any alternative but to take the concerned matter to the parliament. The parliament, therefore, proved its utility with proper skill, and tackled the issue with mastery and expertise. The decision of the parliament could be called a decision according to the sentiment of the people, and this decision forever resolved the issue that had been the bone of contention for ninety years.

FOREIGN POLICY AND THE PARLIAMENT

Legislative activity in connection with foreign policy acquires special significance because of three main reasons. Firstly, vital national questions, especially in a dependent economy with hostile neighbours, are linked up with the conduct of foreign affairs; secondly, the survival of developing countries like Pakistan depends on their ability to balance national interest against international political trends; and thirdly, foreign affairs is considered a special prerogative of the executive.[90]

In Pakistan, legislative discussions concerning foreign affairs have taken one of the following forms:

Foreign Policy Debates

The foreign policy of the country could not be discussed in the parliament through an adjournment motion because it was a wide subject. It was a well-settled principle that the internal or external policy of the country could not be debated upon by means of an adjournment motion. When a member sought to move the adjournment of the house on 6 August 1973 to discuss the foreign policy of Pakistan in light of the cancellation of the president's tour to the US, the speaker observed that minister of state for foreign affairs, Aziz Ahmad, offered to discuss the foreign policy on a day to be fixed in due course. Thereupon, the adjournment motion was withdrawn by its mover.[91] Hence, the offer of the minister of state was not accepted, and the foreign policy was never discussed.

The objectives of the foreign policy debate in the parliament, as mentioned by Bhutto, were not to make enemies. The intent was not to cause deterioration in relations with other states. On the contrary, the objectives were to promote friendship, to foster understanding, to clarify certain issues, and to remove friction and confusion. He categorically declared, 'were it not so, no responsible person would want a foreign policy debate.'[92]

Sharing his experience of the foreign policy debates in the sessions of former assemblies of Pakistan, Bhutto expressed the view that not in a single session had members reflected on the harm that the belief of the world's subservience to Pakistan could cause them. He felt that it had become fashionable to promote distrust and animosity, and not to appreciate friendship and goodwill. He then hoped that the house would be able to look at the course of events with sobriety and a sense of responsibility in order to make constructive contributions.[93]

On 1 April 1974, Khawaja Mohammad Safdar sought to move an adjournment motion in the senate to discuss the failure of the federal government to have the Kashmir issue included in the agenda of the Islamic Summit Conference held in Lahore. The chairman held that the motion apparently related to a matter that was not primarily the concern of the federal government. He ruled that the rules did not permit the matter to be discussed through an adjournment motion.[94]

It was generally felt that the national assembly, at that time, was not competent enough to have a debate on matters relating to foreign policy. On 2 December 1975, Ahmad Raza Kasuri moved an adjournment motion on the reintegration of, and close fraternal ties between Bangladesh and Pakistan. Malik Mohammad Akhtar opposed the motion on the grounds that Bangladesh was a separate country, and it was not in their public interest to discuss the matter. He also contended that it was not an urgent and definite matter of recent occurrence, and was not the primary concern of the federal government. However, Ahmad Raza Kasuri argued that the subject matter of his motion was not disallowed by any of the provisions of rule 80 of the *Rules of Procedure and Conduct of Business in the National Assembly, 1973*. Therefore, a discussion on the motion was permissible. He also stated that he was not proposing any legislation with respect to Bangladesh or its people, and was only suffusing discussion and debate, relating to matters of foreign policy. The speaker disallowed the motion on the grounds that it amounted to interference in the internal affairs of another friendly country which was against the policy of the government. He maintained that it was not the job of the MNAs to discuss statements made by nationals outside their country. He categorically ruled that the matter related to foreign policy could not be discussed through an adjournment motion by commencing debate on the foreign policy in the national assembly; this matter might be taken up later, but not through an adjournment motion.[95]

On 12 December 1975, Ahmad Raza Kasuri proposed to have a debate over foreign policy, but the speaker did not allow it at the time with the argument that the suggestion was premature and would be considered in the next session.[96] On 5 August 1976, a member sought leave of the house of senate to move an adjournment motion to discuss the signing of the agreement with India for running air services between the two countries (as reported in *Nawa-i-Waqt*, 14 July 1976) without getting the Kashmir issue resolved in line with the UN resolutions. The chairman, in disagreement with the mover, observed that the actual signing of the agreement was immaterial. He added that a joint statement regarding agreement between the delegations of the two countries to the resumption of over flights and air-links was placed before the house on 7 July 1976. Therefore, the member had failed to avail the earliest available opportunity to table the motion. Therefore the motion was ruled out of order.[97]

Adjournment motions were often simply used to put matters on record, and it appears that the members, too, were aware about whether or not the motions would be disallowed or would be called out of order. The adjournment motions were often disallowed on some ground or the other. The government too, gained benefits from the motion by explaining its position on it, to some extent, before the motion was ruled out.

The Budget Session Debate

A discussion on foreign policy matters takes place as a result of an opportunity offered by the budget session. However, no discussions on foreign policy took place during the budget session from 1973 to 1977.

Issue-oriented Debate

The issues of foreign policy discussed in the parliament are diverse in nature and of immense national significance or pertaining to relevant national emergencies. The debates on the Simla Accord, the recognition of Bangladesh, and departure from the Commonwealth were some major issues on which the parliament focused within the foreign affairs domain. The following section will focus on the analysis and discussion of all the aforementioned issues relating to foreign affairs.

THE QUESTION HOUR

Legislatives probed into the conduct of foreign policy through questions.[98] In the assembly, various questions were asked relating to matters of foreign policy. For instance, on 12 June 1973, Chaudhry Zahoor Elahi inquired about the resolution of Yugoslavia in the UN for the admission of Bangladesh, and Pakistan's response over it.[99] Maulana Ghulam Ghaus, on 26 June 1973, raised questions concerning agreements between Pakistan and India regarding Kashmir. The same members, on the same day inquired about the names of countries Pakistan had signed defence pacts with. In addition to this, the British government's treatment of Pakistanis in the UK after Pakistan's withdrawal from the Commonwealth came into question in the parliament on 26 June through a bill moved by Mian Gul Aurangzeb.[100] Often, the answers to these questions were short and brief, consisting of one or two lines. One word answers were usually the norm.

Bhutto, as chief executive, overruled the parliament most of the time while formulating foreign policies. Moreover, the foreign ministry executed the foreign policy as the executives wanted it. The US state department attributed the foreign policy of Pakistan (of balanced bilateralism) only to Z.A. Bhutto's credit. In August 1976, the US state department's analysis of Pakistan's foreign policy commented that, 'Bhutto has been trying to compensate for Pakistan's relative political, military and economic weakness by conciliating his neighbours, hedging his bets with the regional and world powers. The same month, in an article in *Pakistan Horizon*, Bhutto described his foreign policy as balanced bilateralism.'[101]

For his part, Bhutto continued to value good relations with the United States, and refrained from anti-US rhetoric, which had been his hallmark during his time as a foreign minister and leader of the opposition in the 1960s.[102]

Bhutto did not take the parliament into confidence and kept the key officials of Pakistan's foreign delegations unaware of important decisions. One such incident took place during the Simla talks. With Indira Gandhi at the peak of her power, Bhutto played a weak diplomatic hand with some skill when the two met during late June in 1972 at Simla. After several days of tough bargaining, Pakistan conceded, as India had long sought to settle all disputes peacefully and bilaterally, including the burning Kashmir issue. According to what Indira Gandhi told the Indian delegation, Bhutto also expressed willingness to settle the Kashmir dispute on the basis of the status quo with the Line of Control being declared as the border, but added that he needed time to gain political acceptance. However, Bhutto mentioned nothing pertaining to such acclaims.[103]

On 8 May 1974, India shook the global scene by detonating an underground nuclear device at the Pokhran test site in the Rajasthan desert.[104] The national assembly discussed the matter on 7 June amid disturbing news of the protests against the Qadianis. When members of the opposition and their leaders in the assembly sought to debate the nuclear explosion through an adjournment motion tabled by no less than five members of the opposition, the Bhutto government welcomed the initiative of the opposition on the grounds, as Bhutto called it, that the opposition 'showed responsibility'. Bhutto said it was the first time since the restoration of democracy in Pakistan that the opposition felt it necessary to close the ranks, and to establish a genuine national outlook towards the impending Indian danger.[105] In short, the parliament arose as a forum where an anti-India debate in support of the government's strict policy on the Indian explosion could take place.

RECOGNITION OF BANGLADESH

The Supreme Court of Pakistan accepted competence of the national assembly regarding the recognition of Bangladesh. On 9 July 1973, a member raised a point of order that the national assembly was not authorized to discuss a resolution for recognition of Bangladesh because both the speaker and members of the house were under oath to protect the sovereignty, solidarity, and integrity of Pakistan, whereas, the resolution sought the approval of the national assembly to the secession of a part of Pakistan. Earlier, this matter was referred to the Supreme Court by the president for advice under Article 187 of the constitution. The opinion delivered by the Supreme Court was that the national assembly could discuss the motion. In view of the verdict by the Supreme Court, the speaker ruled out the point of order.[106] This gave rise to a significant question: why did the parliament not just exercise its authority, without having to seek the support of the president or the Supreme Court's verdict? If the parliament had asserted its powers, the speaker of the national assembly would have started the process himself.

It may be argued that the executive did not wish to take the liability of an unpopular decision, and wanted to get support from other institutions so that the burden of the decision did not lie with him alone. However, that was not the case because ultimately, it was only the parliament that was 'sovereign enough to take the brunt of such a decision'. The Supreme Court could only have provided legal support. Therefore, it may be assumed that the speaker of the parliament did not feel strong enough legally to take the final decision on his own. In fact, it has been the practice in Pakistan's political history that unpopular decisions are sent to be decided by the parliament, and in order to share the responsibility of the decision, the parliament is provided with the support of other institutions. In order to gain popularity, popular decisions were made by the executive alone, without any proper discussion with or without the support of the parliament.[107]

The parliament was used as an institution to gain mandate and support. In July 1973, just before leaving Pakistan for his UK tour, Bhutto stated that he obtained a mandate from the parliament to accord *de jure* recognition to Bangladesh at the appropriate time.[108] However, the appropriate time was already at hand when Khurshid Hasan Meer moved a resolution in the assembly for the normalization of relations and recognition of Bangladesh on 9 July 1973. Ahmad Raza Kasuri opposed the resolution, whereas, Maulana Ghaus Hazarvi supported it along with other government members who spoke fervently in its favour.[109] The resolution was passed; it had now given the government the required mandate to take necessary steps for the recognition of Bangladesh.[110] Consequently, in a meeting with the chief ministers, the federal ministers, the MNAs, and MPAs, Bhutto announced the decision about Bangladesh via television on 22 February 1974.[111]

Bhutto was of the view that he should use the parliament for the decision regarding the recognition of Bangladesh. Bhutto's initial thought was to draft the constitution in such a manner that only a permissive resolution of the national assembly would be enough for the recognition of Bangladesh. I.J.M. Sutherland, the British envoy, was told in Islamabad by Abdul Sattar of the ministry of external affairs that the new constitution had been specifically drafted in such a manner that it was not necessary to have the prior sanction of the national assembly before recognizing Bangladesh. However, a 'permissive resolution' may have been interpreted in a way that Bhutto regarded it as politically desirable, even if not legally essential.[112]

However, he later decided to use the parliament as a scapegoat for making an unpopular decision. J.L. Pumphrey, the British envoy, during a meeting with Bhutto on 12 March 1973, asked whether the new constitution would make it easier for him to put through the recognition of Bangladesh. Shying away from a clear response, Bhutto went so far as to say that he would perhaps seek a permissive resolution from the present assembly; he would rather do this than have to ask the two chambers of the legislature under the new constitution for recognition. He seemed to think that the recognition issue would have to be put before the national assembly, even under the new constitution.[113]

In his address to the assembly, at the time of the approval of the resolution regarding the 'appropriate' time to recognize Bangladesh, Bhutto stated, 'it is obvious that with our POWs in captivity, in light of the talk of bringing some of them to trial in Dacca or anywhere outside Pakistan, the time is not appropriate.'[114]

Exit from the Commonwealth

On 30 January 1972, Bhutto announced Pakistan's departure from the Commonwealth. This step was in consonance with his own published opinion and the election manifesto of his party. The precise reason for Bhutto announcing a unilateral withdrawal of Pakistan from the Commonwealth, soon after he signalled his entry into high office, remains obscure. Perhaps the true reason lay in Bhutto's desire to assert the country's sovereignty and independence, and to demonstrate the fact that Pakistan belonged to Asia and the Third World.[115] This decision was applauded by his supporters as yet another step towards political freedom, as Bhutto was now ready to turn towards more substantial matters in the field of foreign relations.[116] Critics have been of the view that departure from the Commonwealth was a rather irrelevant gesture, and some believe that a decision of such significance should first have been referred to the national assembly.[117] Thus, a significant foreign policy decision was made without the consent or consultation of the parliament.

The Simla Agreement

The Simla Agreement has been extolled by Bhutto's supporters as the acme of diplomatic negotiation, while his critics denounce it as a sell-out on Kashmir. There were whispers of a secret clause reminiscent of the Tashkent Declaration and accusations of burying Kashmir along the new Line of Control.[118]

India agreed to return 5,139 square miles of Pakistani territory seized during the war. The 93,000 Pakistani prisoners of war, however, were not released; in effect India continued to hold them hostage in return for Bhutto's recognition of Bangladesh. This was an action he was, as yet, unwilling to take. The United States welcomed the Simla Agreement 'as an important step towards establishing long lasting peace in South Asia.'[119] Following the agreement, the formal US stance on the Kashmir dispute shifted. Previously, the US had supported the 1948 and 1949 UN resolutions calling for a plebiscite. However, after the Simla Agreement,

Washington indicated that any settlement that India and Pakistan worked out would be acceptable.[120]

The parliament indirectly supported Bhutto in his strategy to pressurize India internationally on the issue of the return of the prisoners of war. On 8 April 1973, the speaker of Pakistan's national assembly read a telegram by the speaker of the Jordanian parliament in which Pakistan's viewpoint was supported. The speaker informed the house that he was going to respond to the telegram with gratitude.[121]

When Z.A. Bhutto left for Simla on 25 May, he called for intellectuals, political leaders, politicians, students, and labour leaders for dialogue. He also had a formal consultation with elective representatives.[122] However, the parliament was left out. The meeting could have been called, but it was not Bhutto's objective to enhance the credibility of the parliament or to invite any suggestions from them. The national assembly initiated consideration of the Simla Agreement at its special session on 10 July 1972. Mian Mahmud Ali Kasuri, the law minister, moved the motion for consideration and said that Pakistan had not compromised on its principles. He said that the agreement emphasizes the establishment of peace and resolution of problems through meaningful bilateral talks on a step-by-step basis, and by withdrawal of forces from each other's territory.[123] Referring to the POWs, Mahmud Kasuri said that international law was very clear on the subject, and India's position was weak. India was duty-bound to repatriate the prisoners of war under the Geneva Convention. The law minister expressed hope that the assembly would adopt the resolution unanimously and show unity on a national issue, despite political differences between the parties.[124]

With reference to the Simla Agreement of July 1972, the national assembly debated the accord for five consecutive days from 10 to 14 July, and some very dynamic conversations took place between its critics and supporters. Most of the criticism was put forward by men who had failed to realize how difficult the position of their negotiators had been. The vast majority of speakers argued in favour of the accord: the only opponents were members of the two right wing Islamic parties (JI and JUP), and one dissident PPP MNA. By and large, the debate in the assembly reflected homogeneity to a great extent. While moving the motion about the Simla Agreement in the national assembly,

Mahmud Ali Kasuri said that the government was not bound under any clause of the constitution to ascertain the opinion of the national assembly before ratifying this agreement. He reminded the house that President Bhutto and his government had, 'tried to ascertain the opinion of the people and their representatives on all fundamental issues at every stage. Therefore, despite there being no constitutional obligation in recognition of the dignity and status of the National Assembly, the agreement was placed before the National Assembly.'[125]

The opinion of the leaders of the three primary opposition parties was as follows. Sardar Sherbaz Khan Mazari[126] pointed out that he felt it was the right step and that they should support it.[127] Mufti Mahmud[128] said that he thought that only this house had the authority to express its opinion regarding important issues facing the country, and that he was happy that the president of Pakistan had taken a step forward by summoning the session and following the democratic ways. Had the agreement been ratified without the consent of the national assembly, it would not have been the decision of the whole nation.[129] Mir Ghaus Bakhsh Bizenjo[130] said that in the present circumstances, he could neither expect nor reach a better agreement.[131] Meanwhile, the JUP and JIP expressed reservations on the Simla Agreement. Maulana Noorani declared the Simla Pact worse than the Tashkent Pact because the former was a declaration of intent while the Tashkent Pact was a binding agreement. He was of the opinion that Pakistan had accepted the aggression of India in East Pakistan.[132]

However, another MNA, Inayat-ur-Rahman Abbasi, refuted Kasuri and stated that the parliament was a democratic and sovereign body, and no government could deny that right. He stressed that 'even if this right is not there, it is in the mind of the President.' He said that it was not fair to say that they were not 'bound to present the agreement for ratification before the house.'[133]

Abdul Hayee Baloch observed that it was the first time that the national assembly was taken into confidence on any issue. He said, 'it was a tradition that all problems of national importance were restricted to private meetings or public meetings where public opinion was generated, and efforts were always made to bypass the National Assembly.' He expressed his pleasure saying 'the beginning of this issue is good.'[134]

Mohammad Hanif Khan said that, undoubtedly, an opportunity was given to every member to express his views and that it was necessary. He said that the MNAs had a constitutional right to express their views or to discuss national issues, but this right had been denied to them for the past twenty-five years.[135]

Mian Gul Aurangzeb said that the national assembly was not a sovereign body yet because members could not discuss what was going on in Karachi. Also, the members could not have a Question Hour or no-adjournment motions. Therefore, he questioned how it was a sovereign body. Khurshid Hasan Meer interrupted him by asking whether or not it was a comparatively better assembly that he was addressing.[136] Maulana Ghulam Ghaus said during the discussion on the Simla Agreement that 'it had proved to be the first time when freedom of speech had been allowed in the session.'[137] The house discussed the Simla issue in detail and every member participated in the debate with great zeal. One of the members said, 'The postmortem of this topic has been made to such an extent that no portion of it is left. It appears that if any member does not speak, he will not retain his membership, and will not remain in his constituency.'[138]

On the last day of the debates, Bhutto, following a three-and-a-half hour long speech, was able to convince the majority of the MNAs that although initially holding a bad hand of cards, he had done the very best with it.[139] The house approved and ratified the accord with an overwhelming majority through a voice-vote.[140]

The session, apart from a few highlights, proved long and wearisome. After initial complaints from opposition members that they were not being allowed to speak, or that their speeches were being curtailed, the chairman (with the president's approval) allowed anyone who wished to speak. The majority did so. However, the speeches were largely irrelevant, often repetitive, frequently interrupted, and delivered in most cases aided and abetted by an unusually effective loudspeaker system). Every morning, when the session commenced, at least an hour would be spent by members either trying to initiate a separate debate on the said crisis (which loomed large all week), or by reading extracts from papers in which they claimed to have been misquoted. This early morning knock-about provided some of the livelier exchanges.[141]

The agreement was something of a triumph for Bhutto. At the end of the 1971 war, there was a defeated, demoralized and truncated Pakistan, large parts of which were occupied by the Indian army. Over 90,000 prisoners of war were in Indian hands. Hence, Bhutto's bargaining position appeared weak, and it seemed likely that he would be forced to accept a settlement on almost any terms. By playing out long negotiations and exploiting international public opinion on the prisoners of war issue, Bhutto was able to build up his own bargaining position to a point where the issue of prisoners of war became an embarrassment for India and a source of friction between India and Bangladesh. As international memories faded, he could isolate Bangladesh in its position of insisting on war crimes trials to the point where it was unlikely that they would ever take place. He also avoided a commitment to accept all the 260,000 Biharis who wished to leave Bangladesh. The agreement, therefore, was much closer to Bhutto's original terms when the negotiations started, than to the terms of India and Bangladesh. His performance over the period of twenty-one months was a striking example of how a tough and skilful negotiator, unhampered by public opinion at home, could make the most of an apparently weak initial bargaining position.[142]

It was Bhutto's achievement that without the recognition of Bangladesh, and without retreating from his position over the proposed trial of certain Pakistanis in Bangladesh, he was able to conclude an agreement of this sort. The inclusion in the agreement of Pakistan's undertaking to accept a 'substantial number' of non-Bengalis who have 'opted for repatriation to Pakistan' was unsatisfactorily vague, and unless there was some undisclosed understanding as to the meaning of 'substantial' and when this program of repatriation was to begin, there was probably room left for profitless bickering[143].

Although the Simla Agreement was made without prior approval or debate over the issue in the parliament, the parliamentarians appeared satisfied over the debate in the house after the agreement was signed. The parliament was contented that a foreign policy affair was discussed in the parliament, and that it had raised the standards of the institution. Nevertheless, the agreement was sealed without prior approval of the parliament, but eventually the government had to take the matter to the assembly. The external affairs of every country are approved and ratified by the parliament because it is a representative institution of the state. However, in Pakistan and India, this practice does not exist in its true spirit. The public representatives should stress that matters of peace be resolved with the partnership of the people. Reading from the pages of history, it is evident that agreements made without the support of the public representatives were bound to fail.

SOCIO-ECONOMIC REFORMS AND THE PARLIAMENT

To the parliament's misfortune, major reforms of social and economic nature were announced by the government without any consultation during the period of martial law, although the assembly could very well have been called for consultation and approval. In addition, it is interesting to note that all the major reforms were made before the formulation of the constitution. The office of the chief martial law administrator and the emergency, which were in force at the time, conferred immense powers to the president, which Bhutto fully used to remove obstacles in the implementation of his policies. In chronological order Bhutto's reforms were announced as follows:

Labour	10 February 1972
Land	1 March 1972
Education	15 March 1972
Police	12 April 1972
Law	13 April 1972 (initial outline only).[144]

This package of major reforms was designed to implement Bhutto's election promises,[145] but due to a parliamentary form of government and the importance of the parliament, it must have been of vital significance to the regime to introduce and implement reforms in consultation with the parliament. However, these consultations were never made.

The reforms were not simple and had significant repercussions on the system. A series of land reforms were introduced on 1 March 1972 through Martial Law Regulation No. 115. They reduced land ceilings to 150 acres of irrigated land or 300 acres of rain-fed land or 12,000 produce index units, plus an additional 200 produce index unit if the owner either owned a tractor or had installed a tube well. The land holdings in excess of the prescribed ceiling were to be resumed without compensation and distributed among the landless cultivators, or those whose holdings were below subsistence level.[146] However, the reforms introduced in 1972 were debated on in the parliament in 1974, when minor amendments in them was a need of the government.[147]

On 3 November 1975, the Land Reforms (Amendment) Bill was again put before the national assembly, and the period of 1972 ordinance was extended. The speaker interrupted the debates and allowed the minister of commerce to present reports of the standing committees that were concerned with other bills. After the presentation of these reports, the house resumed discussion on the Land Reforms (Amendment) Bill,[148] which was passed by the assembly.[149]

By the autumn of 1976, it had become apparent that the land reforms did not produce expected results. To remedy the situation, the PPP government, without consulting the parliament at all, promulgated another Land Reforms Ordinance on 5 January 1976 with three significant features. It reduced the ceiling to 100 acres of irrigated land and allowed compensation to land owners in the form of bonds. Also, it made provision for distribution of resumed land among landless tenants and small land-owners without charge or payment.[150]

Land reforms were made without the consent of the parliament but consultations over the issue were made from the institution from time to time, whenever it was deemed necessary by policymakers. Amendment bills were legitimized by the parliament as the institution appeared to be a mere tool in the hands of the policymakers who used it to legitimatise the reforms.

As far as social reforms were concerned, the government carried out bold and far-reaching economic reforms in the first two years of its stewardship. Under the Economic Reforms Order of 1972, management and control of thirty-one industrial units and ten basic industries was taken over by the government. In addition, the board of industrial management was established to control and supervise their working. These industries included iron and steel, basic metal industries, heavy engineering plants, assembly and manufacturing of motor vehicles, tractor factories, heavy and basic chemical industries, and public utilities like electricity generation and distribution, gas and oil refineries. In addition, the government nationalized life insurance businesses by taking over forty-three Pakistani and four foreign life insurance companies. Moreover, the nationalization of banks, the country's shipping and vegetable oil industries, ginning, and rice husking mills were taken over within the following two years.[151] In 1976, further nationalization under the policy of 'Islamic Socialism' was executed, and the private sector was discouraged.[152]

In Pakistan, some people had seen the Soviet Union's rise to become the second biggest industrial power of the world through state ownership of means of production, distribution, and exchange. Hence, they were greatly excited by Bhutto's nationalization programme. However, an important fact remains that the nationalization, in order to be effective, needed a very honest, ideologically oriented team with an efficient and experienced group of managers. Unfortunately, Pakistan had a dearth of such force. The bureaucrats who had no technical expertise and experience to run nationalized industries were given key positions in the new set up.[153] According to Omar Noman, the state-owned industries in Pakistan became enterprises for political patronage, and were used to pay political debts or accumulate power.[154] The managers of the state enterprises were recruited on the basis of loyalty to the party rather than professional and technical ability. The inevitable consequence was the creation of an inefficient and corrupt public sector.[155]

All the aforementioned steps were taken without the occurrence of any parliamentary activity. No parliamentary committees were established to continue or discontinue these economic reforms. Bhutto, with free will, changed and appointed policy managers without any interference from the parliament. When he wanted to change his policy, he simply replaced the leftist minister of finance, Mubashir Hasan. In doing so, he took advantage of Mubashir's willingness to resign on grounds of ill health, and skilfully managed to convey his sorrow to Mubashir's supporters whilst at the same time persuading the business community that he had made the change in their interests.[156]

The efforts made by the opposition to discuss economic issues, through adjournment motions, were often foiled due to technical reasons. The adjournment motion regarding serious economic situations (caused by a drastic drop in the rate of investment in 1973–4) could not be discussed in the national assembly because it was matter of policy and not a specific issue. Moreover, the argument was that it was not recent, but rather a continuous process and hence could not be discussed through an adjournment motion.[157]

THE BALOCHISTAN GOVERNMENT

Balochistan remained a burning issue throughout the Bhutto era. The controversial arms discovered in the Iraqi embassy on 10 February 1973 gave the government a pretext for the dismissal of the Mengal-led NAP–JUI government. On 16 February 1973, Ataullah Khan Mengal's government was dismissed, and the provincial assembly was suspended as Bhutto proclaimed president's rule in Balochistan.[158] This sparked tribal insurgency which, according to Dr Mubashir, was the worst confrontation so far between the Baloch people and the Government of Pakistan.[159] In April 1973, the provincial government was restored with the Jam of Lasbela[160] as chief minister and Akbar Bugti as governor. Even then, the situation had not normalized. With no options left, the national assembly approved a list of nine members on 8 June 1973[161] to go to Balochistan and make an on-the-spot inquiry into the matter and to submit its report to the house within two weeks.[162] These two weeks were allegedly stretched to over eight months due to government delays and persistent demand by the opposition to discuss Balochistan again. The opposition resented the sheer callousness being shown by the national assembly regarding the affairs of Balochistan, and the way the debate was constantly postponed over and over again until 14 February 1974.[163]

The Baloch opposition did not surrender, hence, army presence had to be reinforced. The result was violent encounters and casualties on an enormous scale. By August 1973, Bugti stated that the problem was no longer one of law and order, but of 'open insurgency', and on 16 August, just two days after the enforcement of the agreed constitution, Bhutto defied his own rules. Consequently, Ghaus Bakhsh Bizenjo (former governor of Balochistan), Ataullah Khan Mengal (an MNA), and Khair

Bakhsh Marri (former chief minister of Balochistan) were arrested on the grounds of a curious spectrum of criminal charges.[164]

In December 1973, the situation in both provinces was by no means tranquil. On 2 December, Abdus Samad Khan Achakzai, a leader of the Pathan community living in Balochistan, was assassinated in Quetta at his residence. This tragic incident had serious and lasting implications. Bhutto, more than once, vehemently cast aside any suggestions of the further dismemberment of Pakistan, but the adoption in 1973 of the High Treason Act, the Private Military Organizations (Abolition and Prohibition) Act, and the Prevention of Anti-National Activities Ordinance suggested the continued presence of fissiparous forces.[165]

At one time during this period, in December 1973, a member sought adjournment of the business of the national assembly, *inter alia*, to discuss the alleged failure of the government of Pakistan to reinstate the lawful Government of Balochistan. The law minister pointed out that, as far as the formation of the provincial government was concerned, the procedure was laid down in the constitution, and therefore, no adjournment motion could be moved to violation of the mandatory provisions of the constitution. The speaker observed that the situation in Balochistan was also prevalent in the month of September, and if the matter had been so urgent, the motion should have been moved earlier. Therefore, he ruled out the motion saying that there could not be an adjournment motion in regards to a continuing process.[166]

The debate in the national assembly on the issue was concluded by Prime Minister Bhutto on 14 February 1974. He contended that the situation in Balochistan was not the creation of this government, and that some members had just tried to oversimplify it. He said, 'As a matter of fact, when this government came into office, we tried to resolve the problem politically.' It is in this connection and in this context that governorships were given to NAP in NWFP and in Balochistan; and it is in this connection that governments were also given to them.

It is not that we were unmindful of the political implications and that we did not know that a political settlement and a political solution were ideal settlements. So, it is not that political efforts have not been made, or that the search for a political solution has not been made. That is factually incorrect, and let me assure you that even today, even in the present circumstances, side by side with the necessary measures that are being taken in Balochistan, we are continuing our search for a political solution.... I do not want to say that it is only a question of fighting the *Sardari* System—here, I would be committing the same mistake that the opposition makes in oversimplifying problems. The *Sardari* System, undoubtedly, is a part of the problem, a very big part of this problem. It is the evolution of the State from primitive feudalism into a modern State.[167]

He also stated:

...the *Sardari* System carries inherent contradictions. There were certain *sardars* who were recalcitrant, and in the past they came into conflict with the government. Subsequently, some of them were tamed or some of them saw the light of reason, and they reconciled themselves to the forces of modernism and realism. There were other *sardars* who from the beginning thought that it would be in the interest of their people to bring about enlightenment and progress and they did not resist the forces of enlightenment.[168]

However, to the government's misfortune, the debates in the national assembly did not come to fruition regarding actions in Balochistan. It also did not play any part in escalating the situation there. The report of the delegation proved to be just a report and a discussion. Hard talks in the assembly also remained insignificant for the development of events in the province.

In the senate, the government kept on evading the discussion on the issue of Balochistan. The evasion became evident at the time of a motion when, on 13 December 1973, a senator brought up the grave situation in Balochistan, as reported in the national press on 9 December. The report stated that thirteen outlaws were killed and four were injured while the troops suffered three causalities (one soldier died and two were left wounded). As soon as the mover finished reading his motion, the minister opposed it. Thereupon, the chairman told the minister that he should state the grounds on which he opposed it. The minister instead suggested that if the mover wanted to say something in favour of the motion, only then would he reply. The chairman, however, did not accept the minister's suggestion and observed that the minister would give reasons for his opposition, and the mover would respond accordingly. However, the minister insisted that it would be better if the mover supported his motion with a statement, as he would respond to that. He declared at the same time that he had no objections to the admissibility of the motion.

The chairman ruled that the merits and facts of the adjournment motion could not be looked into at that stage unless the house was adjourned for debate, and that only technical objections about its admissibility could be raised at that time. The minister expressed that it would not be a debate, and the mover would merely have a right to complete the motion by reading the supporting statement. On this, the chairman questioned the minister's stand, and ruled that such a right did exist under the old set of rules in the national assembly, but was not there in the present rules. The minister objected to the putting of question without the mover's statement and rebuttal. Regardless, the chairman put the question under rule 73 (2). He did this because a majority of the house opposed the move, leading him to inform the mover that the leave to move the motion was not granted to him by the house.[169]

On 20 December 1973, a member wanted to move an adjournment motion to discuss a statement given by the governor of Balochistan, who, while talking to the press on his arrival in Lahore, had said that there was a situation like that of an insurgency in Balochistan. The concerned minister opposed the motion on multiple grounds. He said that it was not a matter of recent occurrence, that the issue did not raise a very important question, that it was a question of law and order, which was primarily the concern of the provincial government, and that the allegation was not based on facts but on a personal opinion of the former governor of Balochistan. The chairman ruled, 'it is a very minor matter, a matter of law and order, which is primarily the concern of the Provincial Government, and, moreover, it is a continuing process, and this even Bugti has said.'[170]

On 18 April 1974, a member sought leave to move an adjournment motion regarding the statement of the governor of Balochistan. He said that Mir Ghaus Bakhsh Bizenjo, Mengal, and Khair Bakhsh Marri had been detained by the Balochistan government and the question of their release was a matter between them and the prime minister. It was alleged in the motion that the governor's statement went against the principles of provincial autonomy as laid down in the constitution.

In reply to the questions put forward by the leader of the opposition about whether or not the governor of Balochistan was an agent or representative of the federal government, and whether it could be denied that he had made that statement as a representative of the said government. The minister for labour and works stated that the governor of Balochistan was not entitled to make such a statement, nor did the governor have the authority to pass orders under the Defence of Pakistan Rules under which the power was vested in the chief minister as executive head of Balochistan.

The chairman observed that it was clear that those three persons had been detained by the provincial government. He went on to make a second point about how they couldn't be released because the prime minister had made a statement earlier giving general details of the decisions taken the other day, such as the withdrawal of the army, continuation of development work, etc. He supposed that the governor probably wanted to convey that before they were released, the prime minister would be consulted or informed of it. The chairman added that the prime minster came into the picture because amnesty had been granted by him, though detention had been ordered by the provincial government. He concluded that amnesty could not be granted by the provincial government. The point in question was how this could be regarded as an encroachment on provincial autonomy.

The next day, when the discussion on the admissibility of the motion was resumed, the minister informed the house that he had spoken to the governor over the phone, and that he had told him that he never meant what had been attributed to him and that his intention was entirely different. He also stated that action would be taken in accordance with the decision taken by the federal government, but it was for the provincial government to decide on the release of detainees. He also stated that the federal government could also release them after they were convicted. Under the constitution, the president could also release them. Therefore, it was a matter between the provincial government and the federal government, and he confirmed that the governor was not involved in it. Amnesty would be granted by the federal government on the recommendation of the provincial chief minister, as there were cases against the detainees for substantive offences. Moreover, the minister added that the statement of the governor did not, in any way, represent the meaning which was being attributed to it by the mover of the motion. The word 'consulted' in particular, was not used at all.[171]

On 30 July 1974, a senator wanted to move an adjournment motion regarding the alleged bombing by the air force on the Bambore Range bordering the district of Kachi, inhabited mainly by Marri tribesmen in the second week of June, causing the death of innumerable people and the destruction of Marri settlements in the region.

The minister, without portfolio, made a statement on behalf of the government, and categorically denied the alleged aerial bombing on Bambore Range or on any other place in Balochistan. He added that the prime minister undertook an extensive tour of Balochistan, and wherever he went, he found conditions to be peaceful. According to the report of the prime minister's tour of these areas published in the *Pakistan Times* on 28 July 1974, a large number of the residents of the Marri area told the prime minster in Mawand that there had been no bombing in the area. Army operations were intended against certain miscreants who harassed the local population and tried to disrupt law and order. The chairman ruled the motion out of order due to lack of proof. [172]

On 30 July 1974, a senator wanted to move an adjournment motion regarding a bomb attack between 12 and 20 June 1974, by the air force on Chamalang Range in the Loralai district of Balochistan, inhabited by the Marri tribe, killing a number of persons and cattle, and razing several Marri settlements to the ground. The mover requested that a deputation be sent to the area to make an inquiry and submit its report to the house, and that the government should agree to hold a full-fledged debate on the Balochistan situation.[173]

Here is an example of the action taken by the senate chairman to apparently give relief to the motion of a senator. On 5 August 1974, a member sought leave of the house to move an adjournment motion to discuss how the government had neither provided Ataullah Mengal, a heart patient, with proper medical treatment nor was he being supplied with newspapers or a radio, causing physical and mental deterioration. During the course of the discussion, the interior minister stated that

Ataullah Mengal had already been examined by a medical specialist, and that he had also been supplied with newspapers that were on the approved list of the jail. He could also be given a radio if he requested it. The chairman instructed the interior minister to note the complaint and look into the matter. The minister assured him that he would inform the provincial government to provide Mengal with the best possible facilities, including medical aid. The mover, being satisfied with the assurance, did not press the motion further.[174] However, Abdul Hayee Baloch claimed that no relief was given to Mengal.[175]

On 6 August 1974, a senator wanted to move an adjournment motion to discuss the failure of the government to investigate the firing in Quetta which took place on 23 July 1974, during the prime minister's visit. In support of the motion, the leader of the opposition contended that as the Federal Security Force, which controlled law and order, was under the federal government, they were concerned with the matter proposed. Therefore, the motion was ruled out of order.[176]

On 6 August 1974, a senator tried to move an adjournment motion to discuss the unwarranted attack by army men on the village of Sheerani in the third week of June, resulting in several casualties, and the destruction of livestock, houses, and crops. However, the minister of state for defence opposed the matter, saying that the occurrence was alleged to have taken place between 16 and 21 June 1974, and there had been a full-fledged debate on the issue in the national assembly on 27 June 1974. Therefore, the motion fell under rule 71 (d) and was not in order.[177]

Again on 6 August 1974, another senator wanted to move an adjournment motion to discuss the government's refusal to permit opposition leaders to visit Chamalang Range and adjoining areas to make an assessment of the damage caused by the bombing. However, the motion was, opposed on the grounds that there had been no bombing. The permission to visit the areas in question was refused by the Government of Balochistan, as alleged by the mover, on the basis of the matter falling within the domain of the provincial government. It was contended in support of the motion that as permission was refused, not only by the provincial government but also by the army, the matter was the concern of the federal government. The chairman observed that the alleged occurrence took place on 2 July. The session commenced on

25 July 1974, and the motion was brought forward on 26 July 1974. Since it was moved late, it could not be regarded as a matter of urgent public importance and was ruled out of order.[178] The minister said that there had been no bombing while the chairman in his observation accepted *prima facie* that the occurrence had taken place on 2 July. In conclusion, the parliament was often kept in darkness.

On 19 November 1974, an adjournment motion was moved in the senate to discuss the failure of the federal government to prevent Afghan nationals from entering Balochistan. The mover alleged that the governor of Balochistan had disclosed in a press conference that about 30,000 Afghan nationals had entered Balochistan, as reported in the *Nawa-i-Waqt* on 19 October 1974. The mover replied that during the last few months, the interior minister had made repeated statements that the government had sealed the Pakistan–Afghanistan border. The statement made by the governor was a fresh disclosure which had come to light all of a sudden, and as such, was a matter of urgent public importance. The chairman observed that he personally felt that the matter was, undoubtedly, of some public importance but that this had been continuing for the last six or seven months. Therefore, it was not urgent and had not created any pressing situation to justify the adjournment of the house for a discussion. The motion was, therefore, ruled out of order.[179]

On 9 March 1976, an adjournment motion regarding the federal government's appointment of four members of the dismissed cabinet of Balochistan to the advisory committee of the governor of the province fell through because its notice was not submitted two hours before the commencement of the sitting.[180] On 16 March 1976, another adjournment motion was not discussed; this was regarding federal government's alleged appointment of dismissed ministers as advisors to the governor of Balochistan, as reported in the *Pakistan Times* on 1 January 1976.

On 5 July 1976, a senator moved an adjournment motion to discuss the alleged unconstitutional order dated 1 July 1976 that suspended the Balochistan government and directed the provincial governor to assume all powers on behalf of the federal government. The motion was opposed by the minister for law and parliamentary affairs on the grounds that it related to a matter which was not specific, and which could be remedied by the legislation. He also added that the Balochistan problem was debated in totality in a meeting of the parliament in a joint sitting on 26 February, and again two months later in the senate. This motion was objected to because of a bar on reviving discussions on a matter which had been discussed in the senate or the assembly within the last six months. Therefore, the motion was ruled out of order on the grounds that such a complicated constitutional point could not be decided by the chairman. If there was anything unconstitutional or illegal in the order passed by the president, it would be challenged in the High Court or Supreme Court only. The senate was not the proper forum to raise discussions over this question.[181]

Thus, neither of the two houses of the parliament could play a reasonable role in the important issue of Balochistan. The individual and opposition members of both the houses tried their best to highlight the issue in the parliament. They also made efforts to use the parliament in support of the opposition's stand in Balochistan. The Baloch parliamentarians also struggled to use the forum to highlight the miseries of the people, and in return, gain political support. However, the government skilfully succeeded in side-lining the institution of the parliament. Sometimes, issues were allowed to be discussed in the parliament, and through those debates, the support was usually in favour of the government. However, as a rule, debates in the parliament were often evaded.

The suspension of the NWFP assembly could also not be discussed in the parliament. Rao Khurshid Ali Khan moved an adjournment motion to discuss the suspension of the provincial assembly of the NWFP, following the murder of Hayat Mohammad Khan Sherpao, a minister of the province. It was opposed by the minister of state for parliamentary affairs, Malik Mohammad Akhtar, on the grounds that the order used to suspend the assembly was issued to save the province from external aggression and internal interference, and that the impugned action of the federal government was justified under clause (3) of article 148 of the constitution. Besides, he contended that it was not a matter of recent occurrence and it also embraced a wide range of issues. The adjournment motion was disallowed on the grounds that it did not relate to any specific issue, and was wide enough to call for a general debate.[182] The ruling was interesting because neither was the matter old nor did it embrace a wide range of issues. It was just that the speaker, who was towing along the lines of the government, did not let issues be discussed in the assembly.

The parliament, during its working period, could not assert its hegemony in the face of other forces, particularly the government, when various vital issues were at hand. The issues were created outside the parliament, and the government often hoodwinked the use of the aforementioned in resolving and deciding issues. Whereas, on other occasions, like the Qadiani issue, the parliament appeared too influential, as it became a committee that listened to concerned parties, and in the end, took the decision to amend the constitution. However, thorough analysis reveals that the parliament was just used for the discussion of issues, without letting the institution assert any hegemony. The parliament showed much activity in the issue; it remained busy a lot of the time. It also appeared as if the whole matter was decided only by the party, but evidence showed that the executive had decided to declare Qadianis as non-Muslims. They only took shelter in the parliament's proceedings because of the sensitivity of the issue. On all other issues, the parliament was clearly following the executive, and was definitely not a decision-making entity free from external influence.

Chapter Six

Establishing Autonomy
Relation of the Parliament with Other Institutions

THE EXECUTIVE'S INFLUENCE OVER THE PARLIAMENT

Classical literature on democracy deals with the function of the legislature as a goal-setting agency for the larger public in terms of policymaking, while the executive is supposed to implement policies on ground. In reality, the influence of the legislature in this regard has been demarcated by the overarching role of the executive. This happens in several ways. The parties in power and the opposition tend to control and manipulate the manner in which their legislators vote (or not) and speak (or choose not to) on the floor of the parliament. In this sense, party leadership operates essentially from outside the legislature to steer legislation, including constitutional amendments.[1]

Domination of the executive is a common fact of political life. The executives are typically powerful institutions which tend to be the major, and sometimes even the sole actors in organized political systems. It is relatively difficult to build a powerful legislature or electorate, or to make them powerful themselves. This is not so with executives.[2]

Pakistan has never been a country where institutions are stronger than personalities. The country has generally done well under authoritarian rule; though much depends on the way in which the authority is exercised.[3] In Pakistan, the parliament is mostly a subordinate legislature. Here, the executive is, without exception, a pre-eminent player on the national political scene as it initiates decisions in party forums, which are translated into laws through the legislative procedure and are then rigidly defined, implemented, and controlled by the bureaucracy. Given the domination of extra-parliamentary forces over the power structure of Pakistan, parliamentary institutions are often considered by political

155

players as necessary accessories of a modern ruling structure. In other words, these institutions legitimize the existing political order. Even if the real power resides outside the legislature, the power holders need to win legal and moral authority by any means possible. Not surprisingly, each of the four military governments tried to fill the gap of legitimacy by creating assemblies through the election process.[4]

It is a well-known fact that Z.A. Bhutto was a strong personality and that the persona of Bhutto as a popular leader of the masses was unrivalled. With the superb craft of an actor, he dominated the political stage, hammering forth a savage attack against his powerless opponents and against the capitalists and the landlords, whose authority was now more imaginary than real. The act comprised a sole performance, with Bhutto as the only actor (and protagonist) of his own drama.[5]

In 1972 there was no one else in the political system of Pakistan who could challenge the position of Z.A. Bhutto. Even the Pakistanis who had been expressing disappointment in Bhutto could not replace him. The British envoy never heard a name suggested for an immediate substitute. In his party, he was unquestionably supreme; there was no match in the national assembly either. There may have been others who had ambition but none had his iron determination and craftiness. He was internationally popular. The idea of Wali Khan, Bizenjo, or Asghar Khan—not to mention Tikka Khan—being entrusted with the destiny of the country would fill any reasonable Pakistani with despair.[6]

More than being the only leader of Pakistan, Bhutto, by nature, believed in the concentration of power within a ruler. According to the secular-minded opposition leader Air Marshal (retd) Asghar Khan, Bhutto was not a democrat by temperament or conviction.[7] As the chief executive of the country, he increasingly acted more like a feudal autocrat rather than a democrat.[8] He gradually became more authoritarian. He used martial law powers to punish several individuals and groups that had crossed his path during his political career. By the time he dismissed the Balochistan government, his critics deemed him an elected civilian strongman who had little patience for the niceties of a parliamentary democracy.[9]

Due to his desire to continue office and to concentrate powers towards himself, Bhutto was reluctant to lift the martial law, so as to strengthen his position while the new constitution came into force. In this way, he could assert his powers without the constitutional restrictions and interruptions from the institutions, which came into being under the provisions of the constitution. Delaying tactics used by Bhutto came to surface when he made his long-awaited announcement on 22 January 1972. It was apparent then that the hopes of the revival of a parliamentary government would not be fulfilled as early as it was expected. The provincial assemblies were scheduled to meet on 23 March 1972, but the national assembly was not to be convened, nor was there to be an early lifting of martial law. These omissions were justified by the same reasons Bhutto had given on 13 January 1972. It was clear that Bhutto was in no hurry to surrender the dictatorial powers he had inherited.[10]

Bhutto might have prolonged martial law out of his desire for concentrating power, but his dilatoriness provoked increasingly urgent clamour amongst the opposition (and even a small number of PPP members) in the press and public sentiment for ending martial law. Khan Abdul Wali Khan, leader of the NAP, spoke darkly of convening provincial assemblies unilaterally. At the same time, forces of law and order seemed in danger of collapse; there were instances of serious unrest, police strikes in certain cities, and frequent clashes between PPP agitators and their political opponents.[11]

It was this disastrous situation in which Bhutto had to turn begrudgingly towards the constitution-making process and towards the parliament. Towards the end of the first day's proceedings in the assembly, he concluded a long speech with a dramatic announcement that, provided the assembly approve the draft of the interim constitution, he would repeal the martial law on 21 April 1972. With this master stroke, he did not lose power or popularity; it was this fear that was compelling him to sustain martial law. The dramatic turn towards the constitution and the parliament virtually silenced the opposition. Bhutto, remaining as powerful as ever, obtained a unanimous vote of confidence which considerably enhanced his reputation and forwarded the interim constitution with only minimal opposition. The latter gave him considerable powers, and also enabled him to claim that he had 'rid the country of the curse of martial law.'[12]

The powers that Bhutto seized during his rule did not come to him as inheritance. On the contrary, he managed to earn these authorities when he was playing a vital role in the formation of the constitution of Pakistan as chief martial law administrator and president from 1971 to 1973. The promulgation of the 1973 constitution perhaps remains to be the greatest achievement of Bhutto, not only in reference to his personal merits, but also in terms of Pakistan's interests. The political bargaining that formed the backdrop of this achievement required Bhutto's special touch. He skilfully coerced different opposition parties and persuaded them to endorse the constitution. The parties eventually came to heel. During the course of negotiations for the constitution, there were threats of walk-outs and boycott of the national assembly. It was only Bhutto who dealt with balancing, negotiating and finally triumphing over all of the adverse controversies which could obstruct a smooth formation of the constitution.[13] This unprecedented role in the formation of the constitution raised people's confidence in Bhutto and upgraded his stature in the politics of Pakistan. This experience made Bhutto more skilful in the concentration of immense power and influence as he confidently started to steer virtually all institutions of the state according to his will.

During progress towards the finalization of the constitution, the opposition was determined to make the executive answerable to the legislature. Similarly, within the PPP, there were members who were inclined towards an effective legislature which could offer them hope of having a say in the affairs of the state.[14] However, Bhutto, determined to control the legislature in order to become more powerful, was more inclined towards a powerful executive.

The draft constitution gave Bhutto almost dictatorial powers to which the NAP was not prepared to agree. Wali Khan stated that he would like the talks to be resumed, and a fresh accord developed. He said that there had been a whispering campaign after the October 1972 accord that the NAP hierarchy had been bribed by guarantees of security of office.[15] Thus, in spite of the opposition against the accumulation of powers in the chief executive, Bhutto administered to converge the powers in the office of the prime minister.

Bhutto preferred an executive-centred presidential form of government, one not too different from the Ayub Khan government (1958–69), but ultimately, he was persuaded to accept a modified parliamentary system[16] where, though the parliament existed, the prime minister was the strong chief executive. The constitution was federal in character, and after much haggling within the cabinet, Bhutto accepted, against his inclinations, that he would be the prime minister, and not continue as president.[17] Previously, Bhutto wanted to retain the presidency, considering its powers, but later he accepted the position of prime minister because of its powerful role of chief executive, according to the new constitution of 1973.

Bhutto did not hesitate to use brutal force to subdue his opponents. There were others who paid a far heavier price for their opposition to Bhutto. These included Dr Nazir Ahmad (JI MNA) from Dera Ghazi Khan, Lahori opposition leader Khawaja Rafiq, deputy speaker of the Balochistan assembly Maulvi Shamsuddin (JUI–NAP), and NAP leader Abdus Samad Achakzai from Quetta.[18]

At the end of the constitution-making process, there was no doubt that Bhutto would enjoy exceptional authority in comparison to his Westminster counterpart.[19] Therefore, the most significant and criticized characteristic of the 1973 constitution was regarding the powers to be enjoyed by the prime minister.[20] Though he lifted martial law in April 1972, Bhutto never came out from this frame of mind. He incorporated his extraordinary powers in the interim constitution of 1972 which vested unprecedented authority in his hands. It took him back to the 1935 India Act under which the chief executive enjoyed total powers. He basked in the sunshine of absolute authority for the next one year under this constitution. On 14 August 1973, he switched from the presidential to the parliamentary form of government and became the strongest prime minister in the history of parliamentary democracy. The head of state (president) was reduced to a position which was in keeping with a parliamentary form of government. The position employed a mere figurehead with no actual powers; all decisions had to be made based on the advice of the prime minister. Any bill of legislation passed by the legislature and assented by the president could not become law unless it was countersigned by the chief executive again.[21]

It was this feature of the most powerful prime minister that made Kamal Azfar believe that every constitution in the history of Pakistan including that of 1973 circumnavigated around an individual. A more unfortunate aspect regarding the 1973 constitution was that the individual in question did not observe the rules of the game made by himself.[22] In Azfar's view, the constitution of 1973 was the first in which the entire executive power was concentrated in the prime minister. This fulfilled the desires of Bhutto to become powerful so that he might overrule all institutions as well as individuals in the political system of Pakistan.[23]

The constitutional powers would have been worthless if Bhutto, or anyone else in his place, had not been able to exercise those powers. But the situations had strengthened Bhutto's position extensively in all respects with an overall majority in both houses; any prime minister from PPP would have little need to worry about getting his policies approved. The fear could only be a sign of discontent in the lower ranks of the party. These dissidents of the party needed increasingly careful handling, particularly when economic matters were discussed.[24]

In order to further secure his position, he added two special features to the 1973 constitution. He made the prime minister's impeachment almost impossible and termed any possible coup as an act of high treason. For the former, the constitution stated that a no-confidence resolution could not be moved against the prime minister unless the successor's name was put forward, or if the assembly was debating an annual budget statement. If the motion was moved at all, it could not be voted upon before the expiry of three days. And if voting did take place, the resolution had to be passed by the majority of the total membership of the national assembly.[25]

Bhutto did not prove to be a weak prime minister. He did not care to work in limits, and nor could the state institutions flourish freely and independently. As the president and chief martial law administrator, he did not pay much regard to democratic institutions like the assembly or the parliament. Bhutto's attitude before the adoption of the constitution and during martial law was almost dictatorial. He concentrated power in his position with the help of different tactics. He reinforced his authority by the appointment of his nominees as governors in all four provinces.

The powers under martial law were even used to unseat a dissident member of his own party.[26] Soon after the adoption of the constitution, it became clear to the opposition that Bhutto did not really intend to abide by the consensus he had reached with them.[27] Not only disregarding the compromises with the opposition outside the parliament, and without the consensus within the assembly, Bhutto did not wish to give the parliament its proper status. On 7 September 1973, opposition leader Wali Khan said during a press conference that 'the reason for the boycott of the national assembly proceedings by opposition was because they felt that the prime minister was 'not ready to give the parliament the status it deserved and was bent upon injuring its dignity under the impression that the Assembly's only job was to endorse his proclamation.'[28]

The persona of Bhutto, as a leader who overpowered the authorities of institutions, was developed in the minds of the opposition as early as 1973. Bhutto was bestowed with an undemocratic title of the 'King of Kings'. On 5 March 1973, during the course of his speech on the constitution bill, opposition leader Abdul Wali Khan referred to the dismissal of the Mengal ministry in Balochistan, and said that the 'orders came from the Imperial Majesty, *Shahinshah* (King of Kings) of Pakistan from Islamabad,' hinting at Z.A. Bhutto. The law minister objected to the use of such words and asked for their withdrawal. The speaker remarked that the rules did not permit ironic expressions against the head of the state. He insisted for the withdrawal of the expressions which, after some argument, was done by the leader of the opposition.[29] This discussion on the comments highlighted the two-fold impressions of Bhutto and the national assembly.

In 1974, Bhutto dominated the federal government just as absolutely as he did his party. With a few exceptions, his entire cabinet consisted of virtually unknown ministers when he came to power.[30] Two of his early critics, Meraj Mohammad Khan and M.A. Kasuri, were ousted before the end of 1972. For a time, the left-wing lobby appeared to be successfully steering him along doctrinaire lines, but when it became apparent that their policies were not only failing to solve the country's economic problems, but even exacerbating them by destroying business confidence, Bhutto dropped two of the lobby's principals, J.A. Rahim and Dr Mubashir Hasan. With the departure of these two, there remained nobody, with the possible exception of Sheikh Rashid, who was likely to oppose Bhutto in any matters of substance.[31]

While the executive's position was being strengthened in rise of the personal stature of Bhutto, the legal and constitutional power of the executive was also enhanced with the help of constitutional amendments. On 24 May 1974, an amendment in the constitution gave the executive sufficient authority to declare any political party illegal if that party proves to be detrimental to the sovereignty or integrity of Pakistan. The modification was intended to protect the prime minister from frivolous changes in party loyalty of the type that had paralyzed governments in the period before Ayub Khan.[32]

Whenever there was the faintest ripple of dissent or protest, the chairman pulled strings like a typical feudal lord. In August 1972, on the least semblance of dissent, he demanded undated letters of resignation from all PPP MNAs, to which only fifty resisted. Thirty of them joined the opposition in condemning the appointment of a high police official.[33] The punishment for non-conformity was not confined to expulsion from the party but would lead to imprisonment or physical assaults. Abdul Hamid Jatoi, a PPP MNA from Dadu, was first involved in fake criminal charges for opposing the party leadership on a police issue, but when those became untenable, he was put under preventive detention.[34]

The national assembly was PPP dominated and, though treated by Bhutto with obvious respect and used most skilfully by him when convenient (as in the matter of Qadianis), it had no real independent power of initiative. The national press, especially the English press, was almost entirely under Bhutto's direct and indirect control.[35]

Bhutto, as the chief executive of Pakistan, continued to accumulate power, and nearing the three-year point, had lost popularity but had gained power. He had full control over his party and the central government, and effective control over the governments of Sindh, Punjab, and the NWFP. In Balochistan, he directed the army which was slowly, and perhaps successfully, seizing control from the sardars. He had the army's backing and was successfully smothering or isolating political opposition.[36] In 1976, Bhutto was virtually unchallenged within his party as well as the government. He had a genuine regard for the desires of the electorate, but paid lip service to democratic institutions;

his style of governance was authoritarian. The continuation of a state of emergency made effective opposition impossible. The press had little freedom of manoeuvre.[37]

In Bhutto's regime, institutions that he once thought were vital to Pakistan's political development continued to languish. Political parties, including the ruling PPP, were in chaos, if not in shambles. The parliament and the provincial legislatures were often adjourned for want of quorums, mainly because the prime minister or the concerned chief minister would not attend, except on rare occasions; and the higher bureaucracy remained demoralized because it had virtually no job security. Student unions and bar associations continued to be vigorous, but they were not institutions of governance. The only institutions prospering in Pakistan in 1976 were the security agencies.[38]

The Bhutto government enjoyed a comfortable majority in the parliament but instead of allowing the parliament to do its job and make law for the land, he adopted the technique of ruling the country through ordinances. He signed 219 ordinances from 1972 to July 1977, at an average rate of one ordinance per week.[39] With minimal opposition in the parliament and unrest on the streets in 1976, Bhutto confidently asked the intelligence agencies for their assessment of the outcome of the general elections to be held soon. The agencies assured him of success in the elections leading Bhutto to seek a fresh mandate by holding general elections in March 1977.[40]

Bhutto did not take the parliamentarians into confidence before decision-making, and often informed them after a certain period of delay. One of the reasons behind this was that a number of MNAs were in the parliament because Bhutto wished it so, and some could not even imagine becoming one without Bhutto's wish.[41] Hence, these Bhutto-sponsored members never dared to suggest any measures for strengthening the institution where they represented the people of their respective constituency. They could not resist the wishes of the executive during their participation in parliamentary procedures.

The national assembly's formation could also be called into question due to the treatment of the members of the assembly from Balochistan. Wali Khan, the opposition leader, said in 1973 that the assembly was not in order because the members from Balochistan had been denied their constitutional right of representing their electorate.[42]

The executive machinery of the country did not regard the parliament to be significant under any circumstances. For instance, privilege of parliamentarians was breached by the executive to such an extent that in a circular dated 23 December 1974, the acting chief minister of Sindh, under the orders of the prime minister had directed that no senator shall visit Lauri Sharif during any religious ceremony or on an occasion like an *Urs*. Over this, J.A. Rahim, on 27 January 1975, raised a question of breach of privilege of all senators from the province. The motion was opposed by the minister for law and parliamentary affairs on the grounds that such a privilege was not available to members of parliament under the constitution, and that the member did not raise the question at the earliest opportunity. The acting chairman agreed with the opposition and the motion was ruled out of order.[43]

The parliamentarians were arrested on the orders of the executive, and their voices could not be raised in the house of which they were elected members and which was supposed to be the most powerful institution of the parliamentary form of government. On 3 March 1976, Maulana Shah Ahmad Noorani raised a question regarding breach of his privilege alleging that on 19 December 1975, he was arrested and detained for about two hours, and the police officials concerned did not comply with the provisions of Rules 64 and 65 of the senate rules. The chairman ruled the motion out of order, observing that the question of privilege was not raised at the earliest opportunity.[44]

On another occasion, the issue of continued harassment of Maulana Shah Ahmad Noorani (senator) by the police, CID and intelligence personnel inside the government hostel was raised as a matter of privilege on 4 March 1976. The minister for finance argued that the allegations were not as specific as they did not name the official or the particular type of harassment caused by him to the senator. He also contended that the motion related to a matter in which the senate could not intervene. On 16 March, the leader of the house moved that the motion be referred to the committee on rules of procedure and privileges. The chairman, consequently and unwillingly, put the motion to the house, which was carried forward. As he allowed the motion to be moved, it was deemed to have been admitted under the rules.[45]

During the democratic period from 1971–7, the executive dominated the state of Pakistan more than any other institution. Z.A. Bhutto was, undoubtedly, a dominating leader and he proved to make the institution of executive as the centre of power as well. The parliament, on the other hand, could not exercise its autonomy free from the control of the executive. The members of the parliament, individually as well as collectively, remained in the shadows, and could not assert their constitutional authorities. Often the executive continued to use the parliament in support of its policies and decisions. The efforts of the opposition in the parliament regarding assertion of the position of legislature were often overshadowed by the executive, though the weakness of the opposition was also a factor in the strength of the executive. The parliament within was too weak to assert its position in front of the powerful executive. It also could not help the executive in the wake of public agitations and military intervention in the government in the form of martial law in 1977.

THE CABINET AND THE PARLIAMENT

Before the Bhutto regime, the cabinet had not been a substantial institution vis-à-vis the chief executive or the parliament. In most cases, the chief executive—be it the prime minister, president or governor general—would be more influential than the cabinet. For instance, Yunus Samad has observed that the supremacy of the planning committee was composed of secretaries from all the ministries over the cabinet from 1947 to 1953, and that in reality, the committee was a parallel cabinet composed of and headed by bureaucrats. All important decisions were reached there, and then presented to the cabinet for approval.[46]

President Ayub also ran the government without challenges to his authority. His government was highly centralized, in terms of law-making and policy decisions.[47] Ayub Khan and a few of his close aides like Manzur Qadir, would also lead the decisions of the cabinet. Despite the presence of able personalities, the cabinet consisted of a group of persons who were, in fact, close to Ayub Khan. Therefore, the cabinet could not be seen working as a powerful institution.

As far as abilities of the ministers were concerned, Bhutto's first team of ministers was unique in several ways. Barring Tridev Roy and Nurul Amin,[48] all the others were members of his political party. Almost all of them had a university education. Five of them had attended institutions of higher learning abroad. Seven out of ten ministers were practicing lawyers and one of them a practicing consulting civil engineer. One was a retired judge of the High Court. Except Jatoi, none of them were big landlords. It was a cabinet of professional men from the middle class, and its sole purpose was to serve Bhutto well during the first year of his government. The team went to work with zeal and dedication.[49]

Hussain Haqqani views that Bhutto's original political team had been replaced by a new team of ministers and advisors from the civil and military establishment. Under the influence of this team, the PPP's secretary general perceived 'Bhutto's tilt toward an obscurantist interpretation of Islam.'[50] This team too formed the cabinet of the chief executive.

However, the parliament was not free from the invisible influence of the cabinet; the prime minister too exerted influence over parliament through the cabinet. On one occasion, the speaker of the national assembly, the custodian of one of the houses of the parliament, did not hesitate to attend the meeting of the cabinet which, in fact, he was not part of. This was critically pointed out in the national assembly on 24 June 1974 by Ahmad Raza Kasuri. He drew the attention of the house to a photograph published in a newspaper, of a cabinet meeting with the speaker sitting next to the prime minister. He observed that the speaker was not a member of the cabinet and had no place in a party meeting or the meeting of the executive; he was above the cabinet. Abdul Qayyum Khan, minister for the interior, giving an explanation in support of the action of the speaker, said that the cabinet could invite any person to attend its meeting. However, he ignored the fact that it lowered the status of the national assembly in front of the cabinet. Another minister, Sheikh Mohammad Rashid, tried to clarify that the prime minister had to discuss the schedule of the budget session and had invited the speaker to attend the meeting.[51]

The speaker observed that he was 'summoned' for briefing on the legislative business of assembly. He was enquired about the timings of the sessions of assembly. The members did not accept the explanations of speaker and stressed the parliament's decisions were made in the meetings of the cabinet.[52] The speaker further informed that from the day he had been elected as speaker, he had not attended any party or public meeting, and neither had he held a press conference.[53] This was an answer to the allegation that the speaker had become partial by attending the meeting of the cabinet, but neither did Kasuri stress (nor did the speaker mention) that the honour and sanctity of the parliament was desecrated at that very moment when the speaker was 'summoned' to attend the meeting of the cabinet.

This encroachment of the cabinet over the position of the custodian of the national assembly took place in the days when Ahmad Raza Kasuri, an active member of the national assembly, made a statement during his visit to England to the effect that the assembly had no legal status, and as such had no respect for the house. The speaker did not let the issue be discussed in the house and called Kasuri in his chamber to 'explain certain matters' which were 'for the benefit of the house' and for 'the benefit of democracy.'[54]

In a parliamentary form of government, ministers are supposed to be answerable to the parliament, and for this purpose their presence in the sessions of the parliament is considered obligatory. But often, the concerned ministers did not deem it necessary to attend the sessions of the national assembly regularly. One instance is that of 28 November 1975, when Begum Nasim Jahan mentioned that the minister-in-charge was not present in the senate during a debate on a bill. The chairman pointed out that the law minister, one minister of state and the parliamentary secretaries were sitting in the house. The chairman remarked that in a democratic government, the cabinet was collectively responsible.[55]

In the meeting of the national assembly held on 28 August 1972, a member sought leave to move a privilege motion alleging a breach of privilege of MNAs. The aggrieved member alleged that Iftikhar Ahmad Tari, a Punjab provincial minister, had threatened him with dire consequences if he raised a point of privilege against the Punjab government, as was done by him earlier in a meeting of the national assembly, when it was working as a constitution-making body. The mover added that what the minister said was a direct threat to the freedom of the elected representatives in the opposition. He produced copies of the newspapers in which the said remarks of Iftikhar Ahmad Tari were published. The minister for education and provincial coordination raised a point of order objecting to the admissibility of the privilege motion on the grounds that the reference was to an incident which occurred when the national assembly was sitting as a constitution-making body. He argued that under the rules this matter should be raised by the member when the assembly sits as a constitution-making body.[56]

It was also contended that the speech of the minister of the Punjab violated the privilege of a member of the national assembly. The matter was decided to be discussed in the house. There was a motion for referring the matter to the privileges committee, but, after getting a sense of the house, the speaker announced that the matter is to be referred to the privileges committee, which will report to the house by 5 September 1972.[57]

ARMY VS THE PARLIAMENT

The military's constitutional mandate in Pakistan (laid down in the constitutions of 1956, 1962, and 1973) is limited to securing the frontiers against external threat and assisting in national emergencies or natural disasters on the request of civilian authorities.[58] Yet somehow, since the independence of the country, the Pakistan military has been the most politically influential institution in the country.[59] Jinnah, soon after independence, chided a young army officer who complained against important posts being entrusted to British officers. Jinnah cautioned the officer not to forget that the armed forces were the servants of the people, 'you do not make national policy; it is we, the civilians, who decide these issues, and it is your duty to carry out these tasks with which you are entrusted.'[60] Despite this advice from the Father of the Nation, military intervention in politics is the most conspicuous feature of Pakistan's political landscape.[61] Pakistan's polity has been under the influence of the military through most of its history; even when it was not in power it has been 'behind the steering wheel.'[62] That is why some view it as the largest political party.[63]

The military considers itself as an alternative institution, capable of contributing to socioeconomic and political development.[64] It is claimed that the military is sucked into governance and politics because it is the most modern and capable institution.[65] Its organizational discipline versus the inefficacy of political institutions is one of the major justifications for political intervention by the army. Socio-political analysts, such as Ayesha Jalal, Saeed Shafqat, Hussain Haqqani, and Hassan Abbas find the army to be extremely manipulative. The general essence of their argument is that the military deliberately acquired multiple roles and weakened the state and its political system for its own interests.[66]

Even its defeat against India in the war of 1971 did not result in the army's withdrawal from politics and civilian affairs.[67] After that, the military rulers, having failed to manage the state, temporarily assumed a low-key profile by allowing Bhutto to run the country.[68] Bhutto, by planting seeds of constitutionalism in Pakistan, by founding PPP, and by ensuring elections, broke the authority of the Pakistan Army in internal Pakistani affairs.[69] Soon after taking control of the country after 1971, he compelled forty-three senior officers of the armed forces to retire; these included two generals, eleven lieutenant generals, ten major generals, one vice-admiral, four rear-admirals, one air marshal, and two air vice marshals. He, ostensibly, took this drastic step to purge the defence forces of what he called Bonapartism.[70] Bhutto also began a campaign to publicise the military's surrender ceremony in Dhaka. The army opposed this campaign vigorously and the news reel of the surrender was not shown again on PTV.[71]

Addressing the nation, Bhutto said, 'Come what may, these Bonapartic influences must be rooted out in the interest of the country; in the interest of the Pakistan of tomorrow; in the interest of the armed forces and the people of Pakistan.'[72] Bhutto even expressed his dissatisfaction with the traditional concept of defence services, and toyed with the idea of a people's army. He said, 'We must take a leaf or two out of North Vietnam's military textbooks. A people's army, rather than a conventional army, is the philosophy that will guide us in our new defence policy.'[73]

As to a military takeover, Article 6 (1) termed abrogation of the constitution as an act of 'high treason' and stated that, 'any person who abrogates, or attempts or conspires to abrogate, subverts or attempts or conspires to subvert the Constitution by use of force or show of force or by other unconstitutional means shall be guilty of high treason.'[74]

Bhutto wanted to bring into his hands all the levers of power, and this was the only time in the turbulent history of military–civil relations that a civilian leader was able to prevail over the leaders of the armed forces.[75] Bhutto's control of the army was revealed with the resignation of the army chief, General Gul Hasan. The coordination between Bhutto and General Gul Hasan, who had replaced General Yahya Khan, did not last long because of the differences between them on several issues. For instance, Bhutto proposed that all army officers should be screened by the police or the intelligence. Gul Hasan rejected this proposal since he was satisfied with the normal vetting process. Bhutto wanted to send the army to Karachi to enforce discipline amongst the restive workforce. Gul Hasan disagreed and asked him to use the police. Bhutto wanted to attend a meeting of promotion and selection board due to sit on 5 February 1972, to replace officer casualties and to retire senior officers; General Gul Hasan did not agree. Towards the end of February 1972, Bhutto asked Gul Hasan to crush the police strike in Peshawar. At the same time, Bhutto asked national security advisor, Major General (retd) Akbar Khan for the same action, who in return, ordered the School of Artillery in Nowshera to dispatch two 25-pounder guns with crews and ammunition to Peshawar. He also ordered some recruits from the Punjab Regimental Centre, undergoing training in Mardan to be dispatched to Peshawar, but General Gul Hasan stopped both attempts.[76]

Soon the time came when Bhutto decided to get rid of Gul Hasan, after he refused to provide a briefing on the contingency planning for all ministers. A few days later, on 3 March 1972, Lt. Gen. Gul Hasan Khan and Air Marshal Rahim Khan were asked to resign from service in a very dramatic way.[77] According to Ghulam Mustafa Khar, both Gul Hasan and Rahim Khan were ready to mount a coup, but the conspiracy was discovered and Bhutto managed to have these men arrested in the President House.[78]

After General Gul Hasan's resignation, General Tikka Khan was appointed chief of army staff. The title 'chief of staff' replaced the title 'commander-in-chief' for all three branches of the armed forces of Pakistan. Air Marshal Zafar Chaudhry was appointed as the first chief of air staff, who replaced Air Marshal Rahim Khan.[79] General Tikka Khan (chief of army staff, 1972–6) emphasized on professionalism and loyalty to the constitution and the civilian authority established there under.[80]

General Tikka Khan's loyalty with the civilian government coincided with Bhutto's hold over other troublemakers in the armed forces. On 30 March 1973, the government announced that fifty-nine military officers had been arrested on charges of plotting to overthrow the government. According to authorities, the arrested officers were planning to overthrow the government during a military march-past ceremony by arresting the president, the governor of Punjab, the ministers and the chief of the army staff. A few weeks later, on 2 May 1973, twelve officers from the air force were arrested on the same charges.[81] The court martial trial of the accused military officers began on 9 July 1973. It was presided over by Major General Ziaul Haq (later general and the president of Pakistan).[82]

Again, there was some resentment over government policies in a small group of the army and air force officers. This came to light when fourteen officers of the Pakistan Air Force, including two group captains, and twenty-one officers of the army including two brigadiers (one of whom was retired) were arrested on charges of conspiring to seize power by arresting top government executives and the top brass of the army.[83] The plan was discovered before it was launched. The chief of air staff, Air Marshal Zafar Chaudhry, ordered a premature retirement of all the fourteen air force officers. Their cases were reviewed by the government. After review, the premature retirement of seven officers was cancelled. The case ended when the ban on reinstating them was lifted. The revision of the air headquarters decision was resented by the chief of air staff. Eventually, he conceded to the civilian leadership's request for his resignation.[84]

The British envoy, in the light of these confusing circumstances, commented that 'the army is the only foreseeable alternative government, but they have shown no desire to repeat the experience of 1958–71.'[85]

General Ziaul Haq, who succeeded Tikka Khan in 1976, initially advised his troops to adhere to their professional roles, and paid tribute to the civilian government for maintaining a deep interest in the modernization of the military.[86] The cooperation of the armed forces or the upper hand of the Bhutto regime over the institution of the armed forces was marred by the new elections when a movement was started to protest against the rigging in elections. This gave the army general a chance to enforce martial law. Thus, the short period of civilian hegemony over the military ended.

Bhutto was temporarily successful in asserting the primacy of the civilian government.[87] He successfully curbed the role of the armed forces in the political permutations of the country and subordinated it to civilian leadership. He also demolished the supremacy of bureaucracy in political affairs by affecting reforms in the civil services. He succeeded in evolving political and economic institutions, yet he failed miserably in embracing democratic norms. This shook the foundations of parliamentary democracy in Pakistan.[88]

While asserting civilian supremacy over the military, the Bhutto government adopted policies to extend the popular support it enjoyed at the time of assumption of power, and endeavoured to lay down the infrastructure for political institutions. These policy measures included the introduction of socio-economic reforms, formulation of the constitution, and the use of the ruling PPP as a major instrument of political mobilization.[89] Bhutto's reforms of the military and bureaucracy were also meant to accumulate power within the office of the prime minister, subsiding the military-bureaucratic elite along with the parliament and the cabinet.[90]

It is worth mentioning that due to Indian designs, it was impossible to decrease the power of the army to its maximum extent. Therefore, Mustafa Khar maintains that Bhutto could not harness the army as was necessary. He reduced its powers in the beginning but could not continue to do so.[91] From the standpoint of Bhutto's relationship with the military, he made the blunder of miscalculating the resilience of the armed forces in thwarting the strategic changes he had brought about in their management. Initially, he seemed to have taken a major step forward in changing the command and control structure of the organization, which granted the prime minister the position of supreme commander of the armed forces.[92]

Bhutto attempted to control the military by stopping the growth of its commercial ventures, which curtailed its financial autonomy. However, these measures were reduced to nothing by the lack of change in the overall tenor of policymaking. He erred by viewing the military as a junior power that could be controlled and utilized for promoting his interests. Hence, he allowed the army to regroup. The military capitalized on Bhutto's dependence on military force for building his personal political power. It emerged, from the ashes of 1971, sufficiently strengthened to prepare for another takeover in 1977.[93] He enjoyed popular support in the early stages of his rule, while the military's reputation had declined dramatically, owing to the East Pakistan debacle. However, Bhutto's assertion of civilian supremacy did not prove durable for three major reasons. First, his efforts to personalize power rather than work towards establishing viable participatory institutions and processes eroded his popular support. Second, in their determination to dislodge Bhutto, some of the opposition leaders made it clear in the later stages of the anti-Bhutto agitation (1977) that they would not challenge the military in the event of his overthrow. Third, the military had recovered from the shock of 1971 by 1977. When the senior commanders found out that the Bhutto regime was discredited and could not survive without their support, they retrieved political initiative.[94]

During the aforementioned situation of conflict between the chief executive and the army, the parliament remained aloof; there were no mentions or discussion about these incidents in the parliament.

How the Assembly Tackled the Army?

Having eliminated the generals whom Bhutto perceived as possible or real rivals, the parliament opted to establish and strengthen civilian control through constitutional means. The parliament's policy was to confine the function of the military to defence and security matters.[95] The parliament was authorized to formulate laws for those found guilty of high treason. In September 1973, the parliament passed a law providing a death sentence or life imprisonment for the subversion of the constitution. The constitution also laid down an oath for the personnel of the armed forces which specifically forbade them to take part in political activities of any kind.[96]

The defence of the country, as well as the institution responsible for the defence, was seldom discussed in the proceedings of the house. On 17 January 1974, Khawaja Safdar (senator) sought leave of the house to discuss the failure of the federal government to provide the Pakistan defence forces with modern weapons in order to enable them to effectively protect the borders against probable Indian aggression in the future. The protection was especially for the Indian armed forces, who had been equipped with the latest and most sophisticated arms including SAM–6. The minister of state for foreign affairs and defence, opposing the motion, assured the mover and the house that there had been no inaction, neglect, or dereliction by the government of duty in ensuring the defence of the country. However, the minister stated that he could not disclose those measures. When the mover asked permission to speak on the admissibility, the deputy chairman of the senate ruled that many things could not be divulged in the house for the sake of public interest. Therefore, he did not permit the adjournment motion to be made. The mover, however, insisted on speaking on the issue. Finding no way to satisfy the mover, the motion was put to the house, which voted not to discuss the motion.[97]

On 3 December 1974, Sardar Sherbaz Khan Mazari wanted copies of the White Paper on Balochistan to be provided to MNAs. Malik Mohammad Akhtar, without making any promises, said that he would supply the document to the members. He reminded them that the White Paper was not an assembly record and could not be treated as such.[98]

On 16 January 1974, Maulana Noorani sought to move an adjournment motion relating to the statement of the army chief, General Tikka Khan, on the installation of latest weapons near the border of the country. The minister of state for defence objected to the adjournment motion, stating that the statement of General Tikka Khan appeared to have been misreported in the newspapers. According to the press, he had announced the induction of modern weapons into the armed forces of the neighbouring country, and not about the installation of the same on the borders of Pakistan. He assured the house that the government was taking necessary measures to meet the situation, but could not disclose details. The objection was upheld by the speaker who ruled the motion out of order, as a discussion thereon would be detrimental to public interest.[99]

On 15 June 1974, during a discussion on the general budget, Abdul Khaliq Khan used the word mercenary to describe the Pakistan Army, and also made allegations of atrocities committed by the army in East Pakistan. An objection was taken under rule 226 (j) of the *Rules of Procedure and Conduct of Business in the National Assembly, 1973* that the words were treasonable, seditious and defamatory. Thereupon, the speaker observed that the words 'mercenary army' shall not be published in the press, but they should remain on record. When a member requested that it should be published in the press to expose such persons, the speaker observed that there was no restriction that the matter relating to the army should be barred from the press. He insisted though that this particular word should neither be released nor expunged. Thereafter, the deputy leader of the house requested that allegations of atrocities on East Pakistanis, which were made by Abdul Khaliq Khan in his speech, should also not be published in the press, since the war commission was inquiring into it, and because it had international complications.[100]

CREATION OF THE FEDERAL SECURITY FORCE

The creation of the Federal Security Force (FSF)[101] was also a controversial issue between the army and the government. The army considered it a parallel institution that might decrease the need and importance of the army. It would also negatively affect the hegemony of the institution. The formation of the FSF was also an act that was committed without the consent of the parliament. The act of the formation of the FSF was not brought to the corridors of the parliament, and was made through a presidential order.

The FSF operated like Bhutto's private *Savak*; it signalled the significance of military force in political discourse. The FSF also deepened the fears of the generals regarding Bhutto's intention to minimize the importance of the military. The establishment of an auxiliary force would ultimately reduce his reliance on the army.[102] The FSF was generally used instead to disrupt opposition meetings and harass government opponents. This expanded the political role of security agencies, and led to the questioning of Bhutto's credentials as a democrat. It also weakened the political foundations of his elected government, making Bhutto more vulnerable to political blunders.[103]

During a general discussion on the budget, Rao Khurshid Ali Khan (MNA) criticized the role of certain federal agencies in connection to the law and order situation in provinces. The interior minister objected that the law and order situation in provinces was the exclusive responsibility of provincial governments, and that the federal government could not be involved in such matters. The speaker held that there were certain federal agencies which could be utilized by the provincial governments for maintaining law and order. As these agencies were financed by the federal government, any incident showing failure on the part of such agencies to maintain law and order in the provinces could be discussed in the house, and criticism to that extent was justified.[104]

On the 17 January 1975, a member sought leave of the house to move an adjournment motion to discuss the use of the FSF by the Punjab government to prevent Air Marshal (retd) Asghar Khan from holding a public meeting in Lahore, on 12 January 1975. He further alleged that the failure of the federal government in dissuading the Punjab government from using the FSF for curbing the civil liberties and fundamental rights of the public had sent a countrywide wave of resentment. The minster for interior opposed the motion on the grounds that it did not primarily concern the federal government and denied allegations about the use of the FSF. He further observed that under the FSF Employment Rules 1974, the FSF, when requisitioned by the provincial government, acted under the orders of the magistrate, who was a provincial officer. He added that law and order was a provincial subject and the federal government had no power under the constitution to give directions or orders to the provincial governments in this respect. The deputy chairman ruled the motion out of order on the grounds of denial of allegations by the minister, and that it did not lie within the domain of the federal government to interfere in matters of law and order.[105]

Pakistani political scientists, Saeed Shafqat and Mohammad Waseem, hold the civil bureaucracy responsible for the relative weakness of civilian institutions and the increase in the military's influence.[106]

The relationship between the army and the government was often governed by the personality of Bhutto. To curtail the hegemony of the power-seeking generals, Bhutto made efforts to weaken the authority of the army over the civil government from inside the army itself. Bhutto, however, did not fully succeed in lowering the institutional supremacy of the army. The defence of the country remained outside the scope of parliamentary affairs. Even the political decisions to obstruct the authority of generals were made without any reference to or from the parliament. The parliament could also not assert its powers in contrast to the army.

CIVIL BUREAUCRATIC OBSTACLES IN THE WAY OF THE PARLIAMENT

The ideal form of democratic rule relies heavily on the functioning of the parliament as an institution that sets goals for the larger public in terms of decision-making and policymaking. In contrast, the bureaucracy is supposed to be a machine that implements the decisions and policies of the government on ground level. Notwithstanding the significance of the legislature in the democratic political system, the powers of the parliament have been restricted by the dominant role of bureaucracy in Pakistan. This encroachment of bureaucracy into the domains of legislation took place due to several factors. One of those factors is related to the fact that the parties in power and opposition tend to control the voting behaviour and the speaking pattern of the legislators on the floor of the parliament. In this way, the leadership of the parties steer the activities of the parliament. The same party leadership, in a democratic setup, also seize command over the bureaucracy, and establish full control over the system.[107]

While this setup has been ideal, Pakistan's functioning has not been very democratic. It has been relatively difficult for its legislature or electorate to assert itself against the all-powerful executive[108] or the bureaucracy. In Pakistan, institutions have never been sufficiently strong and the country has often been governed through authoritarianism.[109] Practically, the parliament remains a subordinate legislature. On the other hand, the executive plays a pre-eminent role in national affairs as compared to that of the parliament. Notwithstanding the forces which originate from outside of the parliament and end up controlling the country, the political players consider the institutions of the parliament an essential segment of modern political structures. The parliament and its subordinate institutions provide legitimacy to the political order.[110] Despite power residing outside the parliament, it is needed by power holders in order to win moral and legal authority. Therefore, it can be claimed that the government is a representative of the masses, and the parliament represents public opinion. It was for this reason that all four military regimes arranged the elections, and created assemblies which granted legitimacy to military rulers.[111]

Since the inception of Pakistan, it was ruled over by an oligarchy formed by the civil and military bureaucracy. The bureaucracy was thus the top-most tier of the country's oligarchic system. Civil and military bureaucracy, however, remained busy in efforts to keep each other at bay. The civil bureaucracy succeeded in these efforts even during the martial law regime.[112] Pakistan inherited, from the British, the equation of power between the legislature and the executive, while the British were the colonial powers that felt the need for a stronger state bureaucracy for the purpose of establishing control over India. Subsequently, this pattern of government persisted and, civil and military bureaucracy succeeded in developing their own interests in controlling the politics of the state. Thus, in the presence of various democratic institutions, they were able to play the ultimate arbitrator's role in the state of Pakistan. Hamza Alavi has described the weakness of Pakistan's political institutions as the crisis of an overdeveloped state.[113]

Pakistan's civil bureaucracy was strong in making and enforcing decisions, however, it did not work alone in its implementation. On the other hand, while ruling over the country, it had close ties with the military. Sometimes, it also happened that both institutions, the military and civil bureaucracy, also came into conflict with each other over control of the country. During the first four years of Pakistan, which ended with the death of Liaquat Ali Khan, civil servants became very close to the chief executive. Though democratic institutions were present, the bureaucrats were attached to the government because both Jinnah and Liaquat Ali Khan relied heavily on the bureaucrats. Jinnah would encourage the top civil servants of various departments (both central and provincial) to directly communicate with him on matters of significance.[114] Former Indian Civil Service (ICS) officers were appointed as governors of three provinces in Pakistan.[115] Two of these governors were so politically strong that they also got the chance to preside over meetings of the cabinet.

In the case of Pakistan, no scholar negates bureaucratic importance and influence in contrast to parliamentary influence and significance. Many scholars have established the notion that before Bhutto, the institution of bureaucracy was stronger than the parliament.

Bhutto enjoyed the support of the masses in a certain way. Therefore, he attempted to exercise control over the bureaucrats with the help of structural changes as well as 'purges'. In this regard, he introduced administrative reforms in 1973. Through these reforms, he made an attempt to establish supremacy of the parliament over bureaucrats. His purpose was the acceptance of the supremacy of political leadership by the bureaucrats, at least at the upper hierarchy of governance. Soofia Mumtaz, was of the opinion that this supremacy of political leadership meant the supremacy of the parliamentarians.[116] In his attempt to subdue the bureaucracy, special guarantees for Pakistan's civil service ensured in the constitutions of 1956 and 1962 were abolished.[117] As a consequence of the war of 1971, the Bhutto regime characterized the former government as corrupt, weak, and inefficient. These allegations towards the former government machinery took practical shape in the form of punitive action against the bureaucracy. Within three months of Bhutto taking control as president, the Removal from Service Regulation 1972 was promulgated under martial law order no. 14. According to press reports at the time, 1828 civil officers were forcibly retired. This number was six times greater than the number of government officers who were removed in 1969. This removal of the officers, particularly the senior ones, weakened the power of the bureaucracy. It weakened at least every cadre of civil superior services. Therefore, the CSP's influence became weak in every way. Gradually, the civil bureaucracy, especially the CSP, became weaker to the extent that it could neither block any effort at change nor could it resist the control of politicians.[118]

Notwithstanding Bhutto's efforts to establish more control over the civil bureaucracy, the latter continued to enjoy its hold on the Pakistani state. As a result, the weakening of the institution of bureaucracy during the early phase of the Bhutto regime was turned into a strength in the later part of this period. During this phase, his 'kangaroo bureaucracy' did not only become stronger but also succeeded in getting a significant share in the government.[119] Bhutto used the civil bureaucracy and the bureaucrats as a tool for enforcement of his personal authoritarian rule against political rivals, especially through police repression.[120] Bhutto made most of the decisions himself, later using civil bureaucracy to implement them. The bureaucracy was tamed by some key bureaucrats whom he trusted and who yielded the power.[121]

According to Mubashir Hasan, by October 1974, for all practical purposes, the stronger personalities from Bhutto's old team were gone; the place of his old political team had been taken by bureaucracy in the persons of Aziz Ahmad, Vaqar Ahmad, Masud Mahmud, Yahya Bakhtiar, and Kausar Niazi.[122] When Ghulam Mustafa Khar asked Bhutto why he had opted for a team consisting of bureaucrats, his reply was that to come into power, he needed a special team of political workers, but to retain power he needed bureaucrats.[123]

Vaqar Ahmad occupied an important post of cabinet secretary, combined with the post of establishment secretary, which made him the most powerful civil servant ever. An implacable foe of the traditional hold of the civil superior service, Vaqar Ahmad played a leading role in alienating what was once called the steel framework of the British Raj.

Dr Mubashir Hasan mentioned a specific case as an example. By the middle of June 1974, Vaqar Ahmad had become all powerful. When the two senior CSP officers, Hasan Zaheer and Masud Mufti, who had been detained in India as prisoners of the 1971 war, finally reached Pakistan, his request for their posting in the ministry of finance was not complied with. He raised the matter with Bhutto. To follow Mubashir's own statement, 'In his comments, Vaqar Ahmad wrote explanatory paragraphs which ended with:

...While every effort is made to meet the wishes of the minister or the ministry, the Establishment Division has to keep requirements of the government as a whole when proposing such appointments.'[124]

On this issue, Bhutto wrote to me: 'How I would feel relieved if this simple fact was realized. Please appreciate my apparent difficulties. I have to take decisions for the whole country. It is not possible to satisfy everyone. Even a saint, or a *Wali*, or a new prophet cannot do it. Hope you do not misunderstand.'

...Time had changed a year earlier, confronted with a similar request from me, the same Vaqar Ahmad would have come to my office with a long list of officers and would have requested me to select those I wanted appointed to the Ministry of Finance. Little did he or Bhutto realize that by then, almost all the ministers were very unhappy with Vaqar and his arrogant attitude.[125]

The ministers confirmed the domination of the bureaucracy while speaking in the parliament. The statements of a common personality or an opposition member could be negated as being biased, but a minister's statements cannot be labelled as biased against the government. The complaint of the minister about the overwhelming rule of bureaucracy could be seen in the proceedings of the senate on 27 February 1976 when a senator moved an adjournment motion to discuss a statement made by the federal communication minister. The statement was published in *Jang* on 23 December 1975. The minister stated that the government was being run as a government-under-bureaucracy, and not as a government of the people, as the name of the party had claimed or as the leaders had labelled. The motion was ruled out of order by the chairman on the same grounds that were often used for the rejection of most adjournment motions; the motion was not concerned with a matter of recent occurrence.[126] Even then, the appearance of the statement in the national press and its echo in the senate indicates the bureaucracy controlled the country. The minister who filed the complaint due to bureaucrats' pressure did not deem it suitable to raise the matter in the parliament because he was sure that he would not get proper support there. On the contrary, he used the medium of press to highlight his concern.

The bureaucrats could misbehave with a parliamentarian publicly. Such misbehaviour on the part of officials or police were mentioned in the parliament on many occasions, especially when privilege motions were moved. One such issue was raised through Sherbaz Mazari's privilege motion on 17 December 1974 in the national assembly. Mazari had alleged that the police had stopped him from seeing the detainees at the Sihala Jail. This act of stopping a parliamentarian had violated his privilege as an MNA. In response to his motion, the minister of state for parliamentary affairs opposed the motion and explained that the privilege of the member had not been violated and thus the house did not need to intervene. The mover was of the view that parliamentarians were representatives of the people, and that public servants did not have the authority to humiliate them. He stressed that the dignity of the MNAs may be recognized, and in this regard, their affiliation with ruling or opposition parties should not be considered at all. The minister of state for parliamentary affairs agreed with the mover, assuring him that the government would look into the grievances of the mover, and in the case that it considers it essential, the defaulting officers would be admonished. The minister also assured the house that he would keep the institution informed about the actions of the government regarding the privilege of one of the members of the institution of the parliament. After the assurance of the minister on the floor of the house, the speaker of the national assembly observed, regarding the privilege of the MNAs that they must be honoured without any discrimination of being in the opposition or treasury benches.[127]

Despite such observations of the speaker and statements of the ministers supporting the point of view, as well as the status of the parliamentarians on some occasions, the bureaucracy could not be subdued altogether and superiority of the parliament over the institution of bureaucracy could not be ensured. Before the first general elections of 1970, political leaders and parties generally accepted the superiority and lawful authority of the bureaucratic elite. The colonial administrative structure, which established the supremacy of the bureaucratic elite, performed satisfactorily with minor irritations, until 1970.[128] If Bhutto had succeeded to cow down the bureaucracy at the beginning of his tenure, he did not manage it with the help of the parliament. The parliament was left out of the power-game, which was being played by Bhutto and the executive machinery called the bureaucracy. Again, during the latter period of the Bhutto government, when he was able to secure cooperation from the bureaucracy, it had no concern with respect to the commanding position of the parliament in comparison with the bureaucracy. In case of comparison of parliamentary and bureaucratic institution, the latter was more dominating in exercising control over the government. The personalities who dominated the government in some way used the institution of bureaucracy as a machine that supported their autocratic rule over the country.

Bhutto did not prove to be a weak prime minister; he also did not care to work within constitutional limits. Moreover, he did not let institutions of the state flourish independently and freely. He, as the president and chief martial law administrator, did not pay much regard to democratic institutions such as the national assembly or the parliament.[129]

There were many occasions when an issue of maltreatment of members of the parliament (at the hands of the opposition) by the police was reported in the parliament through means of privilege motions. Despite such proceedings of the parliament, the members did not succeed in establishing their influence on the institution of bureaucracy. In the first two years of Bhutto's governance, he managed to exercise dominance over the bureaucratic institution. However, it was not the parliament which helped him in managing such dominance over the bureaucracy. On the other hand, the actions as well as the strength of an individual executive could control bureaucratic elements. In the later part of the Bhutto regime, the bureaucracy had to cooperate with the head of the state who was the chief executive, and in fact was also the *boss* of the bureaucracy. This reaffirms the fact that the parliament was not stronger than the bureaucracy.

The parliamentarians themselves were responsible for the bureaucratic hold; and the major cause of bureaucratic dominance was that the parliamentarians were not able to abide by the principles and the spirit of liberal democracy—where respect for law, tolerance of dissent, minorities and opposition groups is a prerequisite, and needed to be developed. The dominant political party, namely the PPP, and her leadership failed to promote a pro-democracy environment—an environment in which plurality of views was encouraged, and conflict of views and values could be resolved through non-violent means.[130]

The first bicameral parliament of Pakistan was not a strong institution in contrast to the mature institution of bureaucracy that had experience as well as capacity of dominance over the system since the colonial period. Neither the ruling political parties nor the powerful chief executive was willing to give larger importance to the representative institutions; nor were the parliamentarians skilled enough to exert supremacy vis-à-vis the bureaucracy. The constitution was framed by the parliament, and it was considered a great performance of the national assembly as a constitution-making body, but decision-making and monitoring of activities regarding bureaucratic functions became difficult for the parliament. The standing committees which were constituted for the purpose of monitoring bureaucracy were present, but were not able to harness bureaucracy which worked regardless of any influences from the parliament. Bhutto's asset was the popular support which he enjoyed at the beginning of his rule. Instead of using mass appeal 'to institutionalize the institutions', in the words of Rizvi, the whole network of the political system was built around his personality.[131]

REDUCTION IN THE POWERS OF THE JUDICIARY

Bhutto's government had moved amendments in the constitution, curtailing the powers and jurisdiction of the superior courts. While comparing the powers of the judiciary in contrast to that of the parliament during the Bhutto regime, Burki viewed that the power of declaring a political party illegal was exercised with the approval of the Supreme Court, and as demonstrated by later events, the court was ready to oblige.[132] The British envoy deduced that the higher courts of the country were made powerless and were unable to protect the lives and the honour of the citizens by the amendments and special ordinances of the government.[133]

The powers of the courts were curtailed by the government with the help of the legislation in the parliament. Bhutto government's decision to curtail the powers and jurisdiction of the courts, preventing them from granting relief to political opponents, particularly in exercise of constitutional jurisdiction under Article 199, came about under the Fourth Amendment.[134] The High Court's power to grant bail was extinguished by the Fifth Amendment in the matter of offences falling under the Defence of Pakistan Rules.[135] The Supreme Court, like the High Court in the provinces, claimed and sometimes displayed proper independence. This was clearly a chronic irritant for Bhutto; while publicly applauded, it was gradually made to erode.[136] This amendment was passed in a very unfortunate manner. The members of the opposition in the national assembly wanted to hold a debate, but they were denied permission to speak, and were physically thrown out of the assembly by the security staff.[137]

A further encroachment on the independence of the judiciary was embodied in the Fifth Amendment to the constitution. The bill was passed by the national assembly on 5 September 1976 by 111 votes. The opposition staged a walkout during the second reading of the bill. It was passed by the senate on 8 September 1976, and became an act on 15 September after receiving assent from the president.[138] Through this amendment, the judiciary was made to feel insecure; it was snubbed, and its powers to punish for contempt of court were curtailed.[139]

This Sixth Amendment to the constitution is another instance of the arbitrary style of working of the chief executive through the parliament. This amendment was passed rather hastily overnight while the national assembly was having its last session before its dissolution. A tenure system was introduced for the first time for a chief justice of a High Court without involving any obligation on the part of the executive to appoint a chief justice on the basis of seniority. The government was also empowered to transfer judges. The Sixth Amendment Act enabled the government to retain the services of a particular person as head of the country's judiciary.[140]

Through the parliament, though, without the consensus between the government and the opposition, the power of the courts was further reduced by excluding a whole range of political offences from their jurisdiction. Special courts and tribunals were created to try these offences. The procedures prescribed for the trial of these offences were loaded against the accused. Of these trials, the Hyderabad trial became widely known, in which Khan Abdul Wali Khan and several other leaders of the defunct NAP were prosecuted in 1975 before a special tribunal.[141]

On many occasions, sub judicial matters were not discussed in the national assembly. Even the speaker, over the issue of the arrest of Agha Shorish Kashmiri, ruled that the national assembly could not discuss the matter that was in court, even if the writ was not admitted; the matter became sub judice as soon as the writ was filed. He contended, '...the discretion contained in Rule 88 (5) was that when a matter was sub judice, no resolution could be moved; and if no resolution could be moved, then no adjournment motion could be moved.'[142] However, on an occasion when the deputy speaker of the national assembly was summoned to court, the assembly reacted violently. The assembly asserted the parliament's supremacy on the grounds that power had been vested in it by the constitution, in an incident when an MNA filed a civil suit with the administrative civil judge in Rawalpindi against the Government of Pakistan, the chairman of the house, and the library committee, challenging the decision of the committee to realize punitive charges from those members who were unlawfully occupying accommodation in the Central Government Hostel. The said member had also filed an application with the court for a stay order, and the administrative civil judge had summoned the deputy speaker in her capacity as chairperson of the committee to appear on 11 June 1974. Ashraf Khatoon Abbasi, the deputy speaker and the chairperson of the house and the library committee moved a privilege motion against the MNA for a civil suit. The mover explained that the decision relating to punitive charges was taken by the committee in exercise of the powers vested under the constitution. Under Article 69 (2) of the constitution, the deputy speaker, being an officer of the national assembly, was not subject to the jurisdiction of any court in respect of the exercise of powers as chairperson of the committee. Thus, by bringing legal proceedings against her, the member of the national assembly had committed a breach of the privilege granted to the assembly under the previously mentioned article of the constitution. Sardar Shaukat Hayat Khan (MNA) deduced that as the high privilege of the whole house was involved, it did not need to be referred to the privileges committee, and could be discussed in the house, and action could be taken against the member.

Thereupon, the house sent the matter to the privileges committee in order to give the accused member an opportunity to defend himself.[143]

The action of the administrative civil judge Rawalpindi was also called into question through the privilege motion for committing a breach of privilege laid down in Article 69 (2) of the constitution, and by summoning the chairman of the committee when the assembly was in session. This was due to the violation of the privileges granted under sections 3 and 4 of the Members of the National Assembly (Exemption from Preventive Detention and Personal Appearance) Ordinance, 1963. The speaker facilitated the moving of the motion. This was because rule 68 (1) of the *Rules of Procedure and Conduct of Business in the National Assembly 1973* dictated that not more than one question of privileges could be raised by the same member in a single sitting. The speaker advised that the second privilege motion should be moved by some other member of the committee in an evening sitting. Accordingly, during the evening sitting, another member moved a verbal motion for the suspension of sub-rule 3 (a) of rule 226 of the rules of procedure which barred discussion on any matter which was sub judice. The privilege motion was referred to the privileges committee to report back within fifteen days.[144]

On another occasion, when there was a matter of the arrest of Mukhtar Rana (MNA) commenting on the superiority of the parliament over the judiciary, Sardar Shaukat Hayat Khan (MNA) said on the floor of the house, '...the Parliament is the mother of all the courts of law and the Sovereign Parliament has, in the past, called upon those people who are keeping a Member of the house in custody to be brought before the Commons, and when the custodians resisted, they compelled them and tried the custodians for contempt. This is the way of the democratic world.'[145]

Contending the supremacy of the assembly, he urged the speaker of the national assembly to order sergeant-at-arms to go and bring back Mukhtar Rana (MNA) who was in custody of the police, to the house. He also stressed that when he was brought to the house, they would decide whether they should try the court of law which tried him.[146]

The courts helped the parliament in extending its powers. Bhutto, before putting the resolution of the recognition of Bangladesh in the assembly, asked the Supreme Court to rule on whether such a resolution was constitutional. The Supreme Court replied that there was no bar on it.[147] It was after this verdict of the Supreme Court, that the parliament acquired the legitimacy to recognize Bangladesh.

POLITICAL PARTIES AND THE PARLIAMENT

The parliament comprised the members who were affiliated with some political parties. Political parties are an integral part of a democratic political system, and a parliament endorses political conditions in which political parties survive and develop easily. In turn, these parties strengthen the parliament. The inter-relationship between political parties and the parliament can be studied with the description of the former within and outside the parliament.

PPP held 85 of the 144 national assembly seats. It, however, commanded majority in only two provinces (Punjab and Sindh). In the NWFP, the PPP secured only three seats out of the 40 of the provincial assembly, and in the case of one of those seats (won by Hayat Mohammad Khan Sherpao), the success of PPP was made possible by the support lent to it by the NAP. In the case of Balochistan, the PPP had not been able to win a single seat out of twenty. In both these provinces, the NAP and the JUI together commanded an absolute majority.[148]

A convention was held in Rawalpindi between 28 February and 1 March 1973, where the United Democratic Front (UDF) was formed, in order to oppose the PPP action in Balochistan. It consisted of JUIP, PDP, PML (Council), PML (Convention), NAP, JUP, JI, and the independent parliamentary group. Led by the Pir Pagara, Sayyid Mardan Ali Shah with Mufti Mahmud as the vice-president, the aims and objectives of the UDF included evolving ways and means to restore democracy, checking dictatorship, and striving for an Islamic democratic and parliamentary constitution.[149]

During the formation of the constitution, the boycott of UDF in the parliament confronted Bhutto with the choice of either coming to terms with the UDF or forcing a federal constitution without agreement, and in the absence of all the representatives of one of the federating units.[150]

The UDF, though comparatively few in number, included all the MNAs from Balochistan.[151] The majority in the national assembly (1973–7) consisted of parties which had both, socialist and secular orientations.[152] Bhutto did not accept any party in the government in any province. Even then, he was forced to accept the presence of these parties in the parliament. Bhutto's strategy was one of circumscribing the NAP's ability to govern with the ultimate goal of replacing NAP governments in both provinces.

In the accord reached in March 1972 between NAP and Bhutto, the right of the NAP to form provincial ministries had been conceded. JUI and NAP had been on the forefront in the campaign for the lifting of martial law and for ending the emergency. Now placed in the provincial seats of power, they faced the unceasing hostility of the central government. Attempts at creating disunity between NAP and JUI, however, proved unsuccessful.[153]

Bhutto pressurized the elected representatives of the political parties to leave their respective opposition parties. However, the members of these parties, both inside and outside the parliament, remained steadfast in their loyalty to their parties, despite immense pressure. The regime also appeared unable to checkmate NAP and JUI on the political plane, despite accusation of unpatriotic behaviour against Khan Abdul Wali Khan, leader of the NAP.[154]

On 8 February, Hayat Mohammad Sherpao who had for the last half a year or so been the *de facto* chief minister of NWFP, with Inayatullah Khan Gandapur as the chief minister in name, and had taken a back seat, was killed in a bomb explosion.[155] Bhutto lost no time in placing the blame squarely on the NAP, and on 9 February, almost the entire top leadership of the party—still at liberty—both in the NWFP and the other provinces, including Wali Khan and Arbab Sikander, were arrested under the Defence of Pakistan Rules. The following day, the NAP was dissolved under the Political Parties Act 1962, and its assets seized.

On 10 February, Bhutto called the assembly back early from a short recess to push through legislation to remove the immunity of MNAs and MPAs (for fifteen days after a session) on the arrest of non-criminal charges, conferred on them in Ayub Khan's time and amend the Political

Parties Act to enable the government to declare a 'foreign aided political party' an unlawful organization.[156]

On 17 February, governor's rule was declared in NWFP for ninety days. Subsequently, three advisors were appointed for the governor— none of them members of the former ministry—and were each allocated comprehensive portfolios. On 21 February, raids on universities throughout the country were lodged, and considerable arms said to have been discovered in the hostels of Peshawar University, and particularly in one housing members of the Pakhtoon Students Federation (a NAP allied body). On 23 February, Nasrullah Khan Khattak, Pakistan's ambassador to Tunis, a Pathan and a PPP supporter, was appointed as president of the NWFP PPP, in Sherpao's place. On 24 February, the government referred a ban on the NAP to the Supreme Court.[157]

The political parties, other than PPP, could not influence the parliament, nor could these parties get any support from it. This was because when the national assembly started functioning, the proclamation of emergency had sapped a number of political parties. NAP, a major opposition political party, led by the leader of the opposition, was banned.[158]

The parliament was a major platform for MNAs to express their grievances. Often, members belonging to political parties of the opposition expressed their concerns about the atrocities with their respective parties on the floor of the assembly. The senate, the chair of the house and the concerned minister would deal with the issue.

On 14 December 1973, a senator sought leave to move an adjournment motion to discuss negligence in providing medical aid that caused the death of Mohammad Siddiq Khan[159] on 7 December 1973. The motion was called inadmissible because the minister stated that the late detainee had a severe heart attack on 7 December to which he succumbed despite all possible medical aid given to him.[160]

On 25 April 1974, a senator sought to raise a discussion on a question of breach of privilege of his party JUI, and submitted that a *Nawa-i-Waqt* edition of 25 March 1974 had misreported matters regarding the national assembly. The report stated that thirteen members of the assembly did not take part in the voting, including some members of the opposition in the NAP. JUI (Mufti Group) and Sardar Shaukat Hayat

Khan also voted in favour of the bill. The senator complained that the misreporting had impaired the position of his party. The chairman ruled out the motion, and observed that if the privilege of a member or of the senate or of a committee was violated, the question could be raised, but there was no provision in the rules for raising a question of breach of privilege of a party.[161]

On 23 August 1974, a member sought leave to move an adjournment motion to discuss the discriminatory treatment meted out to former chief minister of Balochistan, Sardar Ataullah Mengal, and others in Sahiwal Jail under instructions of the federal government. The motion was opposed by the leader of the house on the grounds that the matter was not the concern of the federal government.[162]

On the 13 August 1974, a member sought leave to move an adjournment motion to discuss the indiscriminate arrests of NAP and JUI workers under the Defence of Pakistan Rules by the Zhob district administration on the instructions of the Balochistan government. The chairman ruled out the motion on the grounds that the matter, besides being a provincial subject, was sub judice.[163]

THE RULING PARTY—PAKISTAN PEOPLES PARTY (PPP)

PPP as the ruling party remained a strength of the parliament. However, throughout his tenure, Bhutto showed little concern for institutionalizing the party process. Growing trends of personality-cult and authoritarianism made it obvious that Bhutto was more concerned with short-term gains rather than achieving long-term objectives of party building.[164] The unfortunate stance gradually emerged as Bhutto often stated at party meetings, 'I am the peoples party and they are all my creatures'.[165] Thus, Bhutto's domination over the party exceeded that of Jinnah's over the Muslim League.[166] Bhutto did not encourage elections within the party; instead, he nominated leaders to the central executive committees at national, provincial, and local levels. The membership of the party expanded but the organizational structure declined under personal control.[167]

Bhutto dominated the political machine. The party held about 105 of the 150 seats in the national assembly. PPP also had a large majority in the assemblies of Punjab and Sindh, and controlled the governments in NWFP and Balochistan.[168]

Since PPP came to power, there was constant turbulence in its ranks due to conflicts between the left and right wings, religious and secular parties, provinces, and perhaps more than anything else, conflicts amongst Bhutto's principal lieutenants. This state of disarray continued, and even got worse after three years of the PPP government. The most likely explanation for this was that Bhutto liked it this way. He seemed not to be a prisoner of ideology or preconceptions.[169]

One of the most interesting things about the national assembly session from 14 August to 24 September 1972 was the emergence of a group of PPP MNAs who were prepared to argue against the party on certain issues, and if necessary, to even vote against them. The more obvious PPP rebels were Ahmad Raza Kasuri, Abdul Hamid Jatoi, Abdul Khaliq Khan, and Khurshid Rao (who proved to be relatively quieter than usual during this period). Additionally, on two or three occasions they were joined by about thirty others. They participated in the rejection of M.A. Kasuri's amendments to the constitution on 25 August, the outcry against the appointment of an old government hatchet-man named Najaf Khan to a police appointment on 14 September, and most notably, the signing of a document on 22 September, asking the speaker to call an additional constitutional session to examine the privileges of members. On another occasion, when the PPP members were called on, presumably as a loyalty test, to offer their resignations to party headquarters as blank cheques only to be used if necessary, only some thirty-five out of the eighty-five members complied.[170]

By the end of 1974, the PPP had come to be an organization in which both orthodox and conservative elements had gained prominence, consequent upon the expulsion of leftist and radical elements by virtual immobilization of those who still remained within the party. Rightist and reactionary elements were patronized by Bhutto. On one pretext or the other, Bhutto continued to avoid the issue of holding party elections.[171] Sardar Shaukat Hayat was of the view that Bhutto was running his party on the lines of the Nazis in Germany, where he had organized an equivalent of Brown Shirt hooligans amongst his workers, teaching them the same tactics as Hitler had done.[172]

THE MEDIA AND THE PARLIAMENT

The media, during the entire period of the parliament, did not curtail its autonomy. It is the opinion of a number of observers that not only the parliament but other institutions of the government remained superior to the media. The media was either controlled by the government or required to observe government guidelines. Various devices were used to deny opposition leaders a hearing. Nevertheless, Pakistan was not a totalitarian state.[173] Newspapers of the Pakistan Trust, radio, and television were tightly controlled by the government; the opposition hardly received any publicity, as reported by *The Guardian*.[174]

Devices employed to suppress criticism of the government were familiar. The repressive press laws of Ayub Khan's days were enforced in their full vigour. Permission to newspapers and arid periodicals could be cancelled at will, and editors and publishers were detained under various preventive detention laws or under the Defence of Pakistan Rules. Altaf Gauhar, chief editor of *Dawn*, had attracted the attention of the intelligentsia by his forceful editorials against the government and was imprisoned and forced to resign from his post. Similarly, Muzaffar Qadir, editor of the weekly *Punjab Puch*, was also imprisoned and his paper was ordered to be closed. Altaf Hassan Qureshi, editor of the monthly *Urdu Digest*, Mujibur Rahman Shami, editor of the weekly *Zindagi*, and Mohammad Salahuddin, editor of the daily *Jasarat*, were among those who served long periods of detention and endured suffering, which opposing the government often resulted in. A few papers, critical of the regime, like the daily *Nawa-i-Waqt*, continued to appear. But it had to adopt a moderate tone and suffer financial loss due to a lack of government advertisements. The weekly *Afrasia* was also one of the lucky survivors. It kept criticism alive through its satirical columns.[175]

It was also alleged that the government did not even allow press to report statements of parliamentarians who were in opposition. There was an impression amongst the MNAs of the opposition that their protests did not appear in the press for the simple reason that the press was not allowed to publish such things.[176] Such restrictive measures and tactics were also reported in the parliament, but no action was taken for the freedom of the press. Various parliamentarians raised their voices for the freedom of the press. A member pointed out in the senate that the disturbance of the press conference of the governor of Balochistan on 9 November 1973 and the statement of the governor over it disclosed the hard reality that the national press was completely gagged. Though the motion was ruled out,[177] it managed to express the concern of the parliamentarians for the press as well as the attitude of the government on the press conference of the governor.

On 6 December 1973, a member sought leave of the senate to move an adjournment motion to discuss the imposition of restrictions on the daily *Shahbaz* (Peshawar), as a result of which the paper had been forced to cease publications. The member argued that this was contrary to fundamental rights guaranteed by the constitution. The chairman, however, ruled the motion out of order on the grounds that the matter was not a concern of the federal government.[178]

On 7 December 1973, a senator sought leave of the house to move an adjournment motion to discuss the situation arising out of the orders of the federal government banning the daily *Khyber Mail* for the placement of government advertisements. The chairman ruled the motion out of order in view of the statement given by the minister that forty-seven advertisements were given to them daily in eight days.[179]

The press at the time was concerned with the success of the parliament and commented on the position of the assembly. Rao Khurshid Ali Khan said on the floor of the national assembly that a paper said that it was powerless and oppressed. He considered the comment of the paper an insult to the members of assembly. He said that the force of martial law had crushed the assembly, 'therefore, we [MNAs] are not capable of raising our voice.'[180]

The misreporting on behalf of press that might create confusion about the parliament in the minds of people produced complaints of the parliamentarians. On such occasions, directions were issued to the newspapers that in no way could they negate the directions of the parliament. On 17 April, the minister for labour and works, made a submission that on the Transfer of Property Ordinance (Repeal) Bill 1974, the newspaper had incorrectly reported the proceedings, and published misleading reports. With the exception of one or two newspapers, the others actually omitted to explain the objects and reasons of the bill. It had been reported that Khawaja Mohammad Safdar supported the bill and Shahzad Gul opposed it. In actuality, the opposite was true. The minister felt that it might be a bona fide mistake. The press might not be in a position to understand the bill. The chairman then observed that the speeches of the concerned minister and the members of the opposition were correctly reported only by *The Pakistan Times*. Therefore, he suggested that the other newspapers, especially *Jang*, should toe the line of *The Pakistan Times* and correct the whole affair in the next day's issues.[181]

Sardar Shaukat Hayat Khan, a member from the opposition benches moved a privilege motion complaining that certain news media committed a breach of privilege of the house as well as of the speaker by ignoring directives issued by him for giving full coverage to the proceedings of the house. An objection was raised against the motion on the ground that it was directed against press coverage given to the prime minister's speech. It was contended that no member could be allowed to question the prominence given to his speech relative to that of any other member of the house, because the prime minister, being the chief executive of the federation, should be given due and preferential coverage by the news media.[182]

On 29 March 1974, a member sought leave to move a privilege motion about the alleged misreporting of assembly proceedings by a local newspaper. After hearing views expressed by some members, the speaker warned the newspaper to be careful in the future while reporting the proceedings of the assembly, and observed that the parliament could not, '...force any particular newspaper to publish any particular part thereof. The newspapers have their own rights to publish. They have a right to criticize. We own rights to publish. They have a right to criticize. We cannot shut ourselves in this house and say that we are not subject to any criticism but, so far as the reporting of the proceedings of the assembly is concerned, it has to be reported correctly.'[183]

On 3 June 1974, Ahmad Raza Kasuri (MNA) sought to raise a question of privileges regarding the alleged censoring and curtailment of the proceedings of the national assembly about the Rabwah incident by the ministry of information and broadcasting. However, the ministry denied all allegations. After some discussion, the speaker withheld his consent to the raising of the question, and observed that since the alleged facts were denied by the concerned minister, the matter should end there. He further reminded others that the only embargo that could be placed on the proceeding of the assembly was by the assembly itself through the speaker and not by anyone from outside. The speaker said, 'unless the member had any evidence in support of his allegation, the matter could not, in view of denial of the alleged facts by the Information Minister, be allowed to be perused.'[184]

On 5 November 1975, a privilege motion was moved about the omission of the proceedings of the assembly in the press. The minister concerned quoted a ruling from *The Law of Parliamentary Privileges in India*, wherein, it was held that the omission of proceedings was not regarded as a distortion. This indicated that it was not a breach of privilege, welcoming any suggestions from the mover which would be acceptable. The motion was withdrawn after assurance by the minister.[185]

The parliament, itself, prevented some of its proceedings from publication in the press, and the press often cooperatively obeyed orders. The speaker of the national assembly observed that all documents and records about the Qadiani issue that were in this possession were confidential and secret, and also, members of the press could publish nothing out of any of the records unless the same were officially released by the national assembly secretariat.[186] On 20 June 1974, during a discussion of the federal consolidated fund, the speaker announced:

> I would like to mention that certain remarks about the President were made by Chaudhry Zahoor Elahi. This shall not be reported by the press. I will look into the speech and make an order about the expunction of certain personal remarks. Some reference to the President's expenditure in his personal capacity was made by Chaudhry Zahoor Elahi. Those remarks shall not be reported by the Press. [187]

It remained a practice of the assembly that statements, regardless of whether or not they were made during press conferences, were not made the subject matter of adjournment motions in the national assembly. The speaker, on 16 December 1974, also observed that he would never make newspapers a basis for an adjournment motion because twenty papers will write twenty different narratives regarding the same issue.[188] On 26 November 1975, the speaker observed that the assembly practice for the last three years were that statements made and the press conferences held outside the house were never made the subject matter of an adjournment motion.[189]

RELATIONS OF PARLIAMENTARIANS WITH ONE ANOTHER

The working relationship among the parliamentarians and the parliament's collective response or the response of the authorities of the parliament on the mistreatment against any of the parliamentarians, marks the closeness within it. This is an indicator of the autonomy of the parliament in contrast to other institutions. A sample of such incidents where the parliament's attitude over this closeness could be measured has been studied as under.

On 11 November 1976, a member put forward an adjournment motion for an incident on 30 October 1976. Some unknown persons sealed the walls of the bungalow of Sherbaz Mazari (MNA), beat his servants and broke the panes of the doors and windows of his bungalow. The chairman ruled it out of order on the grounds that a question of law and order was a concern of the province.[190]

The members of the national assembly were very status conscious and they knew the integrity of the house. A paper reporting on the assembly said that, 'It is powerless and oppressed; the fact is that we are not powerless or oppressed. To say so is an insult to the Members of this House. The truth is that the force of the martial law has crushed this assembly.'[191]

When Mukhtar Rana (MNA) was arrested, the house fought against his detention, and in the very first meeting of the national assembly, the treasury as well as opposition members adopted the same position about his detention and release. Sardar Shaukat Hayat Khan (from the opposition) pointed out the matter as being a point of privilege, and that if one looked at previous parliamentary practices, they would find that the parliament is the mother of all courts of law and the sovereign. In the history of parliaments, it has called upon those people who are keeping a member of the house in custody to be brought before the House of Commons, and when the custodians resisted, they compelled them and tried the custodians for contempt. The members of the house reminded the speaker that this chamber was supreme and he was the protector of the rights and privileges of all members.[192] In Mukhtar Rana's arrest case, the parliament was ready to resist the courts also.

In the parliamentary system, the parliamentarians cannot be arrested without the permission of the custodians of the houses of the parliament. On 1 December 1973, Khawaja Safdar (senator) moved a privilege motion about his and Nawabzada Nasrullah Khan's arrest on 6 September 1973 by the superintendent of police (Lahore) from the office of the Pakistan Democratic Party. He was taken under custody to the Civil Lines Police Station, Lahore. He was, however, released after about three hours, while the other person was detained under the Defence of Pakistan Rules. The mover made two points:

(1) The action of the superintendent police amounted to a breach of his privilege, and that of the senate, in as much as he was detained in contravention of the provision of section 3 of the Members of the National Assembly (Exemption from Preventive Detention and Personal Appearance) Ordinance 1963,

(2) The fact of his arrest and subsequent release was not intimated to the senate chairman as required by rules 64 and 65 of the *Rules of Procedure and Conduct of Business in the Senate 1973*. The minister for parliamentary affairs opposing the motion contended that the action of the police in taking Khawaja Mohammad Safdar along with another person in the police van and keeping them for two or three hours, did not amount to arrest or detention, and as such, no breach of privilege had been committed. The argument which he advanced was that since the member had failed to submit his privilege motion at the earliest opportunity, as required under sub-rule 2 of rule 59, the motion was inadmissible.

The senate chairman, contrary to the contention of the ministers, ruled that the arrest or detention under the ordinary law could be seriously challenged. The chairman had no hesitation in holding that Khawaja Mohammad Safdar was placed under arrest. However, he ruled the motion out of order on the grounds that the senator deliberately did not care to lodge his complaint to the house at the earliest time. The chairman also accepted that there could be no manner of doubt that the arresting authority had clearly contravened the mandatory provisions of rules 64 and 65, which enjoin upon him to immediately intimate the arrest and release of the member to the senate chairman. He held the motion in order since this omission on the part of the concerned police official constitutes a breach of the collective privilege of the house.[193] This action of the chairman is an example of the assertion of the rights of the senate.

On 12 December 1973, a member sought leave to raise a question of breach of privilege arising out of the treatment of Mir Mahmood Aziz Kurd (senator), detained in District Jail, Quetta, as a 'B' class prisoner, and the refusal of the Government of Balochistan to accord the senator the requisite status in jail. After hearing lengthy arguments, the chairman observed that the objections raised by the minister prevailed for three reasons, and he did not hold the motion in order. Yet he suggested to the government to consider this question favourably. He requested the minister to consider this question on humanitarian grounds, keeping in view the status of the house and senators. He hoped and trusted that the minister would give due weight to the suggestion that senators should not be treated at a level less than that accorded to other dignitaries.[194] On 13 December 1973, a senator sought to raise the question of the privilege of Mir Mahmood Aziz Kurd, who was arrested in August 1973, and lodged in District Jail, Quetta. The mover sought the medical facilities for Aziz Kurd in jail. On the assurance of the minister that the senator was being provided with the facilities in jail and was labelled 'A' class within three days of his arrest, the mover was satisfied and withdrew his motion.[195]

Torture of J.A. Rahim (senator) by the Federal Security Force on 25 July 1974 could not be accepted as a breach of privilege of a senator or of the senate, because the interior minister happened to be out of town, and he had to convey a request on his behalf that the matter be deferred until his return.[196]

The matter of torture on Abdul Wahid Kurd (senator) during his arrest of eighteen days without heating facilities in a freezing winter was referred to the standing committee on the rules of procedure and privileges on 18 December 1974.[197]

On 27 January 1975, a member raised a question of breach of privilege contending that a police party headed by a deputy superintendent wanted to arrest him without a warrant, and thus, the police was harassing him. After opposition of the mover from the minister for interior and the minister of state for law and parliamentary affairs, the chairman of the senate contended that a question of breach of privilege could only arise if a senator was obstructed in the performance of his duties as a member of the senate. Since no such breach of privilege or obstruction in the performance of his duties as a member was identified, the motion was ruled out of order.[198]

On 13 February 1975, Chaudhri Mohammad Aslam (senator) raised a question of breach of his privilege. He contended that at 10 a.m. that day, on his way to attend the session of the senate, he was stopped at the gate of the premises by the police guard on duty. He identified himself, but the head constable and the assistant sub-inspector misbehaved with him. However, on the intervention of somebody from the watch and ward staff, he was allowed to come in. After some discussion, the chairman held the motion to be in order. [199]

Ahmad Raza Kasuri's (MNA) privilege motion about an attack on him and his father by the Federal Security Force, resulting in the murder of his father on the night of 10 November 1974, was held out of order as the matter, apart from being sub judice, was not primarily the responsibility of the federal government.[200]

On 1 March 1976, a member sought leave to move an adjournment motion to discuss the alleged disappearance of Abdul Hayee Baloch (MNA), as reported in daily *Hurriyat* of 5 February 1976. After some discussion, the chairman ruled the motion out of order on the grounds that it was based on an inference.[201]

On 18 March 1976, an adjournment motion to discuss the whereabouts of Chaudhry Zahoor Elahi (MNA) before the Lahore High Court resulting from the order of the chief minister of Sindh was ruled out of order. The overrule was on the grounds that there was not enough evidence produced by the mover and his supporters to the effect that the

Sindh chief minister had actually issued an order to his home secretary to not to comply with the orders of the High Court.[202]

On 14 April 1976, a member sought leave of the house to move an adjournment motion to discuss a matter arising out of the alleged arrest of two senators (one of whom lead the opposition) from the MNA hostel in Islamabad on 14 April 1976. These arrests were allegedly in connection to some planned cases. The chairman observed that they were arrested in the ordinary course of law and the motion was ruled out of order.[203]

After observation of the aforementioned incidents, it can be concluded that on some occasions, the status of the parliament and parliamentarians against the mistreatment by the authorities was maintained by the competent authority of the parliament. In some cases, it was done even when some rules were disregarded, but equally, on some occasions, the contentions of the parliamentarians were not admitted by the authorities. It is, therefore, easy to maintain that the authorities did not protect the privilege of the parliamentarian through establishment or observation of universal rules, but only occasionally, when the action appeared expedient to them.

TRAINING IN PARLIAMENTARY AFFAIRS

The expert functioning of the members of any institution also increases the autonomy of the institution. In this regard, the competence of the parliament under study can be examined through the study of some sample precedents which marked the expertness or lack thereof of the parliamentarians.

In the national assembly session from 14 August 1972 to 24 September 1972, the behaviour and discipline of the MNAs was not appropriate, particularly on emotional issues. This was, for many of them, their first extended session.[204]

The first day of the long awaited meeting of the country's first elected national assembly on 14 April 1972 began inauspiciously with a noisy and ill-mannered display by two dissident PPP MNAs, Rao Khurshid Ali and Abdul Khaliq Khan. According to a British observer, J.R. Paterson, the MNAs had clearly come to make trouble. In the same session, the Council Muslim League leader, Sardar Shaukat Hayat was manhandled by a PPP mob outside the assembly and the entire opposition staged a short walkout in protest.[205]

The British envoy commented:

>...the session compared favourably with those of the Ayub assembly. The setting and appointments in the Chamber were dignified, not to say lush. Relatively few MNAs were old hands, and an ignorance of rules of procedure was natural; in particular, and every interruption was advanced under cover of 'point of order'. Nurul Amin, who took the chair at first, was ineffective. His successor, Fazal Elahi Chaudhry (an experienced senior deputy speaker in the 1965 assembly), was a considerable improvement.[206]

On 14 April 1972, the level of the speeches of the MNAs, mostly in Urdu, was decent, considering the lack of parliamentary experience. However, there was plenty of repetition and irrelevance. There was only one member who had the will to remind the house of its responsibilities in this exceptional session.[207]

Sometimes, some member appeared oblivious to the rules or behaved against them. On 14 December 1973, when the Finance (Supplementary) Bill 1973, entered the third reading stage, a member wanted to oppose it. The speaker told the member that it was the third reading of the bill, and that he should not discuss any technical defect of the bill at that stage.[208]

In many cases, there was usage of inappropriate words in parliament by some members. For example, during a discussion on the Road Transport Workers (Amendment) Bill 1974, a member uttered some impolite words about the decisions of the house. The speaker thereupon observed that the members should refrain from making such comments about the laws passed by them, and should respect the decisions of the assembly.[209]

Sometimes, such situations happened to mark the ineptness or non-serious attitude of some parliamentarians. When a member moved that a private bill be taken into consideration, it was not opposed. The mover then wanted to speak on the bill but a member objected on the grounds that debate could only be allowed if the bill was opposed. The speaker ruled that even when a bill was not opposed, the mover had to explain its provisions.[210] During a general discussion on the budget, when a member criticized the general administration, the finance minister objected that as the criticism was not related to any item of the budget, it was not permissible. The deputy speaker observed that there was no ruling which could be invoked to restrain any member from making a speech on any subject of his choice or from criticizing government policies, during the budget session.[211]

On 1 June 1974, Mahmood Azam Farooqi raised a question of privilege over a letter handed over to him, while coming to the assembly. It stated that if the Qadianis were not declared a minority by a certain date, the assembly building would be burnt down along with its members. The speaker first remarked that the motion should be definite, and then moved in a proper manner.[212] On 24 June 1974, Khurshid Hasan Meer, a minister rising on a point of order, drew the attention of the speaker to Ahmad Raza Kasuri who was sitting on the arm of his chair, and remarked that this was disrespectful to the chair. The speaker upheld the point of order and observed, 'that is no way of sitting in the parliament'.[213]

During a discussion on the admissibility of an adjournment motion, Malik Mohammad Akhtar rose to a point of order. When Mahmood Azam Farooqi objected to his rising, Malik Mohammad Akhtar said 'nacho nacho' (dance, dance). The former sought a ruling whether the word 'nacho' was parliamentary. The speaker declared that it was an un-parliamentary expression. Thereupon, Malik Mohammad Akhtar withdrew his remarks.[214]

More than the seriousness of the members, the relevance with the business of the parliament is also required for participation in the proceedings of the parliament, which in turn, may raise the autonomy of the house. There were some incidents when the problem of irrelevance appeared. Some examples are quoted here. Once a member criticized the political policies and conditions in the country—such as law and order, political atmosphere, confrontation and the rule of law. Sardar Mohammad Aslam (senator) rose on point of order and asked whether the member was discussing the political situation in the country or the bill.

On 13 December 1973, the deputy chairman of the senate warned a senator, who was speaking on the Employees Bill 1973, to Rule 197 of the rules of procedure not to be irrelevant or indulge in repetition. The senator persisted that the point he was making had not been brought to the notice of this house. The chairman upheld the point of order and said that this was not within the scope of this bill.[215]

On 7 September 1973, when the Federal Public Service Commission Bill 1973, was being explained by the minister without portfolio, Qamar-uz-Zaman Shah (senator) rose on a point of order from a seat other than his own. The deputy chairman asked the member to speak from his own seat.[216] On 11 December 1973, after the admissibility of his adjournment motion regarding the smuggling of Banaspati, Khawaja Mohammad Safdar (senator) began to read from the text of a newspaper. The minister raised a point of order to the effect that no member could keep on reading what he had already said. The mover maintained that it was the government newspaper which gave the news. The minister for law and parliamentary affairs criticized the violation of dignity and decorum of the house by the move, who kept muttering to himself while he was sitting.[217]

The expertness, exactness, relevance and seriousness of the parliamentarians, although appeared absent in some of the cases stated and recorded above, most of the time these elements prevailed over the atmosphere of the parliament, and a majority of the members followed it.

In short, the autonomy of the institution of the parliament was not preserved in face of the institution of the strong chief executive. The army, though initially weakened by the chief executive, remained to be stronger than the parliament. The boundary lines between the judiciary and the parliament had been well defined in the constitution, yet in some important cases, for example, the recognition of Bangladesh, the supremacy of the decision of the judiciary prevailed. The parliament tried to subdue the judiciary through the amendments in the constitution, but these amendments proved the autonomy of the chief executive instead of the parliament. The members of the parliament could not assert much due to their incapacity, inexpertness, and weaknesses.

Chapter Seven

Conclusion

Pakistani historiographers who have written about the institutions of the country have not given much importance to the formation and working of the institution of the parliament. This is why the true tales of Z.A. Bhutto's era and its dimensions remain untold. This study was conducted to fill the gaps that existed in this aspect of the political history of Pakistan. The contents of this book reveal that without studying the institution of the parliament, which is the mother institution in any parliamentary democracy, many dimensions of Pakistan's political history cannot be understood.

Institution building of the parliament of Pakistan between 1971 and 1977 can be discussed in two phases: from its beginning to the adoption of the consensus constitution (1971–3), and the rest of its tenure (1973–7). In the first phase, the parliament remained highly successful and sovereign in carrying out its responsibilities, and members of the parliament performed as parliamentarians are expected to in a democratic parliamentary system. All this was reflected in the process of constitution-making, i.e. debates, participation in the standing committee and working committee, and establishing consensus through refinement of various aspects of the constitution.

The first general elections in Pakistan, held in 1970, on one hand, resulted in a crisis that led to the bifurcation of Pakistan in 1971. On the other hand, it produced the first directly elected national assembly that adopted the 1973 constitution by which the senate of Pakistan was formed, and a bicameral parliament of Pakistan kept functioning until 1977 when fresh elections were arranged. The national assembly, elected under new elections, could not start functioning as the crisis over allegations of rigging in the elections got deeper, and the imposition of martial law delayed, if not altogether, halted the functions of the parliament as well as other democratic institutions of the country.

The first ever directly elected parliament of Pakistan not only provided a constitutional foundation for the subsequent parliaments of Pakistan, but it also continued to pass on traditional values set by previous parliaments in the history of Pakistan, as well as in other democratic countries. There is no point of departure from the assertion made by Sahibzada Farooq Ali Khan, the speaker of the national assembly (1970–7), that it was a runway from which the next assemblies were to take off.[1]

The territories that comprised Pakistan were situated at the fringes of the subcontinent, and a large part of them had never been the epicentre of British rule, and thus had no prior experience with parliamentary work or even the idea of democracy. Therefore, in the early history of Pakistan, known as the first parliamentary era (1947–58), the institution of the parliament could not take firm roots. The parliament was considered a representative of the aspirations of the masses, but it did not get its due position because of an unnecessary delay and postponement of elections, or the implementation of indirect elections.

It was observed that the first decade of Pakistan witnessed the presence of constituent assemblies—ones that could not assert themselves as strong institutions. On the other hand, the bureaucracy and the army strengthened their positions in the socio-political scenario. Despite routine legislative activities, the constituent assemblies could not share power with the chief executive or other institutions of the state. The country continued to be ruled by the nexus of civil and military bureaucrats.

The constitution, which is a basic political handbook of the parliament, could not be framed in time, and even when it was framed, the assembly (or the parliament) would continue operations as if the constitution did not exist. The assembly was dissolved and formed by players who were forces external to the institution of the parliament, and the assemblies could not be shaped as an institution to be reckoned with. Notwithstanding allegations of the doings of external forces, it was also the impotence of the parliament itself that it could not perform the role assigned to it. Whenever the assemblies were dissolved, there was an acceptable reason that the assembly did not perform its duties according to the standards and requirements of the institution.

Then came the decade of martial law (1958–69); the military administration took over, and another style of indirect elections was introduced in the form of 'basic democracies'. This indirect election, once again, impeded the parliament's journey towards becoming the representative institution of the masses. The military and authoritarian rule would not accept the hegemony of a governing institution, which would reduce its sole hold on power. Therefore, the assemblies were directed by the Ayub's dictatorial government. Often, it was only the needs and wishes of the president that were regarded during legislation. The institution of the parliament remained a secondary tool in the hands of the rulers and could not get internal strength.

The assemblies, during Ayub's regime, lost their place and standard as an institution, more so compared to previous assemblies in the parliamentary period. They remained subservient to other institutions and especially to the military. Elections were held, yet these elections were not free from serious allegations of rigging due to indirect electorates. The institution, born as a result of these elections, could not get proper legitimacy or strength. A legislation that would be subject to direct control of the parliament was made, but on the directions of forces external to the parliament. Financial matters, which are monitored by the parliament, were not controlled by the national assembly, and its control over monetary affairs was restricted.

Thus, the process of the institutionalization of parliament has been the focus of this book. However, before the assembly took over, the country witnessed another military rule, which had managed the first direct elections but could not manage to keep the country united. Consequently, the first discussion at the time of oath taking in the house was about what would be done with the other half of the assembly, the members of which were elected from the same elections but had chosen not to join the post-1971 assembly.

The traditions that the new assembly inherited were not encouraging in respect to institutionalization. It was thus very hard for members of the parliament to embrace new traditions, and to establish the parliament as a reasonable and powerful institution. The 'complexity' of any institution is enhanced with the adoption of proper and universal rules, and the regulation and the 'differentiation' of the institution develops through mutual respectful relationships amongst the members of any institution.

The new assembly formulated some rules and regulations similar to those formed by previous assemblies. These rules were utilized to form the framework for the functions of the parliament. New rules and regulations were introduced while the house of the senate—a novel addition in Pakistan—was conceived and invented. The parliament, from 1971–7, can be given the credit of succeeding in maintaining its complexity with the adoption of such rules and regulations, which set a trend and precedent for future parliaments in Pakistan.

However, the complexity achieved by the formation of rules and regulations could not be continued under the influence of the powerful chief executive. The complexity (that worked as the foundation of the parliament) did not continue during its working. Many rules, which were the primary safeguard of the parliament, were neither protected by its members nor cared for by forces external to the institution.

The aspect of differentiation—the affiliations of the members— was remarkable in this assembly, especially in its starting phase and during the period of constitution-making. Altogether diverse ideological grounds, dissimilar political connections, different ethnic entities, various professional backgrounds, and different educational qualifications were present in the assembly, yet they united to bring about consensus on the issues of the construction of the institution of parliament, and the framing of the 1973 constitution.

The differentiation achieved during the initial stages was, unfortunately, lost after the framing of the constitution. The treatment of the opposition by the government and treasury benches, as well as its inability to assert itself through the institution of the parliament, emerged as the two elements, which marred the 'differentiation' achieved in the initial period. The differences among the members increased to such an extent that the institution of the parliament seemed to be divided into two warring factions, especially in its last days. It was this conflict within the parliament, which was highlighted, in the broad political atmosphere of the country after the 1977 elections. The clashes between the opposition and government, which could not be settled in the houses of the parliament, reached the streets of the country, and they caused not only the demise of the institution of the parliament, but also the democratic system in the country.

The sovereignty of the institution—where the institution functions without any interfering influence of external forces and factors—could be observed in the first two years of the assembly's performance as a constituent assembly of Pakistan. During these times, the assembly proved to be sovereign in all respects. External conditions and internal 'complexity' as well as 'differentiation' helped the parliament in practicing and enjoying its 'sovereignty'.

Therefore, the outcome of the sovereignty of the parliament came in the production of the most consensual document—the 1973 constitution. Here, the constituent assembly, that was also providing the country legal legitimacy and political support just after its breakup, was also laying the foundation stones for the institutions of an emergent Pakistan. The future of Pakistan was to claim that it was re-established through the constitution that was framed by the duly elected representatives of the people of Pakistan—namely, the parliament.

After the accomplishment of the task of framing the constitution, the parliament was confronted with the task of maintaining its durability (i.e. the quality of an institution to face challenges and determine its supremacy while resolving issues) and autonomy (where an institution establishes clear boundaries with other institutions of the state, and saves itself from their interception). Unfortunately, in this regard, the parliament did not prove as successful, since it was in its early phases.

A general perception about the workings of the parliament is that external forces, which were not a part of the parliament, weakened the institution to such an extent that it was unable to flourish and develop. It is generally considered that other institutions of the state, for instance, the army, the bureaucracy and the judiciary intervened in the affairs of the parliament and obscured its independent function, leading to its perpetual decline. This assumption led us to form one of the two major hypotheses of this study. However, this hypothesis cannot be confirmed completely. External institutions cannot be held fully responsible for all of its irregularities.

The observation and analysis of the developments lead us to the conclusion that the durability and autonomy of the institution of the parliament during the second half of its life were not completely distorted by forces and factors outside the parliament. On the other hand, the internal weaknesses of the parliament, like its inability to maintain complexity and differentiation, its failure to respond internally to major challenges, and its inefficiency in dealing with other institutions led to its ultimate collapse

The parliament, while working towards establishing its durability, managed to assert its control while responding actively to the Qadiani issue. Only the parliament was in the picture while making the decision to proclaim the Qadianis out of the Islamic sphere. It was only able to play an important role with the help of borrowed strength from outside forces and factors. It just linked itself with the everlasting popular demands and situations within the country. The issue that beefed up outside the parliament was brought in, and decisions engineered outside the parliament were endorsed by the institution.

Except for the apparent active response to the Qadiani issue, the response of the parliament on all other major issues was secondary, delayed, or blurred. Sometimes the issue was decided in accordance with the government's wishes without any productive feedback. It was the duty of the treasury benches to highlight and bring forward issues in the houses of the parliament or at least support the efforts of the opposition in bringing issues to light. Instead, the treasury benches were prone to acting on issues only when orders were given by the ruling executive or governmental machinery, despite calls for consideration from the opposition. Thus, issues regarding the legislation on amendments in the constitution were not generated within the parliament, nor were decisions on crucial issues made through a proper parliamentary process, or with some kind of consensus in the parliament.

The autonomy of the institution could not be preserved by the parliament as there was a very strong chief executive working parallel to it. Being a strong institution in itself, the chief executive, the all-dominating personality of Z.A. Bhutto asserted itself most of the time. As a popular leader, seasoned politician, expert manager of affairs and negotiations, the status of Bhutto could marginalize almost every institution of the state—not just the parliament. The parliament had to follow his lines and, therefore, could not assert its institutional autonomy in the face of such a strong, active, and assertive chief executive. Bhutto, who had been chiselling his influence from the very start, was able to overpower and hijack almost all functions of the parliament. The parliament was often a mere toolbox in the skilful hands of the chief executive.

In the second phase, Bhutto became used to steering the parliament, as he used its utility for the fulfilment of his political gains in the wake of his restrictions on the freedom of press. His dealings with the opposition in an authoritarian manner and control over the judiciary through restrictions over the independent legislation restricted the authority and independence of the judiciary. The parliament was only able to move in the direction pointed out by the ruling party under the leadership of the authoritarian Bhutto.

Also, the powerful chief executive intruded in the boundaries of other institutions of the state. The constant tussle between the institution of the army and the chief executive appeared over numerous issues such as the creation of the FSF, recruitment and promotion policy of army officers, and the use of the military in civil affairs. In the start, the chief executive seemed assertive, though the future looked bleak for the prime minister. The parliament, however, was never able to assert itself before the institution of the army. Decisions regarding armed forces were only conveyed to the parliament—they were never involved in the process.

The parliament could seldom protect its 'autonomy' in the face of the judiciary, bureaucracy, and other institutions. Also, the members of the parliament were rather inexperienced when it came to dealing with other institutions intruding into their domains. The aforementioned, in addition to the lack of institutional capacity, and inability to confront other institutions, resulted in a weak autonomy of the institution.

During as well as after the period of emergence, the universal rules—regulations, which are universally considered essential for the construction of the institution of the parliament—were adopted. Such rules and the close affiliations of the members of the parliament, in respect to party connections, professional closeness, political affinity, and other qualifications, resulted in the complexity of the institution, that is an innate quality of institution-building.

Instead of becoming a source of power for the parliament, the external forces, during this period of the sovereignty of the latter, acquired strength from it. The parliament achieved the status of a source of power for the chief executive, the army, the bureaucracy, and all other state organs. It blessed a nation that was disappointed after the great tragedy of the separation of East Pakistan, with hope and enthusiasm. The war of 1971 had left Pakistan in shambles, as the largest province of Pakistan had been annexed from it, while the remainder of the country was in a state of defeat. During those critical years the rehabilitation of the post-war state, image-building of Pakistan in the international community, and steps towards improving a post-war economy were the need of the hour. The parliament, through its proceedings, provided support to the government in undertaking these issues.

During such perilous times, the parliament set new standards for law-making and crafted new trends in the legislation of Pakistan. Most of all, it laid the foundation for the constitution. The accomplishment of this parliament—the 1973 constitution—became a guiding milestone for the subsequent generations of Pakistan.

The 1973 constitution was a lasting achievement for this parliament, which was framed after twenty-six years of the creation of Pakistan. The prime distinction of the constitution was that it was framed by elected representatives of the peoples of Pakistan, and passed unanimously. All major political parties, groups and units of federation agreed on the constitution. The constitution got such tremendous support of the people and political parties, and became so significant, that even after thirty-seven years of its enforcement, it has remained a consensual constitutional document, despite efforts of two army coups to change it through large amendments.

However, the necessary practices of complexity and sovereignty did not continue in the subsequent tenure. The rules established by the parliament appeared to have been disregarded or used only tactfully for vested interests. Other institutions of the state, particularly the strong executive, came into prominence as the parliament, voluntarily or sometimes begrudgingly, had to surrender its powers.

The crux of the findings shared in this book indicate that the parliament did not lack the basic characteristics of an institution during its emerging period. However, its performance in the later period was shadowed under the prominence of other forces and institutions. The other institutions were not inherently stronger than the parliament, but they were still able to overshadow it due to the weaknesses and shortcomings within the institution of the parliament itself. During the first phase, the parliament achieved prominence by fulfilling expectations associated with it. However, in the later period it did not follow the same procedures and rules which were set and formed by it, resulting in its inefficiency, decline and ultimate failure.

In composition, the feudally-dominated parliament had close affiliations with the feudally dominated PPP. The parliament could not break free from the shackles of the aspirations of PPP, owing to the closeness of the purpose and composition of the party. The consensus between the opposition and the treasury benches that could be seen in the process of constitution-making faded with the lapse of time. Political parties and parliamentarians unconsciously undermined their power by not developing the national assembly into a forum for national debate and a primary source for legislation.

The latter phase witnessed the parliamentarians paying little attention to developing the organs of the parliament into a forum for debating national issues. The parliamentary parties and their leadership paid little attention towards developing their position on specific issues within the respective houses and the committees of the parliament.

Only on the singular occasion of the formulation and approval of the Second Amendment—the declaration of Qadianis as non-Muslims—the unanimous functioning of the parliament came to the forefront. The temporary union of the treasury and the opposition benches soon wore away. Not only the parliament but the strong and secular-minded chief executive had to regard the aspirations of the people influenced by their religious fervour. The leading posture of the parliament seemed to bow before the strong exterior public opinion. The echoes of chanting outside the parliament shook the floor of the house, and the feudal parliamentarians could not resist the overwhelming pressure of the masses. The parliament reflected the aspirations of the people through the constitutional amendment, and proved themselves to be true representatives of the masses though the leading role they played by succumbing to national pressures and desires.

The parliament appeared weak in the formulation of foreign policies as well as the monitoring of foreign affairs, and was not able to influence the decisions of the government regarding the formulation of foreign policy. The foreign office continued to function under policy directions made by the prime minister or the minister of foreign affairs, who often decided without any prior consultation with the parliament or its members.

The resolutions of the parliament regarding foreign policy were taken for granted, while the parliament, itself, did not bother to pass such resolutions. Some unpopular decisions like the acceptance of the Bangladesh and Simla Agreement were, seemingly, put before the parliament in order to scapegoat the institution from the consequences of such a sensitive matter. Similarly, the Kashmir issue had been the core issue in the context of the country's foreign affairs, as well as matters of sentiment within the masses in Pakistan. It was not properly dealt within the debates of the parliament, and various parliamentarians repeatedly pointed out this grievous negligence with respect to an issue of such significance.

Akin to foreign affairs, the parliament could not take hold of matters concerning armed forces. Like the preceding parliaments, the one in focus of this study also remained aloof to the issues of defence, and the government dealt with the forces on its own, alienating the parliament. On the issues of defence, either the parliamentary committees were not formed or if they were, they were not practically influential. Also, in some cases, where they did prove influential, they did not take the whole parliament into confidence and took decisions secretly on behalf of individual members of the committees. The defence ministry was at complete liberty to deal with the issues of the armed forces on their own.

The parliament as a legislative body did considerable work during its span. It passed 361 acts of parliament (legislations) on various issues. Fourteen joint sittings of both the houses of parliament were held, along with thirty-six sessions of the national assembly and seventeen sessions of the senate. All through these sessions, important matters of the state and the society of Pakistan were discussed. During the question-answer sessions, the parliamentarians raised the questions concerning the functions and decisions of the government. They openly and freely criticized the government during their debates, and brought seven amendments in the constitution during its life span. Although, these amendments were of a minor nature, in contrast with the larger work of constitution-making, they reflected the active functioning of the parliament as an institution.

In a nutshell, this book reveals that the parliament faced crises such as the involvement of the military and civil bureaucracy in their lust for power, and the overthrow of the civil governments followed by the failure of the parliament to maintain its viability and utility as a mother institution because of rift, tussle and disunity between the treasury and the opposition factions within and outside the parliament. Even though the parliament had unanimously passed an ideal constitution, which is still in force, it could not protect the same constitution. In fact, the working of the parliament assumed such a mechanism in which the opposition parties had little room for expressing their free will, or exercising freedom of speech during the second phase of the parliamentary life. It was generally perceived by the parliamentarians that Bhutto had assumed an authoritarian character and was controlling the affairs of the parliament. Therefore, when the rigging took place on a small scale (especially locally), it was perceived as an outcome of government command. The negotiations to address the issue between the government and the opposition parties were prolonged because both of them had failed to develop a democratic culture in the parliament. This provided an opportunity to the external forces to grab power.

After close readings of primary sources, I posit that the internal weakness of the parliamentary parties within and outside the parliament brought about the failure of the system in Pakistan. Civil and military bureaucracies were always eyeing situations where they could step in and usurp power. The big opportunity presented itself yet again through the political parties representing the parliament because of their vested interests, and because of the failure of the parliament, as an institution, to promote a democratic culture in order to resolve political issues. Their disunity is quite evident in parliamentary debates and in the general election of 1977. The political parties had failed to develop a political culture. As a result, the parliament began to weaken despite its marvellous take-off in its first phase when it framed the constitution. In fact, the decline in the efficiency of the institution of the parliament provided reason to the military administration (such as General Ziaul Haq's) to topple the elected government of Pakistan in 1977, and, consequently, take Z.A. Bhutto to the gallows. Had the foundations of the institution of the parliament been strong enough, no other institution (not even the military) would have been able to impose martial law, and extend it over a period of years.

Notes

Chapter 1. Institution Building in Pakistan: A Conceptual Framework

1. David Menhennet and John Palmer, *Parliament in Perspective* (London: The Bodley Head, 1967), pp. 9, 13.
2. The Anglo-Saxon era denotes the period of English history between approximately 550 and 1000. The term is also used for the language, now known as Old English that was spoken and written by the Anglo-Saxons.
3. Moyra Grant, *The UK Parliament* (Edinburgh: Edinburgh University Press, 2009), pp. 2–4.
4. Ibid., p. 2.
5. Ibid.
6. M.N. Kaul, S.L. Shakdher, *Practice and Procedure of Parliament* (New Delhi: Metropolitan, 1978), p. vii.
7. Morris-Jones, *Parliament in India* (London: Longmans, 1957), p. 5.
8. Zulfikar Khalid Maluka, *The Myth of Constitutionalism in Pakistan* (Karachi: Oxford University Press, 1995), p. 87; Morris-Jones, *Parliament in India*, p. 46.
9. Maluka, *Myth of Constitutionalism*, p. 114.
10. Morris-Jones, *Parliament in India*, pp. 45–62.
11. Government of India Act 1935, Section 18.
12. C.L. Anand, *The Government of India Act 1935 with a Critical Introduction* (Lahore: Law Publishers, 1939).
13. Hamid Khan, *Constitutional and Political History of Pakistan* (Karachi: Oxford University Press, 2009), p. 23.
14. G.W. Choudhury, *Constitutional Development in Pakistan* (Lahore: The Ideal Book House, 1969), p. 25.
15. S. Qalb-i-Abid, *The Muslim Politics in Punjab 1923–1947* (Lahore: Vanguard, 1992); Chaudhri Muhammad Ali, *The Emergence of Pakistan* (Lahore: Research Society of Pakistan, 2009), p. 27.
16. K.K. Aziz, *Historical Handbook of Muslim India 1700–1947*, Vol. 2 (Lahore: Vanguard, 1995), pp. 434–5.
17. The Plan was announced on 15 May 1946. Muhammad Iqbal Chawla, *Wavell and the Dying Days of the Raj* (Karachi: Oxford University Press, 2011), p. 121.
18. Choudhury, *Constitutional Development*, p. 13.
19. By May 2019, the parliament had passed twenty-six amendments to the constitution.
20. Lawrence Ziring, *Pakistan: The Enigma of Political Development* (Boulder, Colorado: Westview Press, 1980).

21. Veena Kukreja, *Civil–Military Relations in South Asia: Pakistan, Bangladesh and India* (New Delhi Sage Publications, 1991), p. 45.

22. Maleeha Lodhi, 'Pakistan in Crisis', *The Journal of Commonwealth and Comparative Politics* 16 (March 1978), p. 65.

23. Ian Talbot, *Pakistan: A Modern History* (Lahore: Vanguard Books, 1999), pp. 8–9.

24. Hasan Askari Rizvi, *The Military & Politics in Pakistan 1947–1997* (Lahore: Sang-e-Meel Publications, 2000).

25. Mazhar Aziz, *Military Control in Pakistan* (Oxon: Routledge, 2008).

26. Ayesha Siddiqa, *Military Inc.: Inside Pakistan's Military Economy* (Karachi: Oxford University, Press, 2007).

27. Shuja Nawaz, *Crossed Swords: Pakistan, its Army, and the Wars Within* (Karachi: Oxford University Press, 2008).

28. Husain Haqqani, *Pakistan between Mosque and Military* (Lahore: Vanguard, 2005).

29. Ayesha Jalal, *The State of Martial Rule: The Origins of Pakistan's Political Economy of Defense* (New York: Cambridge University Press, 1990).

30. Hamza Ali Alavi, 'Authoritarianism and Legitimation of State Power in Pakistan', in Subrata Kumar Mishra, ed., *The Post-Colonial State in Asia: Dialectics of Politics and Culture* (New York: Harvester Wheatsheaf, 1990), pp. 19–72.

31. Rizvi, *Military and Politics*, p. 13.

32. Aziz, *Military Control in Pakistan*, p. 1.

33. Siddiqa, *Military Inc.*

34. Ibid.

35. Nawaz, *Crossed Swords*, p. xxviii.

36. One of the hypotheses is that the forces outside the parliament affected the working of the parliament as a sovereign body.

37. Ibid., p. 153.

38. Haqqani, *Pakistan between Mosque and Military*, p. 3.

39. Ibid., p. 87.

40. Roger D. Long, *Pacific Affairs*, 64 (Autumn, 1991), pp. 427–8.

−41. Frank Goodnow, *The Civil Service of Pakistan* (New Haven: Yale University Press, 1964).

42. Ilhan Niaz, *The Culture of Power and Governance of Pakistan 1947–2008* (Islamabad: Oxford University Press, 2010).

43. Huma Naz, *Bureaucratic Elites and Political Development in Pakistan (1947–1958)* (Islamabad: National Institute of Pakistan Studies Quaid-i-Azam University, 1990).

44. Ali Ahmed, *Role of Higher Civil Servants in Pakistan* (Dacca: National Institute of Public Administration, 1968).

45. Khalid bin Sayeed, *The Political System of Pakistan* (Kingston: Queen's University, 1966).

46. C. Bhambhari and M. Bhaskaran Nair, 'Bureaucracy in Authoritarian Political System', in S.P. Varma and Virendra Narain, eds., *Pakistan Political System in Crisis: Emergence of Bangladesh* (Jaipur: South Asia Studies Centre, University of Rajasthan, 1972).

47. Charles H. Kennedy, *Bureaucracy in Pakistan* (Karachi: Oxford University Press, 1987).

48. Aminullah Chaudhry, *Political Administrators: The Story of the Civil Service of Pakistan* (Karachi: Oxford University Press, 2011).

49. Goodnow, *Civil Service of Pakistan*, p. 77.

50. Niaz, *The Culture of Power*, pp. 128, 247.

51. Khalid B. Sayeed, 'The Political Role of Pakistan's Civil Service', *Pacific Affairs* 31 (June 1958), p. 137.

52. Tariq Ali, *Pakistan: Military Rule or People's Power* (London: Jonathan Cape, 1970).

53. Badruddin Umar, *The Emergence of Bangladesh: Rise of Bengali Nationalism (1958–1971)* (Karachi: Oxford University Press, 2006).

54. Rasul Bakhsh Rais, *State, Society and Democratic Change in Pakistan* (Karachi: Oxford University Press, 1996).

55. Stanley Wolpert, *Zulfi Bhutto of Pakistan: His Life and Times* (Karachi: Oxford University Press, 2008).

56. Anwar H. Syed, *The Discourse and Politics of Zulfiqar Ali Bhutto* (New York: St. Martin's Press, 1992).

57. Maulana Kausar Niazi, *Zulfikar Ali Bhutto of Pakistan: Last Days* (Online Edition accessed at <http://bhutto.org>).

58. Sheikh Muhammad Rashid, *Juhd-e-Musalsal* (Lahore: Jang Publishers, 2002).

59. Rafi Raza, *Zulfikar Ali Bhutto and Pakistan: 1967–1977* (Karachi: Oxford University Press, 1997).

60. Salmaan Taseer, *Bhutto: A Political Biography* (New Delhi: Vikas Publishing House, 1980).

61. Philip P. Jones, *Pakistan People's Party* (Karachi: Oxford University Press, 2003).

62. Shahid Javed Burki, *Pakistan under Bhutto* (New York: St. Martin's Press, 1980).

63. Matthew Holden Jr., 'Exclusion, Inclusion, and Political Institutions', in R.A.W. Rhodes, Sarah A. Binder, and Bert A. Rockman, eds., *The Oxford Handbook of Political Institutions* (Oxford: Oxford University Press, 2006), p. 182.

64. Kevin T. McGuire, 'The Institutionalization of the U.S. Supreme Court', *Political Analysis* 12 (Spring 2004), p. 129.

65. Nelson Polsby, an American, who wrote the article 'The Institutionalization of the U.S. House of Representatives' in 1968 and achieved fame by providing a model for the study of parliament in the context of institutionalisation. His next contribution is a part of the *Handbook of Political Science* (Reading, Mass.: Addison-Wesley Pub. Co., 1975).

66. P. Gehrlich, 'The Institutionalization of European Parliament', in A. Kornberg, ed., *Legislatures in Comparative Perspective* (New York: David McKay, 1973).

67. W.C. Opello Jr., 'Portugal's Parliament: An Organizational Analysis of Legislative Performance', *Legislative Studies Quarterly* 11 (1986), pp. 291–320.

68. J.R. Hibbing, 'Legislative Institutionalization with Illustrations from the British House of Commons', *American Journal of Political Science* 32 (1988), pp. 681–712.

69. M.I. Mezey, 'Legislatures: Individual Purposes and Institutional Performance', in A.W. Finifter ed., *Political Science: The State of Discipline II* (Washington DC: The American Political Science Association, 1993), p. 354.

70. P. Squire, 'The Theory of Legislative Institutionalization and the California Assembly', *The Journal of Politics* 54 (1992), pp. 1026–54.
71. G.W. Copeland and S.C. Patterson, 'Parliaments and Legislatures', in G.T. Kurian, ed., the *World Encyclopedia of Parliaments and Legislatures* (Washington DC: Congressional Quarterly, 1998), pp. xix–xxxii.
72. P. Norton, 'Introduction: The Institutions of Parliaments' in P. Norton, ed., *Parliaments and Governments in Western Europe* (London: Frank Cass, 1998), pp. 1–15.
73. S.N. Eisenstadt, ed., *Max Weber on Charisma and Institution Building: Selected Papers* (Chicago and London: The University of Chicago Press, 1968).
74. Samuel P. Huntington, *Political Order in Changing Societies* (New Haven and London: Yale University Press, 1968).
75. Robert E. Goodin, *The Theory of Institutional Design* (New York: Cambridge University Press, 1996).
76. Eisenstadt, *Max Weber on Charisma and Institution Building.*
77. Gabriel A. Almond, and Sidney Verba, *The Civic Culture: Political Attitudes and Democracy in Five Nations* (Princeton, New Jersey: Princeton University Press, 1963).
78. Nelson W. Polsby, 'The Institutionalization of the U.S. House of Representatives,' *American Political Science Review* 62 (March 1968), pp. 144–68.
79. Many historical sociologists employ a broad conceptualisation that essentially entails the argument that past events influence future events. James Mahoney, 'Path Dependence in Historical Sociology', *Theory and Society* 29 (2000), pp. 507–48.
80. Samuel P. Huntington, *Political Order in Changing Societies*, p. 2.
81. Ibid., p. 14.
82. Ibid., p. 15; Huntington refers for detail: Philip Selznick's *Leadership in Administration* (New York: Harper and Row, 1957), p. 5.
83. Taiabur Rehman, *Parliamentary Control and Government Accountability in South Asia* (Oxon: Taylor & Francis e-Library, 2007), p. 21.
84. Ibid., p. 22.
85. Hibbing, 'Legislative Institutionalization', p. 681.
86. Ibid.; Chubb 1988; Canon 1989; Brace and Ward 1989; Van Der Slik 1989.
87. Squire, 'Theory of Legislative Institutionalization', p. 1026.
88. Rehman, *Parliamentary Control*, p. 43.
89. McGuire, 'Institutionalization of the US', pp. 130–2.
90. Hibbing, 'Legislative Institutionalization', pp. 684–5.
91. Douglas C. Chaffey, 'The Institutionalization of State Legislatures: A Comparative Study', *The Western Political Quarterly* 23 (March 1970), p. 180.
92. Hibbing, 'Legislative Institutionalization', p. 685.
93. Ibid., pp. 696–7.
94. Ibid., p. 701.
95. Ibid., p. 703.

CHAPTER 2. THE PARLIAMENT IN PAKISTAN: A BRIEF SURVEY

1. *Government of India Act, 1935: Unrepealed Constitutional Legislation* (Karachi: Ministry of Law, Government of Pakistan, 1951), p. 6.
2. Muneer Ahmad, *Legislatures in Pakistan 1947–1958* (Lahore: Punjab University, 1960), p. 8.
3. Inam-ul-Haq Kausar, *Pakistan Movement and Balochistan* (Quetta: United Printers, 1999), pp. 55–79.
4. Establishment of the Pakistan Constituent Assembly, DO 35/5102, TNA London; the first constituent assembly was elected by the provincial legislative assemblies. There were separate electorates for religious communities; one representative was allotted per million people of the population.
5. Nasim Hasan Shah, *Constitution, Law, and Pakistan Affairs* (Lahore: Wajidalis Publisher, 1986), p. 7.
6. Increase and Redistribution of Seats Act, 1949.
7. The name 'East Bengal' was officially changed to 'East Pakistan' in 1955, with the adoption of the One Unit Scheme in West Pakistan and was incorporated in the Constitution of Pakistan 1956, part I, article 2 (a).
8. Mushtaq Ahmad, *Government and Politics in Pakistan* (Karachi: Royal Book Company, 2009), p. 88.
9. Ibid., p. 89.
10. The dissident groups of the Muslim League created smaller parties or factions due to personal grievances or disagreements on party lines. For example: East Pakistan Awami Muslim League, Jinnah Muslim League, Azad Pakistan Party led by Mian Iftikharuddin, Pakistan Peoples Party led by Ghaffar Khan and G.M. Syed.
11. Mushtaq Ahmad, *Government and Politics in Pakistan*, p. 89
12. Some other important members of the assembly included namely Liaquat Ali Khan; Khwaja Nazimuddin; Sir Zafarullah Khan; Sardar Abdur Rab Khan Nishtar; Abdul Ghaffar Khan; A.K. Fazlul Haq; Fazlur Rahman; Jogendra Nath Mandal; Dr Omar Hayat Malik; Maulana Shabbir Ahmad Osmani; Dr Ishtiaq Hussain Qureshi; Kamini Kumar Datta; Malik Mohammad Firoz Khan Noon; Sris Chandra Chattopadhyay; Mian Mumtaz Mohammad Khan Daultana; Mian Mohammad Iftikharuddin; Begum Shaista Suhrawardy Ikramullah; and Sheikh Karamat Ali.
13. Yunas Samad, *A Nation in Turmoil: Nationalism and Ethnicity in Pakistan, 1937–1958* (New Delhi: Sage Publications, 1995), p. 127.
14. *Constituent Assembly Debates*, vol. 1, no. 1 (10 August 1947), p. 1.
15. There were seven nomination papers received by the secretary on behalf of M.A. Jinnah; all nomination papers were valid, and there was no other candidate. *Constituent Assembly Debates*, vol. 1, no. 2 (11 August 1947), p. 11.
16. *Constituent Assembly Debates*, vol. 1, no. 4 (14 August 1947), pp. 49–52.
17. Sikandar Hayat, *The Charismatic Leader: Quaid-i-Azam Mohammad Ali Jinnah and the Creation of Pakistan*, rev. ed. (Karachi: Oxford University Press, 2008), p. 316; he mentions that the Muslim nation recognised him as a charismatic leader,

revered him as the Quaid-i-Azam, and nominated him as the Governor General of Pakistan.

18. Khurshid Ahmad Khan Yusufi, ed. *Speeches, Statements and Messages of the Quaid-i-Azam*, vol. 4 (Lahore: Bezm-e-Iqbal, 1996), p. 2601.

19. Zulfikar Khalid Maluka, *The Myth of Constitutionalism in Pakistan* (Karachi: Oxford University Press, 1995), p. 125.

20. *Constituent Assembly Debates*, vol. v (12 March 1949), p. 101.

21. Twenty-Four member committee consisting of the president of the assembly and the following members: Sir Mohammad Zafarullah Khan; Ghulam Mohammad; Sardar Abdur Rab Khan Nishtar; Khwaja Shahabuddin; Pirzada Abdus Sattar; Fazlur Rahman; Jogendra Nath Mandal; Dr Omar Hayat Malik; Maulana Shabbir Ahmad Osmani; Dr Ishtiaq Hussain Qureshi; Kamini Kumar Datta; Begum Jahan Ara Shahnawaz; Malik Mohammad Firoz Khan Noon; Sris Chandra Chattopadhyay; Mian Mumtaz Mohammad Khan Daultana; Maulana Mohammad Akram Khan; Mian Mohammad Iftikharuddin; Khan Sardar Bahadur Khan; Dr Mahmud Husain; Begum Shaista Suhrawardy Ikramullah; Prem Hari Burma; Nazir Ahmad Khan; Shaikh Karamat Ali; and Liaquat Ali Khan.

22. Basic Principles Committee, *Interim Report*, 7 September 1950 (Karachi: Din Mohammadi Press, 1950).

23. United Kingdom High Commissioner (UKHC) Karachi to Percivale Liesching, Commonwealth Relations Office (CRO) London, 9 September 1952, DO 35/2252, The National Archives (TNA) London.

24. Ibid.

25. Keith Callard, *Pakistan: A Political Study* (London: George Allen & Unwin, 1957), p. 38.

26. Basic Principles Committee, *Interim Report*.

27. *Constituent Assembly Debates*, vol. viii, no. 6 (21 November 1950), pp. 181–185; Herbert Feldman, *A Constitution for Pakistan* (Karachi: Oxford University Press, 1955), p. 28.

28. Hamid Yusaf, *Pakistan: A Study of Political Developments 1947–97* (Lahore: Sang-e-Meel Publications, 1999), p. 47.

29. Mian Iftikharuddin and Sardar Shaukat Hayat Khan set up the Azad Pakistan Party on 10 November 1950 after their expulsion from the PML for their criticism of the PML government's policies. Kausar Parveen, *The Politics of Pakistan Role of the Opposition 1947–1958* (Karachi: Oxford University Press, 2013), p. 128

30. UKHC in Pakistan to CRO London, 23 December 1952, DO 35/5048, TNA London.

31. CAP, Debates, vol. xii, no. 2 (22 December 1952).

32. Parveen, *Politics of Pakistan*, p. 234.

33. UKHC Pakistan to CRO, OPDOM, no. 19, Part 2, 13 May 1949, DO 142/424, TNA London.

34. Yunas Samad, 'South Asian Muslim politics, 1937–1958,' PhD Dissertation, St. Antony's College (Oxford: Oxford University, 1991).

35. The remaining five were Sir Mohammad Zafarullah Khan, Mushtaq Ahmad Gurmani, Sardar Bahadur Khan, Dr Ishtiaq Hussain Qureshi, Dr A.M. Malik.

36. Yusaf, *Study of Political Developments*, p. 55.

37. The proclamation is reported on page 251 in the reported judgment *Federation of Pakistan vs Maulvi Tamizuddin Khan*, PLD 1955 FC 240.

38. The Government of India (Fifth Amendment Bill), *Constituent Assembly Debates*, 21 September 1954, p. 571.

39. Wayne Ayres Wilcox, *Pakistan: The Consolidation of a Nation* (New York: Columbia University Press, 1963), p. 179.

40. Yusaf, *Study of Political Developments*, p. 58.

41. Constitutionally the custodian of the house was called the president. Later, the custodian of the house was called the speaker.

42. Government of India Act 1935, with Indian Independence Act, 1947.

43. *Federation of Pakistan vs Maulvi Tamizuddin Khan*, PLD 1955 FC 240 (Cornelius being the dissenting judge); Tamizuddin Khan, *The Test of Time: My Life and Days* (Dhaka: University Press Limited, 1989).

44. Rupert Emerson, *Representative Government in South-East Asia* (Cambridge: Harvard University Press, 1955), pp. 6–12.

45. Safdar Mahmood, *Pakistan Political Roots and Development* (Karachi: Oxford University Press), p. 169.

46. Mushtaq Ahmad, *Government and Politics* (Karachi: Royal Book Company, 2009), p. 103.

47. Mohammad Waseem, *Politics and the State in Pakistan* (Lahore: Progressive, 1989), p. 127.

48. Ahmad, *Government and Politics*, pp. 103–4.

49. Hamid H. Kizilbash, *Pakistan Foreign Policy and the Legislature* (Lahore: South Asian Institute, University of the Punjab, 1976), p. 7.

50. The corrections made by Jenning on the final draft of the constitution are shown in his handwriting in the *Jennings Papers*, Institute of Commonwealth Research, London B/XV/4-S, British Library, London.

51. Yusaf, *Study of Political Developments*, p. 57.

52. Some bills were very large, for example, the *Pakistan Air Force Act*. It was 206 sections on 54 pages; the bill was passed without discussion (DO 35/5048, TNA London).

53. Ahmad, *Government and Politics*, pp. 92–7.

54. Hamid Khan, *Constitutional and Political History of Pakistan* (Karachi: Oxford University Press, 2009), p. 87.

55. Waseem, *Politics and the State*, p. 127.

56. G.W. Choudhury, *Constitutional Development in Pakistan* (Lahore: The Ideal Book House, 1969), p. 93.

57. Ahmad, *Government and Politics*, p. 105.

58. The Muslim League had only 25 seats; all except 2 were from West Pakistan.

59. The representative character of this assembly was, however, gradually diluted as the new elections to provincial assemblies of Sindh (1951), Punjab (1952), NWFP

(1953), and East Bengal (1954). Especially in East Bengal, the United Front put the Muslim League into a rout. (Waseem, *Politics and the State*, p. 127).

60. Choudhury, *Constitutional Development*, p. 93.

61. Herbert Feldman, *Revolution in Pakistan: A Study of the Martial Law Administration* (Karachi: Oxford University Press, 2001), p. 25.

62. Notification no. F.42-1/55- cons. 3 October 1955, *The Gazette of Pakistan*.

63. Tariq Ali, *Pakistan: Military Rule or People's Power* (London: Jonathan Cape, 1970), pp. 67–8.

64. Choudhury, *Constitutional Development*, p. 96.

65. Yusaf, *Study of Political Developments*, p. 66.

66. Ibid.

67. UKHC Karachi to Percivale Liesching, CRO London, 3 November 1952, DO 35/2252, TNA London.

68. Ahmad, *Government and Politics*, p. 107.

69. Kizilbash, *Pakistan Foreign Policy*, p. 7.

70. *Dawn*, 9 October 1958.

71. Samad, *Nation in Turmoil*, p. 212.

72. Ali, *Pakistan: Military Rule*, p. 87.

73. Hamza Alavi, 'Army and Bureaucracy in Pakistan', *International Socialist Journal* 3, no. 14 (March–April 1966), pp. 140–181.

74. When Iskandar Mirza was ousted on 27 October, Ayub Khan also took the oath as prime minister of Pakistan but he worked less than one day in this capacity before dissolving the post altogether.

75. M. Rafique Afzal, *Political Parties in Pakistan 1958–1969*, vol. 1 (Islamabad: NIHCR, 2002), p. 70; see also, Allen McGrath, *Destruction of Pakistan's Democracy* (Karachi: Oxford University Press, 1996), p. 52; Khalid Bin Sayeed, *The Political System of Pakistan* (Kingston: Queen's University, 1966), p. 411; K.K. Aziz, *Party Politics in Pakistan 1947–1958* (Lahore: Sang-e-Meel, 2007), p. 14; and Mahmood, *Pakistan: Political Roots*, p. 68, they criticised the step taken by Liaquat Ali Khan.

76. Waseem, *Politics and the State*, p. 121.

77. Mohammad Ali Bogra was serving as ambassador in USA when he was appointed the prime minister of Pakistan.

78. Except Liaquat Ali Khan, no prime minister sought a vote of confidence from the assembly.

79. Maluka, *Myth of Constitutionalism*, p. 169.

80. McGrath, *Destruction of Pakistan's Democracy*, Chapter 8.

81. *Dawn*, 18 December 1959. Ayub Khan appointed an eleven-member constitution commission on 17 February 1960 under the chairmanship of Justice Shahabuddin.

82. The recommendations of the Shahabuddin Commission were not accepted by Ayub Khan. Later, Justice Shahabuddin declined to accept the high civil award of Hilal-e-Pakistan, because his recommendations were not accepted.

83. Justice Mohammad Shahabuddin elaborated his viewpoint in detail in his book, *Recollections and Reflections* (Lahore: PLD Publishers, 1972), p. 128.

84. The constitution of 1962 was promulgated by a presidential decree. Chaudhry Mohammad Ali, *The Task Before Us* (Lahore: Research Society of Pakistan, 1974), p. 101.

85. Government of Pakistan, *The Constitution of the Republic of Pakistan 1962* (Karachi: Inter Services Press, 1962), p. 11.

86. Hamid Khan, *Constitutional and Political History*, p. 145.

87. Under the 1962 constitution, elections were held on a non-party basis since the constitution maintained the ban on political parties.

88. 'Parliamentary History,' National Assembly of Pakistan, accessed from http://www. na.gov.pk/en/content.php?id=75.

89. Mushtaq Ahmad, *Government and Politics*, p. 235.

90. Shahabuddin, *Recollections and Reflections*, p. 140.

91. M. Rafique Afzal, 'Constitutional Development in Pakistan, 1958–1969', *Journal of Research Society of Pakistan* 19 (1982), p. 76.

92. The Eighth Amendment, passed in December 1967, electoral college of basic democrats was expanded to 120,000.

93. Iftikhar Ahmad, *Pakistan General Elections: 1970* (Lahore: South Asian Institute Punjab University, 1976), p. 21.

94. Article 60 of the National & Provincial Assemblies First Election Order, 1962.

95. 'Parliamentary History,' National Assembly of Pakistan, http://www.na.gov.pk/ en/content.php?id=75.

96. Mushtaq Ahmad, *Government and Politics*, pp. 237–8.

97. Saleem M.M. Qureshi, 'Party Politics in the Second Republic of Pakistan', *Middle East Journal*, Vol. 20, no. 4 (Autumn, 1966), pp. 456–72.

98. Rashiduzzaman, 'National Assembly of Pakistan', *Pacific Affairs* (Winter, 1969–70), pp. 486–7.

99. Sardar Bahadur Khan who was a veteran politician and brother of Ayub Khan played the role of opposition leader.

100. Mushtaq Ahmad, *Government and Politics*, pp. 239, 244.

101. Ibid., pp. 235–6.

102. Afzal, *Political Parties*, p. 234.

103. Ibid., pp. 236–41.

104. Ibid., pp. 242–4.

105. Ali, *Pakistan: Military Rule*, p. 87.

106. Afzal, *Political Parties*, pp. 244–6.

107. British High Commission Karachi to Arthur Bottomley, Secretary of State for Commonwealth Relations, CRO London, 24 April 1965, DO196/504, TNA London.

108. The Combined Opposition Parties, an alliance of five political parties: Council Muslim League, National Awami Party, Awami League, Jamaat-e-Islami and Nizam-i-Islam Party.

109. Sharif Al-Mujahid, 'The Assembly Elections in Pakistan', *Asian Survey* 5 (November 1965), pp. 538–51.

110. Ayub Khan formulated this party after a convention of Muslim Leaguers. He was the president up to 1970.

111. Rafique Afzal, *Political Parties*, vol. 2, p. 261.

112. British High Commission Karachi to Arthur Bottomley, Secretary of State for Commonwealth Relations, CRO London, 24 April 1965, DO196/504, TNA London.

113. Mushtaq Ahmad, *Government and Politics*, pp. 246–7.

114. British High Commission Karachi to Arthur Bottomley, Secretary of State for Commonwealth Relations, CRO London, 24 April 1965, DO196/504, TNA London.

115. Mushtaq Ahmad, *Government and Politics in Pakistan*, p. 248.

116. Afzal, 'Constitutional Development', pp. 61–81.

117. Mushtaq Ahmad, *Government and Politics*, p. 249.

118. Act IV of 1965, PLD 1965 Central Statutes 76.

119. Hamid Khan, *Constitutional and Political History*, p. 170.

120. Constitution (Sixth Amendment) Act, 1966. Act II of 1966, PLD Central Statutes 147.

121. The Constitution of the Republic of Pakistan 1962.

122. Hamid Khan, *Constitutional and Political History*, pp. 175–6.

123. Mushtaq Ahmad, *Government and Politics in Pakistan*, p. 248.

124. Ibid., p. 249.

125. *National Assembly Debates*, vol. 2 (1969), p. 1475.

126. *Dawn*, 1 February 1969.

127. Rizvi, *Military and Politics*, p. 126.

128. Rashiduzzaman, 'National Assembly of Pakistan', pp. 482–3.

129. Ibid., p. 484.

130. Data gathered from the Summary of the Work done by the National Assembly of Pakistan and Summary of the Business Transacted by the National Assembly (Rawalpindi: Government of Pakistan Press, published from 1962 to 1969), cited by Rashiduzzaman, 'National Assembly of Pakistan', pp. 483–5.

131. Ibid., p. 485.

132. Ibid., pp. 485–6.

133. Ibid., p. 482.

134. *The Pakistan Times*, 23 January 1965; Sayeed, *Political System*, p. 107.

135. Sharif Al-Mujahid, 'Assembly Elections in Pakistan', p. 538.

136. Sayeed, *Political System*, p. 109.

137. Rashiduzzaman, 'National Assembly of Pakistan', pp. 492–3.

138. Samad, *Nation in Turmoil*, p. 212.

139. Afzal, 'Constitutional Development', pp. 61–81.

140. Altaf Gauhar, *Ayub Khan: Pakistan's First Military Ruler* (Lahore: Sang-e-Meel Publications, 1996).

141. Constitutionally the speaker of national assembly should have been appointed as president in case of the resignation of the president.

142. Mushtaq Ahmad, *Government and Politics*, p. 96; Mahmood, *Pakistan: Political Roots*, p. 364.

Chapter 3. Formation, Complexity, and Differentiation of Parliament

1. Differentiation refers to the 'common understanding of members of the institution'. *See*, Nelson W. Polsby, 'The Institutionalization of U.S. House of Representatives,' *The American Political Science Review* 62, no. 1 (March 1968), pp. 144–168.

2. J.A. Rahim, *Outline of a Federal Constitution for Pakistan* (Lahore: Pakistan People's Party Political Series, 1969), p. 53.

3. Hasan Mohammad, *General Elections in Pakistan* (Lahore: Mavra Publishers, 2012), p. 95.

4. Three hundred would be elected to fill the general seats and thirteen to fill seats reserved for women.

5. Herbert Feldman, *Omnibus: The End & the Beginning* (Karachi: Oxford University Press, 1974), p. 58.

6. This age limit was set in place even though the election commission had no way of ascertaining a voter's exact age.

7. Feldman, *Omnibus*, p. 62; The Delimitation of Constituencies Order (No. 3) 1970 was promulgated on 11 April 1970.

8. M. Rafique Afzal, *Political Parties in Pakistan 1958–1969*, vol. 1 (Islamabad: NIHCR, 2002), p. 23.

9. G.W. Choudhury, *The Last Days of United Pakistan* (London: C. Hurst & Company, 1974), p. 95.

10. Ibid.

11. Legal Framework Order 1970, article 25.

12. These elections were unusual in several ways. They were the first general elections on the basis of adult franchise. There was no party in power to defend the policies of the government. It was bound to be a free-for-all affair to all of the political parties, each emphasizing its own objectives. Twenty-five parties were identified as separate political entities by the election commission. Ten were national, nine were based in West Pakistan, and six were based in East Pakistan. There were also no alliances with any party. None of the parties contested for all seats throughout the country.

13. On November 1970, a 100-mph tropical cyclone washed over scores of coastal islands and devastated the densely populated delta region. An estimated 500,000 people were killed in the disaster.

14. Mohammad Waseem, *Democratization in Pakistan: A Study of the 2002 Election* (Karachi: Oxford University Press, 2006), p. 32.

15. Iftikhar Ahmad, *Pakistan General Elections: 1970* (Lahore: South Asian Institute Punjab University, 1976), pp. 53–4.

16. Mohammad Waseem, *Politics and the State in Pakistan* (Lahore: Progressive Publishers, 1989), p. 256.

17. Mir Ghaus Bakhsh Bizenjo, *In Search of Solutions: An Autobiography* (Karachi: Pakistan Study Centre, University of Karachi, 2009), p. 141.

18. Tariq Ali, *Can Pakistan Survive?* (New York: Penguin Books, 1983), p. 83.

19. In the western provinces, there were 798 candidates for 138 seats and in East Pakistan 781 candidates ran for 162 seats; 316 independent candidates, 203 from West Pakistan and 113 from East Pakistan, also took part in the elections. *Report on General Elections Pakistan 1970–71* (Islamabad: Election Commission, Government of Pakistan, 1972), pp. 204–5.

20. Craig Baxter, 'Pakistan Votes—1970,' *Asian Survey* (March 1971), pp. 210–12.

21. Initially, Awami League won 151 seats out of 153. A month later, it won the remaining nine postponed contests.

22. Iftikhar Ahmad, *Pakistan General Elections*, p. 79; the Awami League won in all but two constituencies from where Nurul Amin Khan, a veteran politician, and Raja Tridev Roy, chief of the Chakma tribe returned victorious.

23. In their editorial comments, several newspapers were of the view that Pakistan had come of age as a result of the 1970 elections. See *Pakistan Times*, 10 December 1970 and *Dawn*, 11 December 1970.

24. Iftikhar Ahmad, *Pakistan General Elections*, p. 86.

25. Ikram Azam, *Pakistan's Security and National Integration* (Rawalpindi: The London Book Co., 1974), p. 62.

26. Sartaj Aziz, *Between Dreams and Realities* (Karachi: Oxford University Press, 2009), p. 45.

27. Hasan Mohammad, *General Elections in Pakistan*, p. 106.

28. Mir Ghaus Bakhsh Bizenjo, *In Search of Solutions: An Autobiography* (Karachi: Pakistan Study Centre, University of Karachi, 2009), p. 144.

29. Ghulam Mustafa Khar, interview, 13 June 2012, Khar House, 478 Meer Street, Lahore.

30. Stanley Wolpert, *Zulfi Bhutto of Pakistan: His Life and Times* (Karachi: Oxford University Press, 2008), p. 146.

31. Unlike previous occasions, Yahya Khan did not broadcast the statement himself, instead, it was read out on his behalf; Badruddin Umar, *The Emergence of Bangladesh: Vol. 2: Rise of Bengali Nationalism (1958–1971)*, p. 284.

32. Rafi Raza, *Zulfikar Ali Bhutto and Pakistan 1967–1977* (Karachi: Oxford University Press, 1997), p. 142.

33. Rizwan Ullah Kokab, 'Pakistani Leadership and Separatist Movement in East Pakistan,' PhD diss. (University of Punjab, 2012), p. 265

34. Ian Talbot, *Pakistan A Modern History* (Lahore: Vanguard Books, 1999), p. 202.

35. *Dawn*, 21 December 1971.

36. Sardar Shaukat Hayat Khan, *The Nation that Lost its Soul* (Lahore: Jang Publishers, 1995), p. 339.

37. *Dawn*, 15 April 1972.

38. President's Order No. 11 of 1972. *PLD 1972 Central Statutes*, p. 434. Under this order, the national assembly as provided in the Legal Framework Order 1970 came into existence. The business of the assembly was restricted to expressing a vote of confidence for the president of Pakistan, continuance of martial law till 14 August 1972, framing of an interim constitution, and appointment of a committee of the

assembly to prepare a draft for the permanent constitution no later than 1 August 1972 for submission to the national assembly.

39. From West Pakistan 144 and from East Pakistan 2.

40. Hamid Khan, *Constitutional and Political History of Pakistan* (Karachi: Oxford University Press, 2009), p. 254.

41. Baxter, 'Pakistan Votes', p. 213.

42. Lawrence Ziring, 'Pakistan: A Political Perspective,' *Asian Survey* 15 (July 1975), p. 641.

43. Ziring, 'Pakistan: A Political Perspective', p. 633.

44. Elliot L. Tepper, 'The New Pakistan: Problems and Prospects,' *Pacific Affairs* 47 (Spring 1974), pp. 65–6.

45. Baxter, 'Pakistan Votes', p. 213.

46. The Interim Constitution 1972.

47. Hamid Khan, *Constitutional and Political History*, p. 255.

48. Ibid., p. 264.

49. *National Assembly Debates*, vol. 5, no. 35, 27 July 1974, p. 430.

50. Ibid., vol. 3, no. 2, 31 May 1974, p. 26.

51. Ibid., vol. 4, no. 16, 17 June 1974, p. 274.

52. Hamid Khan, *Constitutional and Political History*, p. 278.

53. Constitution of Pakistan 1973, art. 70, 71.

54. Craig Baxter, 'Constitution Making: The Development of Federalism in Pakistan,' *Asian Survey* (December 1974), pp. 1081–82.

55. *National Assembly Debates*, vol. 6, no. 1, 29 October 1975, p. 57.

56. *Senate Debates*, 16 March 1976, pp. 396–403.

57. *National Assembly Debates*, vol. 1, no. 1, 16 January 1974, p. 27.

58. *Who is Who in the National Assembly*, National Assembly of Pakistan, Record and Biographies.

59. Kamal Azfar, *Pakistan Political and Constitutional Dilemmas* (Karachi: Pakistan Law House, 1987), p. 159.

60. Nabeela Afzal, *Women and Parliament in Pakistan 1947–1977* (Lahore: Pakistan Study Centre, University of the Punjab, 1997), p. 82.

61. *National Assembly Debates*, vol. 1, no. 3, 17 April 1972, p. 399.

62. According to art. 50 of the constitution, the parliament of the federation of Pakistan consisted of two houses, namely, the national assembly and the senate. The election to the senate was a prerequisite for the promulgation of the constitution.

63. The Constitution of Pakistan 1973, art. 59 (1).

64. Notification No. F.24 (1)/73-Pub, 10 June 1973.

65. Government of Pakistan, *First Senate of Pakistan* (Islamabad: Senate Secretariat, 1980).

66. *Dawn*, 17 July 1973; C.R. Budd, British Embassy Islamabad to Foreign and Commonwealth Office (FCO) London, 18 July 1973, FCO 37/1339, TNA London.

67. According to article 272 (b) of the 1973 constitution.

68. Government of Pakistan, *First Senate of Pakistan* (Islamabad: Senate Secretariat, 1980).

69. These rules were notified by the Senate Secretariat on 28 July 1973.

70. Government of Pakistan, *First Senate of Pakistan* (Islamabad: Senate Secretariat, 1980).

71. Ibid., pp. 81–90.

72. The Constitution of Islamic Republic of Pakistan 1973.

73. Senate of Pakistan, *Rules of Procedure and Conduct of Business in the Senate 1973* (Islamabad: Printing Corporation of Pakistan Press, 1973), pp. 58–63.

74. National Assembly of Pakistan, *Rules of Procedure and Conduct of Business 1973* (Islamabad: Printing Corporation of Pakistan Press, 1988), Chapter XI.

75. *Senate Debates*, 15 April 1976, pp. 127–37.

76. Ibid., 6 August 1974, pp. 227–8.

77. Ibid., 1 April 1974, p. 3.

78. *National Assembly & Senate Debates* (Joint Sitting), 10 December 1975.

79. Government of Pakistan, *First Senate of Pakistan*, pp. 74–5.

80. *National Assembly Debates*, vol. 6, no. 4, 3 December 1974, p. 150.

81. C.R. Budd, British Embassy Islamabad to Foreign and Commonwealth Office (FCO) London, 18 July 1973, FCO 37/1339, TNA London.

82. Ibid.

83. Ibid., pp. 59–60.

84. J.R. Paterson, British Embassy Islamabad to FCO London, 28 September 1972, FCO 37/1137, TNA London.

85. Ibid.

86. *National Assembly Debate*, vol. 3, no. 6, 5 June 1974, p. 250.

87. Bizenjo, *In Search of Solutions*, p. 204.

88. *National Assembly Debates*, vol. 6, no. 5, 4 November 1975, p. 272.

89. Sherbaz Khan Mazari, *A Journey to Disillusionment* (Karachi: Oxford University Press, 1999), p. 345.

90. Ibid., p. 342.

91. Ibid., p. 350.

92. Kaul & Shakdher, *Practice and Procedure: With Particular Reference to the Lok Sabha* (New Delhi: Metropolitan Book Co., 2001).

93. Ibid.

94. Hamid Yusuf, *The Return of the Politicians* (Lahore: Afrasia Publications, 1980), p. 139.

95. Rao Khurshid Ali Khan, MNA, *National Assembly Debate*, vol. 1, no. 1, 14 April 1972, p. 11.

96. *National Assembly Debate*, vol. 1, no. 1, 14 April 1972, p. 11.

97. Yusuf, *Return of the Politicians*, p. 140.

98. British Ambassador Islamabad to FCO London, 'Mr Bhutto's Internal Position,' 10 December 1974, FCO 37/1498, TNA London.

99. Shaukat Hayat Khan, *Nation that Lost*, p. 340.

100. J.R. Paterson, British Embassy Islamabad to FCO London, 28 September 1972, FCO 37/1137, TNA London.
101. Ibid., 7 February 1975, FCO 37/1652, TNA London.
102. *National Assembly Debates*, vol. 4, no. 1, 26 May 1975, p. 19.
103. Ibid., vol. 7 no. 13, 17 November 1975, p. 117.
104. British Embassy Islamabad to O.W. Everett, FCO London, 25 November 1975, FCO 37/1653, TNA London.
105. C.R. Budd, British Embassy Islamabad to O.W. Everett, FCO London, 10 July 1975, FCO 37/1652, TNA London.
106. J.R. Paterson, British Embassy Islamabad to P.C. Drew, FCO London, 7 February 1975, FCO 37/1652, TNA London.
107. Ibid.
108. C.R. Budd, British Embassy Islamabad to O.W. Everett, FCO London, 3 June 1975, FCO 37/1652, TNA London.
109. Ibid.
110. Ibid.
111. Ibid.
112. C.R. Budd, British Embassy Islamabad to O.W. Everett, FCO London, 10 July 1975, FCO 37/1652, TNA London.
113. Ibid., 3 June 1975, FCO 37/1652, TNA London.
114. Ibid.
115. Ibid.
116. Ibid.
117. *National Assembly Debate*, vol. 7, no. 12, 14 November 1975, p. 27.
118. Ibid., vol. 7, no. 18, 24 November 1975, p. 384.
119. A.R. Murray, British Embassy Islamabad to O.W. Everett, FCO London, 3 December 1975, FCO 37/1653, TNA London.
120. Ibid.
121. Mazari, *Journey to Disillusionment*, p. 353.
122. Ibid.
123. Ibid., p. 371.
124. Ibid., p. 372.
125. Shahid Javed Burki, *Pakistan: Fifty Years of Nationhood* (Lahore: Vanguard, 1999), p. 47.
126. India, Pakistan and Bangladesh Association, 'Confidential Report on Pakistan,' April 1975, FCO 37/1652, TNA London.
127. J.R. Paterson, British Embassy Islamabad to O.W. Everett, FCO London, 5 March 1975, FCO 37/1655, TNA London.
128. *Senate Debates*, 12 November 1975, pp. 11–30; and 13 November 1975, pp. 97–108.
129. Ibid., 12 April 1976, pp. 5–9.
130. Ibid., 16 April 1974, pp. 487–8.

CHAPTER 4. SOVEREIGNTY OF PARLIAMENT AS A CONSTITUENT ASSEMBLY

1. According to art. 271 of the constitution, the tenure of the first national assembly was to begin from the day of its commencement and continue until 14 August 1977.

2. Mohammad Waseem, 'Functioning of Democracy in Pakistan,' in Zoya Hasan, ed., *Democracy in Muslim Societies: The Asian Experience* (New Delhi: Sage Publications, 2007), p. 213.

3. Hamid Khan, *Constitutional and Political History of Pakistan* (Karachi: Oxford University Press, 2009), p. 254.

4. The first general elections were held on 7 March 1973 in Bangladesh.

5. Hamid Khan, *Constitutional and Political History*, p. 254.

6. Ibid.

7. Saeed Shafqat, 'Democracy and Political Transformation in Pakistan,' in Soofia Mumtaz, Jean-Luc Racine and Imran Anwar Ali, eds., *Pakistan: The Contours of State and Society* (Karachi: Oxford University Press, 2002), p. 215.

8. Burki, *Pakistan: Fifty Years*, p. 46.

9. *Dawn*, 16 January 1972.

10. *Dawn*, 25 January 1972.

11. *Dawn*, 7 February 1972.

12. *Dawn*, 19 February 1972.

13. PPP's negotiating team consisted of Mahmud Kasuri, Rafi Raza, Hafeez Peerzada, Mustafa Jatoi, Hayat Sherpao, and Kausar Niazi. NAP was represented by Abdul Wali Khan, Ghaus Bakhsh Bizenjo, Arbab Sikandar, and Khair Bakhsh Marri. The JUI was represented by Mufti Mahmud and Ghulam Ghaus Hazarvi.

14. *The PPP–NAP–JUI: The Tripartite Accord, March 6 1972, Basic Document and Background Material* (Islamabad: 1972, Directorate General of Films and Publications, Ministry of Information & Broadcasting).

15. A.A. Halliley, Office of the British Representative Islamabad to R.T. Fell, FCO London, 4 February, 1972, FCO 37/1136, TNA London.

16. *The PPP–NAP–JUI: The Tripartite Accord.*

17. Ibid.; Press Information Department Govt. of Pakistan (handout, 6 March 1972).

18. Mubashir Hasan, *The Mirage of Power* (Karachi: Oxford University Press, 2000), p. 88.

19. Sayyid A.S. Pirzada, *The Politics of the Jamiat Ulema-i-Islam Pakistan 1971–77* (Karachi: Oxford University Press, 2000), p. 60.

20. *Pakistan Times*, 9 March 1972.

21. President's Order No. 11 of 1972, PLD 1972 Central Statues Part, p. 434.

22. In the first setting of national assembly, 142 members took the oath.

23. *Asma Jilani vs. The Government of Punjab*, PLD 1972 SC 139, http://www.seamonitors.org/id37.html.

24. It is a misconception that Bhutto lifted martial law after the decision of the court in the Asma Jilani case. Bhutto was announcing the lift of martial law on 14 April

1972 while the case was decided on 20 April 1972 by Supreme Court. For details, see Malik Muhammad Saeed, *The All Pakistan Decisions* (Lahore: Church Road, 1972), p. 139.

25. *National Assembly Debates*, vol. 1, no. 3, 17 April 1972, p. 397. Most of amendments were related to the correction of misprinting or elaboration; there was no major amendment. In the 27th Amendment, provinces were allowed the teaching of provincial languages in addition to the Urdu language, pp. 271–278, 392.

26. *National Assembly Debates*, vol. 1, no. 1, 14 April 1972, p. 56.

27. Williams, *Pakistan under Challenge*, p. 136.

28. *National Assembly Debates*, vol. 1, no. 3, 17 April 1972, p. 397. Rao Khurshid Ali Khan, treasury MNA from Sahiwal, voted against the resolution.

29. Interim Constitution 1972.

30. Masud Ahmad, *Pakistan: A Study of its Constitutional History 1857–1975* (Lahore: Research Society of Pakistan, 1978), p. 174.

31. L.F. Rushbrook Williams, *Pakistan under Challenge* (London: Stacey International, 1975), p. 136.

32. Craig Baxter et al., *Government and Politics in South Asia* (Boulder: Westview Press, 1993), p. 210.

33. The Interim Constitution 1972, art. 137, 138 and 139.

34. Williams, *Pakistan under Challenge*, p. 137.

35. Zulfikar Khalid Maluka, *The Myth of Constitutionalism in Pakistan* (Karachi: Oxford University Press, 1995), p. 232.

36. *National Assembly Debates*, vol.1, no. 1 (14 April 1972), p. 24.

37. Ibid., vol. 1, no. 1, 14 April 1972, pp. 55, 62.

38. The committee comprised the following members: Mumtaz Ali Bhutto, Ghulam Mustafa Jatoi, Abdul Hafeez Pirzada, Syed Qaim Ali Shah Jilani, Dr Mrs Ashraf Khatoon, Ghulam Mustafa Khar, Ghulam Hussain, Begum Nasim Jahan, Mubashir Hasan, Malik Mohammad Akhtar, Malik Meraj Khalid, Maulana Kausar Niazi, Khurshid Hasan Meer, Sheikh Muhammad Rashid, Mufti Mahmud, Mir Ghaus Bakhsh Bizenjo, Amirzada Khan, Abdul Qayyum Khan, Mohammad Haneef Khan, Prof. Ghafoor Ahmad, Maulana Shah Ahmad Noorani Siddiqi, Niamatullah Khan Shinwari, Sardar Shaukat Hayat Khan, and Mian Mumtaz Daultana

39. *National Assembly Debates*, vol. 1, no. 3, 17 April 1972, p. 399.

40. Maluka, *Myth of Constitutionalism*, p. 239.

41. *National Assembly Debates*, vol. 1, no. 2, 16 August 1972, p. 53.

42. Ibid., vol. 1, no. 2, 16 August 1972, p. 21.

43. Ibid., vol. 2, no. 1, 1 December 1972, p. 73. Following were the signatories of the said document: Z.A. Bhutto (PPP), Abdul Qayyum Khan (QML), Ghaus Bakhsh Bizenjo (NAP), Arbab Sikander (NAP), Mufti Mahmud (JUI), Shaukat Hayat (CML), Jamaldar Khan (Tribal MNAs), Maulana Shah Ahmad Noorani (JUP), Ghafoor Ahmad (JI), and Sherbaz Khan Mazari (Independent). *National Assembly Debates*, vol. 2, no. 1, 21 October 1972.

44. Rafi Raza, *Zulfikar Ali Bhutto and Pakistan 1967–1977* (Karachi: Oxford University Press, 1997), p. 176.

45. *National Assembly Debates*, vol. 2, no. 1, 31 December 1972, p. 6.

46. *The Pakistan Times*, 21 October 1972.

47. Raza, *Zulfikar Ali Bhutto*, p. 176.

48. Ibid.

49. *The Gazette of Pakistan*, 31 December 1972.

50. 'Report of the Constitution Committee,' *National Assembly Debates*, vol. 2, no. 1, 31 December 1972; Notification No. F. 23 (8) 72-Legis., *The Gazette of Pakistan*, 31 December 1972.

51. The entire proceedings have been tape-recorded and available before the national assembly.

52. Notification No. F. 23 (8) 72-Legis., *The Gazette of Pakistan*, 31 December 1972.

53. *National Assembly Debates*, vol. 2, no. 1, 31 December 1972, p. 5.

54. FCO 37/1333, TNA London.

55. Notably by M.A. Kasuri (PPP), Sardar Shaukat Hayat Khan (PML), Shah Ahmad Noorani (JUP), Professor Ghafoor Ahmad (JI), Amirzada Khan (NAP), Mufti Mahmud (JUI), and Wali Khan.

56. *National Assembly Debates*, vol. 2, no. 1, 31 December 1972; J.R. Paterson, British Embassy Islamabad to D.H. Doble, FCO London, 4 January 1973, FCO 37/1333, TNA London.

57. Opposition's six points: An end to the campaign of the vilification of the opposition parties by the government. An assurance by the PPP that in the event of the rejection of a budget, the prime minister would either seek a vote of confidence or resign; or dissolve the assembly and hold fresh elections. In the event of the dissolution of the assembly, the prime minister should resign his office, and an impartial or national government should be set up to cover the period of the elections. Soon after the passage of the new constitution, impartial elections should be held under an impartial election commission and a national or non-party government, to bring the two houses to their new strengths. If the two-thirds majority for a vote of no confidence in the prime minister is to be retained, the Political Parties Act should be repealed. There should be an arrangement for complete freedom of the judiciary and the election commission.

58. J.R. Paterson, British Embassy Islamabad to D.H. Doble, FCO London, 24 January 1973, FCO 37/1333, TNA London.

59. Ibid.; Sardar Shaukat Hayat Khan, *The Nation that Lost its Soul* (Lahore: Jang Publishers, 1995).

60. Raza, *Zulfikar Ali Bhutto*, p. 176.

61. Choudhury, 'New Pakistan's Constitution,' p. 10.

62. Leonard Binder, *Religion and Politics in Pakistan* (Berkeley: University of California, 1963).

63. Choudhury, 'New Pakistan's Constitution,' p. 11.

64. *National Assembly Debates* vol. 2, no. 18, 2 February 1973.

65. J.R. Paterson, British Embassy London to D.H. Doble, FCO London, 24 January, 1973, FCO 37/1333, TNA London.

66. Abdul Hafeez Khan, *The Conspiracies against Pakistan and The Women in the Lives of Politicians* (Karachi: Royal Book Company, 1991), p. 79.

67. Maluka, *Myth of Constitutionalism*, p. 241.

68. J.R. Paterson, British Embassy Islamabad to D.H. Doble, FCO London, 8 March 1973, FCO 37/1338, TNA London.

69. British Ambassador at Islamabad to the Secretary of State for Foreign and Commonwealth Affairs London, 16 August 1973, FCO 37/1334, TNA London. The UDF was composed of the NAP, PML, JUI, JUP, PDP, KT, and some independent MNAs.

70. *The Pakistan Times*, Lahore, 3 March 1973. Major participant parties were JUP, JUI, NAP, JIP, PDP, United Muslim League and Khaksar Tehreek.

71. *The Pakistan Times*, Lahore, 21 March 1973.

72. Akhtar Hussain, 'Politics of Alliances in Pakistan 1954–1999,' PhD Thesis (Islamabad: National Institute of Pakistan Studies, QAU, 2008), p. 80.

73. *The Pakistan Times*, Lahore, 25 March 1973.

74. British Ambassador at Islamabad to the Secretary of State for Foreign and Commonwealth Affairs London, 16 August 1973, FCO 37/1334, TNA London.

75. Williams, *Pakistan under Challenge*, p. 144.

76. J.R. Paterson, British Embassy Islamabad to D.H. Doble, FCO London, 14 March 1973, FCO 37/1333, TNA London.

77. Ibid.

78. Ibid.

79. *The Pakistan Times*, 31 March 1973.

80. Ibid., 2 April 1973.

81. Ibid., 3 April 1973.

82. Ibid., 5 April 1973.

83. Ibid., 7 April 1973.

84. Ibid., 8 April 1973.

85. Ibid., 11 April 1973.

86. J.R. Paterson, British Embassy Islamabad to D.H. Doble, FCO London, 14 March 1973, FCO 37/1333, TNA London.

87. British Ambassador in Islamabad to the Secretary of State for Foreign and Commonwealth Affairs London, 16 August 1973, FCO 37/1334, TNA London.

88. Aziz Ahmad, Mahmud Ali, and Akbar Khan were not MNAs, but they were ministers of the state, and thus, not threatened by the original time-bar. J.R. Paterson, British Embassy Islamabad to D.H. Doble, FCO London, 9 March, 1973, FCO 37/1333, TNA London.

89. *Pakistan Bulletin*, 15 March 1973, FCO 37/1333, TNA London.

90. Burki, *Pakistan: Fifty Years*, p. 46.

91. Z.A. Bhutto, speech at luncheon of the Foreign Press Association and the Diplomatic and Commonwealth Writers' Association, London, 24 July 1973, FCO 37/1355, TNA London.

92. Ibid.

93. Hasan, *Mirage of Power*, p. 214.

94. J.R. Paterson, British Embassy Islamabad to D.H. Doble, FCO London, 11 April 1973, FCO 37/1333, TNA London.

95. Hamid Yusaf, *Pakistan: A Study of Political Developments 1947–97* (Lahore: Sang-e-Meel Publications, 1999), p. 151.

96. *National Assembly Debates*, vol. 2, no. 36, 10 April 1973, p. 2473.

97. *Nawa-i-Waqt*, 11 April 1973.

98. *National Assembly Debates*, vol. 2, no. 36, 10 April 1973, p. 2449.

99. *Nawa-i-Waqt*, 13 April 1973.

100. Ibid.

101. Ibid.

102. William Crawley, 'Pakistan Constitution Agreement,' Central Current Affairs Talks External Broadcasting, 11 April 1973, FCO 37/1333, TNA London.

103. They were Ali Ahmad Talpur, Abdul Hameed Jatoi, Abdul Khaliq, Mahmud Ali Kasuri, Ahmad Raza Kasuri, Makhdoom Noor Muhammad, Nawab Khair Bux Marri, and Abdul Hayee Baloch. *Nawa-i-Waqt*, 13 April 1973.

104. Baloch, *interview*, 18 April 2012.

105. Ibid.

106. *Nawa-i-Waqt*, 13 April 1973.

107. The Constitution of 1973, Art. 96.

108. Asghar Khan, *We've Learnt Nothing from History* (Karachi: Oxford University Press, 2005), p. 76.

109. Williams, *Pakistan under Challenge*, p. 149.

110. Stanley Wolpert, *Zulfi Bhutto of Pakistan: His Life and Times* (Karachi: Oxford University Press, 2008), p. 213.

111. Khan, *Constitutional and Political History*, p. 271.

112. Pakistan Press Comments on the adoption of the Constitution, 11 April 1973, FCO 37/1333, TNA London.

113. *Nawa-i-Waqt*, 11 April 1973.

114. *Jang*, 12 April 1973.

115. Pakistan Press Comments on the adoption of the Constitution, 11 April 1973, FCO 37/1333, TNA London.

116. Ibid.

117. Ibid.

118. *Nawa-i-Waqt*, 12 April 1973.

119. Pakistan Press Comments on the adoption of the Constitution, 11 April 1973, FCO 37/1333, TNA London.

120. *National Assembly Debates*, vol. 2, no. 36, 10 April 1973, p. 2462. The 1973 constitution was adopted after necessary amendments on 10 April 1973, and it came into effect on 14 August 1973.

121. Herbert Feldman, 'A Survey of Asia in 1973: Part II,' *Asian Survey* 14 (February 1974), pp. 136–42.

122. Ahmad, *Pakistan: A Study*, p. 178.

123. Yusaf, *Pakistan*, p. 152.

124. Ian Talbot, *Pakistan: A Modern History* (Lahore: Vanguard Books, 1999), p. 229.

Chapter 5. Parliament's Durability: Efficiency on National Issues (1973–7)

1. Michel Ameller, *Parliaments* (London: Casell & Company, 1966), p. 174.
2. For example, the changes in article 17 and article 199, British Embassy Islamabad to Foreign and Commonwealth Office (FCO) London, 25 November 1975, FCO 37/1652, The National Archives (TNA) London.
3. Hamid Khan, *Constitutional and Political History of Pakistan* (Karachi: Oxford University Press, 2009), p. 293.
4. British Embassy Islamabad to Foreign and Commonwealth Office (FCO) London, 25 November 1975, FCO 37/1652, The National Archives (TNA) London.
5. MNAs, Mufti Mahmud, Chaudhry Zahoor Elahi, Zulfikar Bajwa and Malik Suleman got injured; they showed their wounds in the press conference a day after the incident. *Nawa-i-Waqt*, 15 November 1975.
6. Khan, *Conspiracies against Pakistan*, p. 72; through the Fourth Amendment Act 1975, besides amending ten articles, the first schedule to the constitution was substituted and an amendment was also made in the fourth schedule. It was also laid down that certain orders shall cease to have effect after a specific period.
7. Abdullah Malik, *Dastan Khanwada-i- Mian Mahmud Ali Kasuri* (Lahore: Jang Publishers, 1995), pp. 438–9.
8. *The Pakistan Times*, 26 March 1969.
9. *Nawa-i-Waqt*, 24 November 1971.
10. Khan, *Conspiracies against Pakistan*, p. 72.
11. Herbert Feldman, 'A Survey of Asia in 1973: Part II,' *Asian Survey* 14 (February 1974), pp. 136–42.
12. Article 232 of the 1973 constitution.
13. *Nawa-i-Waqt*, 6 September 1973.
14. Parliament of Pakistan (Joint Sittings), *Debates*, Official Reports, 4 March 1974.
15. *Nawa-i-Waqt*, 4 March 1974.
16. Mufti Mahmud, Khawaja Safdar, Shaukat Hayat, Ahmad Raza Kasuri, Ali Ahmad Talpur, Sherbaz Mazari, Shah Ahmad Noorani, Khurshid Ali Khan, Maulana Abdul Haq, Mrs Jennifer Qazi, Kamran Khan, Hashim Ghazi, and some others.
17. *Nawa-i-Waqt*, 5 March 1974.
18. *National Assembly Debates*, vol. 2, no. 16, 12 February 1975, p. 275. By the same amendment, powers of the executive were extended in relation to preventive detention. The government could now keep a person in detention without trial for an indefinite period of time.
19. *National Assembly Debates*, vol. 2, no. 16, 12 February 1975, p. 254.
20. Ibid., p. 250.
21. Ibid., pp. 251–2.
22. Ibid., p. 252.
23. *National Assembly Debates*, vol. 2, no. 16, 12 February 1975, pp. 259–60.
24. Ibid., p. 271.
25. Ibid., p. 275.

26. Ibid., pp. 281–7.
27. Ibid., p. 275.
28. Sayyid A.S. Pirzada, *The Politics of the Jamiat Ulema-e-Islam Pakistan 1971–77* (Karachi: Oxford University Press, 2000), p. 118.
29. A quality of the institution to face the challenges and determine its supremacy while resolving the issues.
30. A special bulletin issued by a mosque in London on a letter by Abdul Qadir Zaigham on 2 June 1974. See FCO 37/1499.
31. *National Assembly Debates*, vol. 3, no. 5, 4 June 1974, pp. 167–70.
32. *Nawa-i-Waqt*, Lahore, 31 May 1974.
33. The issue was discussed for the first time in the newly elected national assembly on 14 April 1972 when Maulana Shah Ahmad Noorani, speaking on the interim constitution, demanded to incorporate the definition of a Muslim in the constitution. However, during constitution-making, the ulema did not focus on the Qadiani issue. At that time, their prime demand was to declare Islam state religion.
34. *National Assembly Debates*, vol. 3, no. 2, 31 May 1974, pp. 33–9; *National Assembly Debates*, vol. 3, no. 3, 1 June 1974, pp. 78–84.
35. Rules of Procedure, National Assembly of Pakistan 1973, rule no. 84, *Restriction on a number of motions* (Islamabad: Printing Corporation of Pakistan Press, 1988), p. 26.
36. Mr Justice K.M.A. Samdani was appointed as enquiry officer on 31 May 1974, and Assistant Advocate General Mr Kamal Mustafa Bokhari was to assist him.
37. *National Assembly Debates*, vol. 3, no. 2, 31 May 1974, pp. 33–9; *National Assembly Debates*, vol. 3, no. 3, 1 June 1974, pp. 78–84.
38. *National Assembly Debates*, vol. 3, no. 4, 3 June 1974, p. 130.
39. Ibid., p. 126.
40. Ibid., p. 128.
41. Ibid., pp. 129–30.
42. *National Assembly Debates*, vol. 3, no. 5, 4 June 1974, pp. 153, 170.
43. Ibid., p. 172.
44. Rafi Raza was special assistant to Prime Minister Zulfikar Ali Bhutto, and as a member of several cabinet committees, he was involved in all major political and diplomatic developments at the time.
45. Rafi Raza, *Zulfikar Ali Bhutto and Pakistan 1967–1977* (Karachi: Oxford University, Press, 1997), p. 294.
46. Allah Wasaya, *Parliament mein Qadiani Shikast* (Lahore: Ilm-o-Irfan Publishers, 2000), p. 18.
47. Letter of Ahmadi Movement in Islam, FCO 37/1499, TNA London.
48. Memorandum 'The Ahmadi Problem,' 12 September 1974, FCO, 37/1501, TNA London.
49. *See*, the report of his address in *Dawn* and *Pakistan Times*, 14 June 1974.
50. Rafi Raza, *Zulfikar Ali Bhutto and Pakistan 1967–1977*, p. 294.

51. Pirzada, *Politics of the Jamiat Ulema-e-Islam*, pp. 119, 145; *The Pakistan Times*, 10 June 1972.

52. *The Pakistan Times*, 10 June 1974.

53. Ibid., 11 June 1974.

54. Pirzada, *Politics of the Jamiat Ulema-e-Islam*, p. 119.

55. Satish Kumar, *The New Pakistan* (New Delhi: Vikas Publishing House, 1978), p. 92.

56. *The Pakistan Times*, Lahore, 13 June 1974.

57. *Nawa-i-Waqt*, Lahore, 10 June 1974.

58. *National Assembly Debates*, vol. 4, no. 26, 30 June 1974, p. 1306. The twenty-two members came from various parties. Four were from JUI, three from JUP and PML each, two from JI and NAP each, and five Independents.

59. Interview, Shah Ahmad Noorani, *Anwar-e-Raza* (quarterly) vol. 4, no. 4, 2010, p. 201. Noorani's statement remains unsubstantiated. However, it seems more believable that public response and religious sentiments on the finality of the Prophet (PBUH) convinced Bhutto that he should support public opinion and win popularity. Therefore he, shrewdly, supported the resolution.

60. Ambassador in Islamabad to Secretary of State, Foreign and Commonwealth Affairs, London, Diplomatic Report no. 350/74, 'The Ahmadiyya Issue,' 24 September 1974, FCO 37/1501, TNA London.

61. *National Assembly Debates*, vol. 5, no. 39, 7 September 1974, pp. 559–62.

62. Ambassador in Islamabad to the Secretary of State, Foreign and Commonwealth Affairs, London, Diplomatic Report no. 350/74, 'The Ahmadiyya Issue,' 24 September 1974, FCO 37/1501, TNA London.

63. The media was directed not to publish, broadcast, or telecast anything beyond the official version. Handout of 1 July 1974, Press Information Department (PID), Islamabad. *Pakistan Times*, 2 July 1974.

64. *National Assembly Debates*, vol. 5, no. 39, 7 September 1974, pp. 559–62.

65. Ambassador in Islamabad to the Secretary of State, Foreign and Commonwealth Affairs, London, Diplomatic Report no. 350/74, 'The Ahmadiyya Issue,' 24 September 1974, FCO 37/1501, TNA London.

66. *National Assembly Debates*, vol. 5, no. 39, 7 September 1974, pp. 559–62.

67. Ibid., p. 560.

68. Ibid.

69. Ibid., pp. 560–61

70. Ibid., p. 561

71. Ibid.

72. Ibid., pp. 559–65.

73. Ibid.

74. Ibid.

75. British Embassy Islamabad to FCO London, 9 September 1974, FCO 37/1501, TNA London.

76. Pirzada, *Politics of the Jamiat Ulema-e-Islam*, p. 124.

77. *The Pakistan Times*, 11 September 1974.

78. G.W. Choudhury, 'New Pakistan's Constitution, 1973,' *Middle East Journal* 28 (Winter 1974), p. 11.

79. *National Assembly Debates*, vol. 5, no. 39, 7 September 1974, p. 575.

80. British High Commissioner Islamabad to FCO London, 'Pakistan and the Qadiani Question,' 9 September 1974, FCO 37/1501, TNA London.

81. Ibid.

82. FCO 37/1651

83. British High Commissioner Islamabad to FCO London, 'Pakistan and the Qadiani Question,' 9 September 1974, FCO 37/1501, TNA London.

84. Husain Haqqani, *Pakistan between Mosque and Military* (Lahore: Vanguard, 2005), p. 107.

85. *National Assembly Debates*, vol. 5, no. 39, 7 September 1974, p. 565.

86. Ibid., p. 566.

87. Ibid.

88. Ibid., p. 568.

89. Ibid., p. 569.

90. Hamid H. Kizilbash, *Pakistan Foreign Policy and the Legislature* (Lahore: South Asian Institute, University of the Punjab, 1976), p. 15.

91. *National Assembly Debates*, vol. 4, no. 5, 6 August 1973, p. 259.

92. Bhutto addressed the parliament on 21 December 1973. Government of Pakistan, *Prime Minister of Pakistan Zulfikar Ali Bhutto, Speeches & Statements*, vol. 1 (Islamabad: Directorate General of Films and Publications Ministry of Information & Broadcasting, Government of Pakistan, 2010), p. 196.

93. Ibid.

94. *Senate Debates*, 1 April 1974, p. 3.

95. *National Assembly Debates*, vol. 8, no. 24 (2 December 1975), p. 84.

96. Ibid., vol. 8, no. 31, 12 December 1975, pp. 331–2.

97. *Senate Debates*, 5 August 1976, pp. 83–7.

98. Kizilbash, *Pakistan Foreign Policy*, p. 16.

99. *National Assembly Debates*, vol. 3, no. 15, 12 June 1973, p. 891.

100. Ibid., vol. 3, no. 27, 26 June 1973, 1982.

101. Zulfikar Ali Bhutto, 'Bilateralism: New Directions,' *Pakistan Horizon*, 29 (Fourth Quarter 1976), pp. 3–59.

102. Dennis Kux, *The United States and Pakistan, 1947–2000: Disenchanted Allies* (Karachi: Oxford University Press 2001), p. 207.

103. Ibid., p. 208.

104. Ibid., p. 211.

105. Z.A. Bhutto, *National Assembly Debates*, vol. 3, no. 8, 7 June 1974, p. 300.

106. *National Assembly Debates*, vol. 3, no. 38, 9 July 1973, p. 2731.

107. This happened in the case of the recognition of Bangladesh, the Simla Agreement and OIC.

108. Z.A. Bhutto, speech at luncheon of the Foreign Press Association and the Diplomatic and Commonwealth Writers' Association, London, 24 July 1973, FCO 37/1355, TNA London.

109. *National Assembly Debates*, vol. 3, no. 38, 9 July 1973, pp. 2715–7.

110. Ibid., vol. 3, no. 38, 9 July 1973, pp. 2761, 2790.

111. *The Pakistan Times*, 23 February 1974.

112. I.J.M. Sutherland, South Asian Department, FCO to Eric Norris, 20 March 1973, FCO 37/1333, TNA London.

113. J.L. Pumphrey, British Embassy Islamabad to I.J.M. Sutherland, South Asian Department, FCO, 14 March 1973, FCO 37/1333, TNA London.

114. India, Pakistan and Bangladesh Association, 'Confidential Report on Pakistan,' August 1973 FCO 37/1350, TNA London.

115. Yusuf, *Return of the Politicians*, p. 132.

116. Asghar Khan, *We've Learnt Nothing*, p. 65

117. British Ambassador Islamabad to Secretary of State FCO, Diplomatic Report no. 182/72, 17 February 1972, FCO 37/1141, TNA London.

118. Yusuf, *Return of the Politicians*, p. 133; the talk of a secret clause was lent substance by a statement made in the Indian parliament by Indian Foreign Minister Mr Vajpayee in 1978 that there was a secret understanding between Indira Gandhi and Z.A. Bhutto on Kashmir. *See*, Z.A. Suleri, 'A Secret Deal on Kashmir,' *The Pakistan Times*, Lahore, 3 May 1978. It is more likely that the agreement had no more a secret clause than the Tashkent Declaration had.

119. *Washington Post*, 2, 3, 4 July 1972.

120. 'Indo-Pakistani Pact Welcomed by the US,' *Washington Post*, 4 July 1972, cited by Kux, *United States and Pakistan*, p. 208.

121. *Nawa-i-Waqt*, 9 April 1973.

122. Malik Mohammad Akhtar, *National Assembly Debates*, vol. 2, no. 2, 11 July 1972, p. 89.

123. Press release Embassy of Pakistan London, FCO 37/1149, TNA London.

124. *National Assembly Debates*, vol. 2, no. 2, 11 July 1972; FCO37/1149, Press release Embassy of Pakistan, London.

125. Mahmud Ali Kasuri, *National Assembly Debates*, vol. 2, no. 1, 10 July 1972, p. 22.

126. Independent MNA elected from NW-89 Dera Ghazi Khan.

127. *National Assembly Debates*, vol. 2, no. 1, 10 July 1972, p. 51.

128. Leader of the JUI, elected from NW-13, D.I. Khan, later nominated for Leader of the Opposition. (Ex-Chief Minister NWFP).

129. *National Assembly Debates*, vol. 2, no. 1, 10 July 1972, p. 55.

130. National Awami Party's MNA elected from NW-138, Kalat, (former governor of Balochistan).

131. *National Assembly Debates*, vol. 2, no. 2, 11 July 1972, p. 108.

132. Ibid., vol. 2, no. 1, 10 July 1972, p. 46.

133. Inayatur Rahman Abbasi, *National Assembly Debates*, vol. 2, no. 1, 10 July 1972, p. 44.

134. Abdul Hayee Baloch, *National Assembly Debates*, vol. 2, no. 4, 13 July 1972, pp. 537–38.

135. Mohammad Hanif Khan, *National Assembly Debates*, vol. 2, no. 5, 14 July 1972, p. 644.

136. *National Assembly Debates*, vol. 2, no. 1, 10 July 1972, p. 153.

137. Maulana Ghulam Ghaus, *National Assembly Debates*, vol. 2, no. 2, 11 July 1972, p. 123.

138. Mohammad Amir Khan, *National Assembly Debates*, vol. 2, no. 4, 13 July 1972, p. 470.

139. Williams, *Pakistan under Challenge*, p. 138.

140. *National Assembly Debates*, vol. 2, no. 5, 14 July 1972, p. 724.

141. J.R. Paterson, British Embassy Islamabad to D.H. Doble, FCO London, 17 July 1972, FCO 37/1149, TNA London.

142. G.B. Chalmers, South Asian Department to Eric Norris, FCO, 6 September 1973, FCO37/1349, TNA London.

143. Feldman,' Survey of Asia,' p. 140.

144. Memorandum, 'Mr Bhutto's First Four Months,' FCO 37/1136, TNA London.

145. Ibid.

146. Khan, *Conspiracies against Pakistan*, p. 76.

147. *National Assembly Debates*, vol. 2, no. 6, 1 April 1974, pp. 318–21.

148. Ibid., vol. 6, no. 4, 3 November 1975, pp. 205–12.

149. Bulletin no. 298, The Budget and Economy, 3 July 1972, FCO 37/1156, TNA London.

150. Khan, *Conspiracies against Pakistan*, p. 77.

151. Ibid., p. 73.

152. Country Assessment Sheet, December 1976, FCO 37/2041, TNA London.

153. Khan, *Conspiracies against Pakistan*, p. 74.

154. Omar Noman, *The Political Economy of Pakistan 1947–1985* (Taylor & Francis, 1988).

155. Khan, *Conspiracies against Pakistan*, p. 74.

156. Ambassador in Islamabad to Secretary of State, Foreign and Commonwealth Affairs, London, Diplomatic Report no. 404/74, 'Mr Bhutto's Internal Position,' 10 December 1974, FCO 37/1498, TNA London.

157. *National Assembly Debates*, vol. 6, no. 11, 12 December 1974, pp. 456–7.

158. *The Pakistan Times*, 17 February 1972.

159. Hasan, *Mirage of Power*, p. 168.

160. Jam Ghulam Qadir Khan (April 1973–December 1975).

161. The nine members were: Abdul Hafeez Pirzada, Mohammad Hanif Khan, Mir Ghaus Bakhsh Bizenjo, Prof. Ghafoor Ahmad, Sardar Sherbaz Khan Mazari, Nemat Ullah Khan Shinwari, Chaudhry Jahangir Ali, Chaudhry Abdul Wahid and Chaudhry Mohammad Aslam.

162. *National Assembly Debates*, vol. 3, no. 13, 8 June 1973, p. 794.

163. Sardar Sherbaz Khan Mazari, *National Assembly Debates*, 14 February 1974, vol. 1, no. 21, p. 664.

164. Feldman, 'Survey of Asia,' p. 137.

165. Ibid., p. 137.

166. *National Assembly Debates*, 13 December 1973, pp. 630–3.

167. Bhutto's speech on the floor of the national assembly, 14 February 1974, *Speeches & Statements*, p. 284.
168. Ibid.
169. *Senate Debates*, 13 December 1973, pp. 235–45.
170. Ibid., 20 December 1973, pp. 322–8.
171. Ibid., 18 April 1974, pp. 556–65; 19 April 1976, pp. 579–86.
172. Ibid., 30 July 1974, pp. 120–30.
173. Ibid., pp. 130–3.
174. Ibid., 5 August 1974, pp. 187–95.
175. Baloch, interview, 18 April 2012.
176. *Senate Debates*, 6 August 1974, pp. 223–6.
177. Ibid., 6 August 1974, pp. 227–8.
178. Ibid., 6 August 1974, pp. 229–36.
179. Ibid., 19 November 1974, pp. 19–21.
180. Ibid., 9 March 1976, pp. 338–40.
181. Ibid., 5 July 1976, pp. 146–58.
182. *National Assembly Debates*, vol. 3, no. 22, 2 April 1975, p. 85.

CHAPTER 6. ESTABLISHING AUTONOMY: RELATION OF THE PARLIAMENT WITH OTHER INSTITUTIONS

1. Mohammad Waseem, *Democratization in Pakistan: A Study of the 2002 Election* (Karachi: Oxford University Press, 2006), p. 30.
2. Robert C. Fried, *Comparative Political Institutions* (New York: Macmillan Co., 1966), p. 7.
3. British Ambassador Islamabad to Secretary of State FCO (1973) Diplomatic Report No. 392/73, 16 August, FCO 37/1334, TNA London.
4. Waseem, *Democratization in Pakistan*, p. 32.
5. Hamid Yusuf, *The Return of the Politicians* (Lahore: Afrasia Publications, 1980), p. 147.
6. FCO, Diplomatic Report No. 411/72, 2 August 1972, FCO 37/1136, TNA London.
7. Mohammad Asghar Khan, *Generals in Politics* (New Delhi: Vikas, 1983), p. 48.
8. Dennis Kux, *The United States and Pakistan, 1947–2000: Disenchanted Allies* (Karachi: Oxford University Press, 2001), p. 220.
9. Hussain Haqqani, *Pakistan: Between Mosque and Military* (Lahore: Vanguard Books, 2005), p. 102.
10. FCO, Memorandum, Diplomatic Report No. 282/72, 24 April 1972, FCO 37/1136, TNA London.
11. Ibid.
12. Ibid.
13. Salmaan Taseer, *Bhutto: A Political Biography* (New Delhi: Vikas Publishing House, 1980), p. 155.

14. Yusuf, *Return of the Politicians*, p. 136.
15. British Embassy Islamabad, J.R. Paterson, Tour Notes, 17–21 January 1973. FCO37/1338, TNA London.
16. Shahid Javed Burki, *Pakistan: Fifty Years of Nationhood* (Lahore: Vanguard, 1999), p. 46.
17. Taseer, *Bhutto: A Political Biography*, p. 155.
18. Siddiq Salik, *State and Politics A Case Study of Pakistan* (Lahore: Al-Faisal Nashran, 1997), p. 132
19. British Ambassador in Islamabad to Secretary of State FCO, Diplomatic Report No. 392/73, 16 August 1973, FCO 37/1334, TNA London.
20. Ibid.
21. Constitution of Islamic Republic of Pakistan 1973, art. 7; Salik, *State and Politics*, p. 128.
22. Kamal Azfar, *Pakistan: Political and Constitutional Dilemmas* (Karachi: Pakistan Law House, 1987), p. 159.
23. Ibid., p. 87.
24. British Ambassador in Islamabad to Secretary of State FCO, Diplomatic Report No. 392/73, 16 August 1973, FCO 37/1334, TNA London.
25. Constitution of Pakistan, 1973, art. 96, clauses 1–5.
26. Yusuf, *Return of the Politicians*, pp. 128–31; Mukhtar Rana, MNA from NW-49, Lyallpur was disqualified on 10 April 1972.
27. Burki, *Pakistan: Fifty Years*, p. 47.
28. British Embassy Islamabad to D.H. Doble, FCO, 10 September 1973, FCO37/1339, TNA London.
29. *National Assembly Debates*, 5 March 1973, pp. 625–30.
30. FCO, Diplomatic Report No. 404/74, 10 December 1974, FCO 37/1498, TNA London.
31. Ibid.
32. Burki, *Pakistan: Fifty Years*, p. 46.
33. Gilbert T. Brown, *Pakistan's Economic Development after 1971 Pakistan: The Long View* (Durham, NC: Duke University Press, 1977), p. 173.
34. Salik, *State and Politics*, 130.
35. Foreign and Commonwealth Office (FCO), Diplomatic Report No. 404/74, 10 December 1974, FCO 37/1498, TNA London.
36. FCO, Diplomatic Report No. 404/74, 10 December 1974, FCO 37/1498, TNA London.
37. Notes on Pakistan, Visit of the M. Thatcher to India and Pakistan, FCO 37/1787, TNA London.
38. Haqqani, *Pakistan: Between Mosque and Military*, p. 109.
39. K.M. Arif, *Khaki Shadows* (Karachi: Oxford University Press, 2002), p. 286.
40. Mohammad Ayub, *An Army, Its Role and Rule: A History of the Pakistan Army from Independence to Kargil, 1967–1999* (Pittsburgh: Rose Dog Books, 2005), p. 361.
41. Khar, interview, 13 June 2012.

42. British Embassy Islamabad to D.H. Doble, FCO, 10 September, 1973, FCO37/1339, TNA London.

43. *Senate Debates*, 27 January 1975, pp. 112–22.

44. *Senate Debates*, 3 March 1976, pp. 143–7.

45. *Senate Debates*, 4 March 1976, pp. 220–35; 5 March 1976, p. 391; 16 March 1976, pp. 273–80.

46. Hamza Alavi, 'Authoritarianism and Legitimization of State Power in Pakistan,' in Subrata Kumar Mishra, ed., *The Post-Colonial State in Asia: Dialectics of Politics and Culture* (New York: Harvester Wheatsheaf, 1990), p. 127.

47. Mushtaq Ahmad, *Government and Politics in Pakistan*, p. 179.

48. Both were non-Awami League members of the national assembly and were elected in 1970 from East Pakistan.

49. Mubashir Hasan, *Mirage of Power* (Karachi: Oxford University Press, 2000), p. 17.

50. Haqqani, *Pakistan: Between Mosque and Military*, p. 106.

51. *National Assembly Debates*, vol. 4, no. 21, 24 June 1974, p. 833.

52. *National Assembly Debates*, vol. 4, no. 21, 24 June 1974, p. 834.

53. Ibid., p. 834.

54. Ibid., p. 878.

55. *National Assembly Debates*, vol. 8, no. 22, 28 November 1975, pp. 5–6.

56. *National Assembly Debates*, 28 August 1972, pp. 520–9.

57. Ibid.

58. Ayesha Siddiqa, *Military Inc.: Inside Pakistan's Military Economy* (Karachi Oxford University Press, 2007), p. 59.

59. Iftikhar H. Malik, *State and Civil Society in Pakistan: Politics of Authority, Ideology and Ethnicity* (London: MacMillan Press, 1997), p. 71.

60. Syed Shahid Hussain, *What was Once East Pakistan* (Karachi: Oxford University Press, 2010), p. 64.

61. Hasan Askari Rizvi, 'The Military: Role Enhancement and the Political Process,' in Abbas Rashid, ed., *Pakistan Perspectives on State and Society* (Lahore: Society for the Advancement of Education 2004), p. 117.

62. Malik, *State and Civil Society*, p. 71.

63. Siddiqa, *Military Inc.*, p. 59.

64. Ibid., p. 64.

65. Hasan Askari Rizvi, *Military & Politics in Pakistan 1947–97* (Lahore: Sang-e-Meel Publications, 2000), p. 207.

66. Siddiqa, *Military Inc.*, p. 65.

67. Stephen P. Cohen, *The Future of Pakistan* (Lahore: Vanguard Books, 2012), p. 54.

68. Malik, *State and Civil Society*, p. 73.

69. Ashok Kapur, *Pakistan in Crisis* (London: Routledge, 2006), p. 106.

70. Malik Ghulam Mustafa Khar, interview, 13 June 2012; Salik, *State and Politics*, p. 124.

71. Shuja Nawaz, *Crossed Swords: Pakistan its Army, and the Wars Within* (Karachi: Oxford University Press, 2008), p. 323.

72. Bhutto's address to the nation on 4 March 1972. The text of Bhutto's broadcast available *The Pakistan Times*, 5 March 1972.

73. Siddiq Salik, *State and Politics: A Case Study of Pakistan*. (Lahore: Al-Faisal Nashran, 1997), p. 126.

74. Ibid., p. 129.

75. Shahid Javed Burki, 'Politics of Power and its Economic Imperatives: Pakistan 1947–99,' in Anita M. Weiss and S. Zulfikar Gilani, eds., *Power and Civil Society in Pakistan* (Karachi: Oxford University Press, 2003), p. 137.

76. Ayub, *An Army*, pp. 355–6; Nawaz, *Crossed Swords*, ch. 13.

77. Gul Hassan Khan, *Memoirs* (Karachi: Oxford University Press, 1993), p. 368.

78. Khar, interview, 13 June 2012.

79. Ayub, *An Army*, p. 356.

80. Rizvi, *Military and Politics*, p. 220.

81. Ayub, *An Army*, p. 358.

82. Ibid., p. 359.

83. *The Pakistan Times*, 1 and 3 April 1973

84. Rizvi, *Military and Politics*, p. 221.

85. Notes on Pakistan, visit of Margaret Thatcher to India and Pakistan, FCO 37/1787, TNA London.

86. Rizvi, *Military and Politics*, p. 221.

87. Rizvi, 'Military: Role Enhancement,' p. 119.

88. Zulfikar Khalid Maluka, *The Myth of Constitutionalism in Pakistan* (Karachi: Oxford University Press, 1996), p. 253.

89. Rizvi, *Military and Politics*, p. 224.

90. Tahir Kamran, *Democracy and Governance in Pakistan* (Lahore: South Asia Partnership, 2008), p. 88.

91. Khar, *Interview*, 13 June 2012.

92. Siddiqa, *Military Inc.*, p. 80.

93. Ibid.

94. Rizvi, 'Military: Role Enhancement,' p. 119.

95. Saeed Shafqat, *Civil-Military Relations in Pakistan* (Lahore: Westview Press, 1997), p. 168.

96. Rizvi, *Military and Politics*, 215.

97. *Senate Debates* (17 January 1974): 55–60.

98. *National Assembly Debates*, vol. 6, no. 4 (3 December 1974): 150.

99. *National Assembly Debates*, vol. 1, no. 1 (16 January 1974): 20.

100. *National Assembly Debates*, vol. 4, no. 14 (15 June 1974): 106.

101. FSF was created in September 1972. It was headed by a retired police officer, Haq Nawaz Tiwana, with a budget of Rs 5,000,000. Eventually, Tiwana was replaced by another police officer Masood Mahmud. (Hasan, *Mirage of Power*, 268.)

102. Siddiqa, *Military Inc.*, p. 81.

103. Haqqani, *Pakistan between Mosque*, p. 110.

104. *National Assembly Debates*, vol. 4, no. 14, 13 June 1975, p. 482.

105. *Senate Debates*, 17 January 1975, pp. 28–32.

106. Siddiqa, *Military Inc.*, p. 67.

107. Waseem, *Democratization in Pakistan*, p. 30.

108. Robert C. Fried, *Comparative Political Institutions* (New York: Macmillan, 1966), p. 7.

109. British Ambassador Islamabad (1973) to Secretary of State FCO, Diplomatic Report No. 392/73, 16 August, FCO 37/1334, The National Archives (TNA) London.

110. Mahboob Hussain and Rizwan Ullah Kokab, 'Institutional Influence in Pakistan, Bureaucracy, Cabinet and Parliament,' *Asian Social Science* 9, no. 7, June 2013, p. 176.

111. Waseem, *Democratization in Pakistan*, p. 30.

112. Hamza Alavi, 'Politics of Ethnicity in India and Pakistan,' in Hamza Alavi and John Harriss, eds., *Sociology of Developing Societies South Asia* (Hampshire: Macmillan, 1988), p. 242.

113. Siddiqa, *Military Inc.*, pp. 67–8.

114. S.S. Hamid, *Early Years of Pakistan* (Lahore: Ferozsons, 1993), p. 71; R. Islam, *The Bangladeshi Liberation Movement* (Dhaka: The University Press, 1987), p. 12; K.B. Sayeed, 'The Political Role of Pakistan's Civil Service,' *Pacific Affairs* 31, p. 131; S.N. Kaushik, *Pakistan Under Bhutto's Leadership* (New Delhi: Uppal Publishing House, 1985), p. 41.

115. Sir Frederick Bourne (East Pakistan), Sir Robert Francis Mudie (Punjab), Sir George Cunningham (NWFP).

116. Saeed Shafqat, 'Democracy and Political Transformation in Pakistan,' in Soofia Mumtaz, Jean-Luc Racine, and Imran Ali, eds., *Pakistan: The Contours of State and Society* (Karachi: Oxford University Press, 2002), p. 215.

117. Robert La Porte, *Power and Privilege: Influence and Decision-Making in Pakistan* (New Delhi: Vikas, 1976), p. 117.

118. C.H. Kennedy, *Bureaucracy in Pakistan* (Karachi: Oxford University Press, 1987), p. 80.

119. Brief of the visit of Margret Thatcher, Leader of the Opposition, to India and Pakistan, FCO 37/1787, The National Archives London, 1976.

120. Yusuf, *Return of the Politicians*, pp. 131, 139.

121. Brief of the visit of Margret Thatcher, Leader of the Opposition, to India and Pakistan, FCO 37/1787, The National Archives London, 1976.

122. Mubashir Hasan, p. 277.

123. Ibid.

124. Ibid., p. 270.

125. Ibid., p. 271.

126. *Senate Debates*, 27 February 1976.

127. *National Assembly Debates*, vol. 6, no. 15, 17 December 1974.

128. Saeed Shafqat, 'Democracy and Political Transformation in Pakistan,' in Soofia Mumtaz, Jean-Luc Racine, and Imran Anwar Ali, eds., *Pakistan: The Contours of State and Society* (Karachi: Oxford University Press, 2002), p. 215.

129. Yusuf, *Return of the Politicians*, pp. 128, 131.

130. Shafqat, 'Democracy and Political Transformation,' p. 214.

131. Rizvi, *Military and Politics*, p. 231.

132. Burki, *Pakistan: Fifty Years*, p. 47.

133. M.A. Zaheer Afridi, Pukhtoon Baluch Action Committee International to Home Secretary British Government, 27 February 1977, FCO 37/2068, TNA London.

134. Hamid Khan, *A History of the Judiciary in Pakistan* (Karachi: Oxford University Press, 2016), p. 163.

135. Constitution (Fourth Amendment) Act, 1975, Act LXXI of 1975, PLD 1975 Central Statutes 337.

136. Ambassador in Islamabad to Secretary of State, Foreign and Commonwealth Affairs, London, Diplomatic Report No. 404/74, 'Mr Bhutto's Internal Position,' 10 December 1974, FCO 37/1498, TNA London.

137. *Dawn*, 15 November 1975.

138. Constitution (Fifth Amendment) Act, 1976, Act LXII of 1976, PLD 1976 Central Statutes 538.

139. Khan, *A History of the Judiciary in Pakistan*, p. 166.

140. Constitution (Sixth Amendment) Act, 1976, Act LXXXIV of 1976, PLD 1977 Central Statutes 46.

141. Yusuf, *Return of the Politicians*, p. 143; ironically, this amendment legally prevented Bhutto from engaging a foreign counsel during his trial for murder.

142. *National Assembly Debates*, 21 August 1972, pp. 209–10.

143. *National Assembly Debates*, vol. 4, no. 21, 24 June 1974, pp. 870–2.

144. Ibid., pp. 900–2.

145. *National Assembly Debates*, vol. 1, No. 1, 14 April 1972, p. 15.

146. Ibid.

147. India, Pakistan and Bangladesh Association, 'Confidential Report on Pakistan,' August 1973, FCO 37/1350, TNA London.

148. Ibid., p. 132.

149. Sayyid A.S. Pirzada, *The Politics of the Jamiat Ulema-i-Islam Pakistan 1971–77* (Karachi: Oxford University Press), p. 88.

150. Ambassador in Islamabad to Secretary of State, Foreign and Commonwealth Affairs, London, Diplomatic Report No. 392/73, '1973 Constitution of Pakistan,' 16 August, 1973, FCO 37/1334, TNA London.

151. Ibid.

152. Azfar, *Pakistan Political*, p. 86.

153. Yusuf, *Return of the Politicians*, p. 145.

154. Ibid., p. 145.

155. J.R. Paterson, British Embassy Islamabad to Miss P. Drew, FCO London, 11 February 1975, FCO 37/1655, TNA London.

156. Ibid.

157. J.R. Paterson, British Embassy Islamabad to O. W. Everett, FCO London, 26 February 1975 FCO 37/1655, TNA London.

158. Abdul Hafeez Khan, *The Conspiracies against Pakistan and the Women in the Lives of Politicians* (Karachi: Royal Book Company, 1991), p. 73.

159. General Secretary of NWFP UDF, and finance secretary of provincial NAP.

160. *Senate Debates*, 14 December 1973, pp. 282–6.

161. *Senate Debates*, 25 April 1974, pp. 695–6.

162. *Senate Debates*, 23 August 1974, pp. 593–8.

163. *Senate Debates*, 13 August 1974, pp. 405–8.

164. Kaushik, *Pakistan under Bhutto's Leadership*, p. 127.

165. Lawrence Ziring, 'Pakistan: A Political Perspective,' *Asian Survey* 15, no. 7 (1975), p. 632.

166. Kaushik, *Pakistan under Bhutto's Leadership*, p. 128.

167. Shafqat, *Democracy and Political Transformation*, p. 31.

168. Country Assessment Sheet, December 1976, FCO 37/2041, TNA London.

169. Ambassador in Islamabad to Secretary of State, Foreign and Commonwealth Affairs, London, Diplomatic Report No. 404/74, 'Mr Bhutto's Internal Position,' 10 December 1974, FCO 37/1498, TNA London.

170. J.R. Paterson, British Embassy Islamabad to D.H. Doble, FCO London, 28 September 1972, FCO 37/1137, TNA London.

171. Kaushik, *Pakistan under Bhutto's Leadership*, p. 130.

172. Sardar Shaukat Hayat Khan, *The Nation that Lost its Soul* (Lahore: Jang Publishers, 1995), p. 340.

173. Country Assessment Sheet, December 1976, FCO 37/2041, TNA London.

174. M.A. Zaheer Afridi, Pukhtoon Baluch Action Committee International to Home Secretary British Government, 27 February 1977, FCO 37/2068, TNA London.

175. Yusuf, *Return of the Politicians*, 140.

176. *National Assembly Debates*, vol. 1, no. 1, 14 April 1972, p. 16.

177. *Senate Debates*, 4 December 1973, pp. 53–6.

178. Ibid., 6 December 1973, pp. 101–2.

179. Ibid., 7 December 1973, pp. 109–11.

180. *National Assembly Debates*, vol. 1, no. 1, 14 April 1972, p. 14.

181. *Senate Debates*, 17 April 1974, pp. 509–13.

182. *National Assembly Debates*, vol. 4, no. 4, 29 May 1975, p. 95.

183. Ibid., vol. 2, no. 5, 29 March 1974.

184. Ibid., vol. 3, no. 4, 3 June 1974, p. 117.

185. Ibid., vol. 6, no. 6, 5 November 1975, pp. 313–21.

186. Ibid., vol. 5, no. 39, 7 September 1974, pp. 574–5.

187. Ibid., vol. 4, no. 19, 20 June 1974, pp. 686–90.

188. Ibid., vol. 6, no. 14, 16 December 1974, pp. 567–75.

189. Ibid., vol. 7, no. 20, 26 November 1975, pp. 481–5.

190. *Senate Debates*, 11 November 1976, pp. 34–7.

191. *National Assembly Debates*, vol. 1, no. 1, 14 April 1972, p. 14.

192. Ibid., vol. 1, no. 1, 14 April 1972, p. 15.

193. *Senate Debates*, 1 December 1973, pp. 7–16; 4 December 1973, pp. 47–9.

194. Ibid., 12 December 1973, pp. 214–24.

195. Ibid., 13 December 1973, pp. 230–3.
196. Ibid., 25 July 1974, p. 9.
197. Ibid., 18 December 1974, pp. 502–4.
198. Ibid., 27 January 1975, pp. 126–31.
199. Ibid., 13 February 1975, pp. 618–26.
200. Ibid., 19 September 1974, pp. 14–19.
201. Ibid., 1 March 1976, pp. 64–7.
202. Ibid., 18 March 1976, pp. 472–87.
203. Ibid., 14 April 1976, pp. 95–109.
204. J.R. Paterson, British Embassy Islamabad to D.H. Doble, FCO London, 28 September 1972, FCO 37/1137, TNA London.
205. Ibid., 29 April 1972, FCO37/1138, TNA London.
206. Ibid.
207. Ibid.
208. *National Assembly Debates*, 14 December 1973.
209. Ibid., vol. 4, no. 35, 27 July 1974, p. 395.
210. Ibid., vol. 6, no. 7 (6 November 1975, pp. 341–82.
211. Ibid., vol. 4, no. 17, 17 June 1975, pp. 637–9.
212. Ibid., vol. 3, no. 3, 1 June 1974, p. 77.
213. Ibid., vol. 4, no. 21, 24 June 1974, p. 897.
214. Ibid., 30 November 1973, p. 293.
215. *Senate Debates*, 13 December 1973, p. 259.
216. Ibid., 7 September 1973, p. 22.
217. Ibid., 11 December 1973, pp. 186–187.

CHAPTER 7. CONCLUSION

1. Sahibzada Farooq Ali, *Jamhooriyat Sabr Talb* (Lahore: Takhleeqat, 2006), p. 213.

Bibliography

PRIMARY SOURCES

Unpublished

The National Archives, Kew Garden London UK

Dominion Office Record

DO 142/424, *High Commissioner Office Report*, 1949
DO 35/2252, *Pakistan Constitution Drafting*, 1949
DO 35/2253, *Pakistan Constitution, Position of the Governor General*, 1949
DO 35/5102, *Establishment of Pakistan*, 1953
DO 35/5048, *Proceedings of the Pakistan Constituent Assembly*, 1952
DO 35/5120, *Composition and Proceedings of Second Constituent Assembly*, 1955
DO 196/504, *Elections in Pakistan*, 1965

Foreign and Commonwealth Office Records

FCO 37/1136, *Reports on Political Situation in Pakistan*, 1972
FCO 37/1137, *Reports on Political Situation in Pakistan*, 1972
FCO 37/1138, *Activities of Political Parties in Pakistan*, 1972
FCO 37/1141, *Withdrawal of Pakistan from the Commonwealth*, 1972
FCO 37/1149, *Negotiations for a Post-War Settlement Between Pakistan and India*, 1972
FCO 37/1156, *Economic Situation in Pakistan*, 1972
FCO 37/1333, *Constitution of Pakistan*, 1973
FCO 37/1334, *Constitution of Pakistan*, 1973
FCO 37/1335, *Constitution of Pakistan: Enclosure*, 1973
FCO 37/1338, *Internal Situation in Pakistan*, 1973
FCO 37/1339, *Internal Situation in Pakistan*, 1973
FCO 37/1349, *Political Relations Between Pakistan and India*, 1973
FCO 37/1350, *Political relations between Pakistan and India*, 1973
FCO 37/1355, *Visit of President Bhutto of Pakistan, to the UK, 23–25 July*, 1973
FCO 37/1498, *Internal Situation in* Pakistan, 1974
FCO 37/1499, *Issue of Atrocities Committed Against Ahmadiyya in Pakistan*, 1974
FCO 37/1501, *Issue of Atrocities Committed Against Ahmadiyya in Pakistan*, 1974
FCO 37/1652, *Internal Situation in Pakistan*, 1975
FCO 37/1655, *Political Situation in the North West Frontier Province of Pakistan*, 1975
FCO 37/1787, *Visit of Margaret Thatcher, Leader of the Opposition, to India and Pakistan*, 1976
FCO 37/2041, *Country Assessment Sheet on Pakistan*, 1977

FCO 37/2068, *Human Rights in Pakistan*, 1977
Jennings Papers, Institute of Commonwealth Research, London B/XV/4-S

Published

Official Publications

Documents of the Parliament of Pakistan

National Assembly of Pakistan Debates, Official Reports (Karachi: Printing Corporation of Pakistan Press)

Vol. 2 (1969): 1475
Vol. 1, No. 1 (14 April 1972): 11, 14, 15, 56
Vol. 1, No. 3 (17 April 1972): 397
Vol. 2, No. 1 (10 July 1972): 55, 153
Vol. 2, No. 2 (11 July 1972): 123
Vol. 2, No. 4 (13 July 1972): 470, 537–38
Vol. 2, No. 5 (14 July 1972): 644
Vol. 1, No. 2 (16 August 1972): 21
Vol. 2, No. 1 (1 December 1972): 73
Vol. 2, No. 1 (31 December 1972): 5
Vol. 2, No. 18 (2 February 1973)
Vol. 2, No. 36 (10 April 1973): 2473
Vol. 3, No. 38 (9 July 1973): 2731
Vol. 4, No. 5 (6 August 1973): 259
Vol. 1, No. 1 (16 January 1974): 20
Vol. 1, No. 21 (14 February 1974): 664
Vol. 2, No. 6 (1 April 1974): 318–21
Vol. 3, No. 2 (31 May 1974): 26, 33–39
Vol. 3, No. 3 (1 June 1974): 77
Vol. 3, No. 4 (3 June 1974): 117, 130
Vol. 3, No. 5 (4 June 1974): 172
Vol. 3, No. 6 (5 June 1974): 250
Vol. 3, No. 8 (7 June 1974): 300
Vol. 4, No. 14 (15 June 1974): 106
Vol. 4, No. 16 (17 June 1974): 274
Vol. 4, No. 19 (20 June 1974): 686–690
Vol. 4, No. 21 (24 June 1974): 833, 897, 900–902
Vol. 4, No. 35 (27 July 1974): 395, 430
Vol. 5, No. 39 (7 September 1974): 559–62, 574–575
Vol. 6, No. 4 (3 December 1974): 150
Vol. 6, No. 11 (12 December 1974): 456–457
Vol. 6, No. 14 (16 December 1974): 567–575

Vol. 6, No. 15 (17 December 1974): 658
Vol. 6, No. 17 (19 December 1974): 760
Vol. 2, No. 16 (12 February 1975): 275
Vol. 3, No. 22 (2 April 1975): 85
Vol. 4, No. 1 (26 May 1975): 19
Vol. 4, No. 4 (29 May 1975): 95
Vol. 4, No. 14 (13 June 1975): 482
Vol. 4, No. 17 (17 June 1975): 637–39
Vol. 6, No. 1 (29 October 1975): 57
Vol. 6, No. 5 (4 November 1975): 272
Vol. 6, No. 6 (5 November 1975): 313–321
Vol. 6, No. 7 (6 November 1975): 341–82
Vol. 7, No. 12 (14 November 1975): 27
Vol. 7, No. 13 (17 November 1975): 117
Vol. 7, No. 18 (24 November 1975): 384
Vol. 7, No. 20 (26 November 1975): 481–485
Vol. 8, No. 22 (28 November 1975): 5–6
Vol. 8, No. 24 (2 December 1975): 84

Senate of Pakistan Debates, *Official Reports* (Karachi: Printing Corporation of Pakistan Press)

(7 September 1973): 22
(1 December 1973): 7–16
(4 December 1973): 53–56
(6 December 1973): 101–102
(7 December 1973): 109–111
(11 December 1973): 186–187
(12 December 1973): 214
(13 December 1973): 230–233
(14 December 1973): 282–286
(20 December 1973): 322–328
(17 January 1974): 55–60
(1 April 1974): 3
(16 April 1974): 487–488
(17 April 1974): 509–513
(18 April 1974): 556–565
(25 April 1974): 695–696
(25 July 1974): 9
(30 July 1974): 120–130
(5 August 1974): 187–195
(6 August 1974): 223–226, 227–228
(13 August 1974): 405–408
(23 August 1974): 593–598

(19 September 1974): 14–19
(19 November 1974): 19–21
(18 December 1974): 502–504
(17 January 1975): 28–32
(27 January 1975): 112–122, 126–131
(13 February 1975): 618–626
(12 November 1975): 11–30
(1 March 1976): 64–67
(3 March 1976): 143–147
(4 March 1976): 220–235
(5 March 1976): 391
(9 March 1976): 338–340
(16 March 1976): 273–280, 396–403
(18 March 1976): 472–487
(12 April 1976): 5–9
(14 April 1976): 95–109
(15 April 1976): 127–137
(19 April 1976): 579–586
(5 July 1976): 146–158
(5 August 1976): 79–82, 83–87
(11 November 1976): 34–37

Government of Pakistan. *The First Senate of Pakistan*. Islamabad: Senate Secretariat, 1980.
National Assembly of Pakistan. *Decisions of the Chair, Vol. 4, 1972–1975*. Islamabad: Printing Corporation of Pakistan Press, 1976.
National Assembly of Pakistan. *Rules of Procedure and Conduct of Business 1973*. Islamabad: Printing Corporation of Pakistan Press, 1988.
National Assembly of Pakistan. *Who is Who in National Assembly of Pakistan*. Islamabad: Printing Corporation of Pakistan Press, 1976.
Parliament of Pakistan (Joint Sittings). *Debates*. Official Reports, 1973–1977.
Senate of Pakistan. *Decisions of the Chair, Part I & II, 1973–1977*. Islamabad: Printing Corporation of Pakistan Press, 1978.
Senate of Pakistan. *Rules of Procedure and Conduct of Business in the Senate 1973*. Islamabad: Printing Corporation of Pakistan Press, 1973.

Constitutions, Acts, and Notifications

Anand, C.L. *The Government of India Act 1935 with a Critical Introduction*. Lahore: Law Publishers, 1939.
Government of India Act, 1935: Unrepealed Constitutional Legislation. Karachi: Ministry of Law, Government of Pakistan, 1951.
Government of Pakistan. 'Legal Framework Order.' 1970.
———. Notification No. F. 24(1)/73-Pub. 10 June 1973.

_____. *Gazette of Pakistan.* 'Constituent Assembly of Pakistan.' 1951.

_____. *Gazette of Pakistan.* 'Constituent Assembly of Pakistan.' 3 October 1955.

_____. *Gazette of Pakistan.* 'National Assembly of Pakistan.' 1964.

_____. *Gazette of Pakistan.* 'National Assembly of Pakistan.' 31 December 1972.

_____. *Gazette of Pakistan.* 'National Assembly of Pakistan.' 1977.

Handout of 1 July 1974, Press Information Department (PID), Islamabad.

Ministry of Law and Parliamentary Affairs, Government of Pakistan. 'Increase and Redistribution of Seats Act, 1949.' Constitutional Documents. Vol. 3, 1964.

_____. *Unrepealed Constitutional Legislation, Independence Act, 1947.* Karachi: Govt. of Pakistan Press and Publications, 1951.

PLD 1972, Supreme Court, 139.

President's Order 11 of 1972. PLD 1972 Central Statutes.

President's Order No. 11 of 1972, PLD 1972 Central Statues Part, 434.

The Constitution of the Islamic Republic of Pakistan 1973. Islamabad: National Assembly Government of Pakistan Press, 2010.

The Constitution of the Republic of Pakistan 1962. Karachi: Government of Pakistan Press, 1962.

The West Pakistan, Constitutional Manual, Vol. 1. *The Constitution of Pakistan 1956.* Lahore: Government Printing, 1958.

Reports

Basic Principles Committee. *Interim Report.* Karachi: Din Muhammadi Press, 1950.

Government of Pakistan. *Report on General Elections Pakistan 1970–71.* Islamabad: Election Commission, 1972.

Report of the Constitution Committee. *National Assembly Debates*, vol. 2, no. 1. 31 December 1972.

Speeches and Statements

Government of Pakistan, *Prime Minister of Pakistan Zulfikar Ali Bhutto Speeches & Statements*, vol. 1. Islamabad: Directorate General of Films and Publications Ministry of Information & Broadcasting Government of Pakistan, 2010.

Yusufi, Khurshid Ahmad Khan, ed. *Speeches, Statements and Messages of the Quaid-i-Azam.* Vol. 4. Lahore: Bezm-e-Iqbal, 1996.

Autobiographies and Memoirs

Ali, Chaudhri Muhammad. *The Emergence of Pakistan.* Lahore: Research Society of Pakistan, 2009.

_____. *The Task Before Us.* Lahore: Research Society of Pakistan, 1974.

Arif, K.M. *Khaki Shadows.* Karachi: Oxford University Press, 2002.

Aziz, Sartaj. *Between Dreams and Realities.* Karachi: Oxford University Press, 2009.

Bizenjo, Mir Ghaus Bakhsh. *In Search of Solutions: An autobiography.* Karachi: Pakistan Study Centre, University of Karachi, 2009.

Gauhar, Altaf. *Ayub Khan: Pakistan's First Military Ruler*. Lahore: Sang-e-Meel Publications, 1993.

Hasan, Mubashir. *The Mirage of Power*. Karachi: Oxford University Press, 2000.

Kaul, Maheshwar Nath and S.L. Shakdher. *Practice and Procedure: With Particular Reference to the Lok Sabha*. New Delhi: Metropolitan Book Co., 2001.

Khan, Gul Hassan. *Memoirs*. Karachi: Oxford University Press, 1993.

Khan, Muhammad Asghar. *Generals in Politics*. New Delhi: Vikas, 1983.

Khan, Sahibzada Farooq Ali. *Jamhooriyat Sabr Talb*. Lahore: Takhleeqat, 2006.

Khan, Sirdar Shaukat Hyat. *The Nation that Lost its Soul*. Lahore: Jang Publishers, 1995.

Khan, Tamizuddin. *The Test of Time My Life and Days*. Dhaka: University Press Limited, 1989.

Mazari, Sherbaz Khan. *A Journey to Disillusionment*. Karachi: Oxford University Press, 1999.

Niazy, Kausar. *Last Days of Premier Bhutto*. Ebook. http://bhutto.org/Acrobat/Last%20 Dayf%20of%20Premier%20Bhutto.pdf

Rashid, Sheikh Muhammad. *Juhd-e-Musalsal*. Lahore: Jang Publishers, 2002.

Raza, Rafi. *Zulfikar Ali Bhutto and Pakistan 1967–1977*. Karachi: Oxford University Press, 1997.

Shahabuddin, Muhammad. *Recollections and Reflections*. Lahore: P.L.D. Publishers, 1972.

Agreements

The PPP-NAP-JUI, The Tripartite Accord, 6 March 1972, basic document and background material. Islamabad: Directorate General of Films and Publications, Ministry of Information & Broadcasting, 1972.

Interviews

Baloch, Abdul Hayee. Interview by researcher. 18 April 2012. Executive Club, University of the Punjab, Lahore.

Hasan, Mubashir. Interview by the researcher. 10 August 2011. Gulberg, Lahore.

Khar, Ghulam Mustafa. Interview by the researcher. 13 June 2012. Khar House, 478 Meer Street, Lahore.

SECONDARY SOURCES

Biographies, Books, and Chapters

Afzal, M. Rafique. *Political Parties in Pakistan 1947–1958*, vol. 1. Islamabad: NIHCR, 2002.

_____. *Political Parties in Pakistan 1958–1969*, vol. 2. Islamabad: NIHCR, 2000.

_____. *Political Parties in Pakistan 1969–1971*, vol. 3. Islamabad: NIHCR, 1998.

Afzal, Nabeela. *Women and Parliament in Pakistan 1947–1977*. Lahore: Pakistan Study Centre, University of the Punjab, 1997.

Ahmad, Iftikhar. *Pakistan General Elections: 1970*. Lahore: South Asian Institute Punjab University, 1976.

Ahmad, Masud. *Pakistan A Study of its Constitutional History 1857–1975*. Lahore: Research Society of Pakistan, 1978.

Ahmad, Muneer. *Legislatures in Pakistan 1947–1958*. Lahore: Punjab University, 1960.

Ahmad, Mushtaq. *Government and Politics in Pakistan*. Karachi: Royal Book Company, 2009.

Ahmed, Ali. *Role of Higher Civil Servants in Pakistan*. Dacca: National Institute of Public Administration, 1968.

Alavi, Hamza Ali. 'Authoritarianism and Legitimization of State Power in Pakistan.' In *The Post-Colonial State in Asia: Dialectics of Politics and Culture*, ed. Subrata Kumar Mishra, 19–72. New York: Harvester Wheatsheaf, 1990.

————. 'Politics of Ethnicity in India and Pakistan.' In *Sociology of Developing Societies South Asia*, ed. Hamza Alavi and John Harriss, 222–246. Hampshire: Macmillan, 1988.

Ali, Tariq. *Can Pakistan Survive?* New York: Penguin Books, 1983.

————. *Pakistan: Military Rule or People's Power*. London: Jonathan Cape, 1970.

Almond, Gabriel A. and Sidney Verba. *The Civic Culture: Political Attitudes and Democracy in Five Nations*. Princeton: Princeton University Press, 1963.

Ameller, Michel. *Parliaments*. London: Casell & Company, 1966.

Ayub, Muhammad. *An Army, Its Role and Rule: A History of the Pakistan Army from Independence to Kargil, 1967–1999*. Pittsburgh: RoseDog Books, 2005.

Azam, Ikram. *Pakistan's Security and National Integration*. Rawalpindi: The London Book Co, 1974.

Azfar, Kamal. *Pakistan Political and Constitutional Dilemmas*. Karachi: Pakistan Law House, 1987.

Aziz, K.K. *Historical Handbook of Muslim India 1700–1947*, vol. 2. Lahore: Vanguard, 1995.

————. *Party Politics in Pakistan 1947–1958*. Lahore: Sang-e-Meel, 2007.

Aziz, Mazhar. *Military Control in Pakistan*. Oxon: Routledge, 2008.

Baxter, Craig, Yogendra K. Malik, Charles H. Kennedy, Robert C. Oberst. *Government and Politics in South Asia*. Boulder: Westview Press, 1993.

Bhambhari, C. and M. Bhaskaran Nair. 'Bureaucracy in an Authoritarian Political System.' In *Pakistan Political System in Crisis*, eds. S.P. Varma and Virendra Narain. Jaipur: South Asia Studies Centre, University of Rajasthan, 1972.

Binder, Leonard. *Religion and Politics in Pakistan*. Berkeley: University of California, 1963.

Brown, Gilbert T. *Pakistan's Economic Development after 1971*. In *Pakistan: The Long View* eds. Lawrence Ziring, Ralph Braibanti, and W. Howard Wriggins. Durham, N.C.: Duke University Press, 1977.

Burki, Shahid Javed. *Pakistan: The Continuing Search for Nationhood*. San Francisco: Westview Press, 1991.

————. 'Politics of Power and its Economic Imperatives: Pakistan 1947–99.' In *Power and Civil Society in Pakistan*, eds. Anita M. Weiss and S. Zulfiqar Gilani. Karachi: Oxford University Press, 2003.

_____. *Pakistan under Bhutto*. New York: St. Martin's Press, 1980.

_____. *Pakistan: Fifty Years of Nationhood*. Lahore: Vanguard, 1999.

Callard, Keith. *Pakistan: A Political Study*. London: George Allen & Unwin, 1957.

Chaudry, Aminullah. *Political Administrators: The Story of the Civil Service of Pakistan*. Karachi: Oxford University Press, 2011.

Chawla, Muhammad Iqbal. *Wavell and the Dying Days of the Raj*. Karachi: Oxford University Press, 2011.

Choudhury, G.W. *Constitutional Development in Pakistan*. Lahore: The Ideal Book House, 1969.

_____. *The Last Days of United Pakistan*. London: C. Hurst & Company, 1974.

Cohen, Stephen P. *The Future of Pakistan*. Lahore: Vanguard Books, 2012.

Copeland, G.W. and S.C. Patterson. 'Parliaments and Legislatures.' In *World Encyclopedia of Parliaments and Legislatures*, ed. G.T. Kurian, 12–18. Washington D.C.: Congressional Quarterly Inc., 1998.

Emerson, Rupert. *Representative Government in South-East Asia*. Cambridge, MI: Harvard University Press, 1955.

Feldman, Herbert. *A Constitution for Pakistan*. Karachi: Oxford University Press, 1955.

_____. *Omnibus: The End & the Beginning*. Karachi: Oxford University Press, 1974.

_____. *Revolution in Pakistan: A Study of the Martial Law Administration*. Karachi: Oxford University Press, 2001.

Fried, Robert C. *Comparative Political Institutions*. New York: Macmillan, 1966.

Gehrlich, Peter. 'The Institutionalization of European Parliament.' In *Legislatures in Comparative Perspective*, ed. A. Kornberg. New York: David McKay, 1973.

Goodin, Robert E. *The Theory of Institutional Design*. New York: Cambridge University Press, 1996.

Goodnow, Frank. *The Civil Service of Pakistan*. New Haven: Yale University Press, 1964.

Grant, Moyra. *The UK Parliament*. Edinburgh: Edinburgh University Press, 2009.

Haqqani, Hussain. *Pakistan between Mosque and Military*. Lahore: Vanguard Books, 2005.

Hayat, Sikandar. *The Charismatic Leader: Quaid-i-Azam Mohammad Ali Jinnah and the Creation of Pakistan*. Karachi: Oxford University Press, 2008.

Holden, Jr., Matthew. 'Exclusion, Inclusion, and Political Institutions.' In *The Oxford Handbook of Political Institutions*, ed. R.A.W. Rhodes, Sarah A. Binder, and Bert A. Rockman, 163–190. Oxford; New York: Oxford University Press, 2006.

Huntington, Samuel P. *Political Order in Changing Societies*. New Haven; London: Yale University Press, 1968.

Hussain, Syed Shahid. *What was Once East Pakistan*. Karachi: Oxford University Press, 2010.

Jalal, Ayesha. *The State of Martial Rule: The Origins of Pakistan's Political Economy of Defense*. New York: Cambridge University Press, 1990.

Jones, Philip P. *Pakistan Peoples Party*. Karachi: Oxford University Press, 2003.

Kamran, Tahir. *Democracy and Governance in Pakistan*. Lahore: South Asia Partnership, 2008.

Kapur, Ashok. *Pakistan in Crisis*. London: Routledge, 2006.

Kaul, M.N. and S.L. Shakdher. *Practice and Procedure of Parliament*. New Delhi: Metropolitan, 1978.

Kausar, Inam-ul-Haq. *Pakistan Movement and Balochistan*. Quetta: United Printers, 1999.

Kaushik, Surendra Nath. *Pakistan under Bhutto's Leadership*. New Delhi: Uppal Publishing House, 1985.

Kennedy, Charles H. *Bureaucracy in Pakistan*. Karachi: Oxford University Press, 1987.

Khan, Abdul Hafeez. *The Conspiracies against Pakistan and the Women in the Lives of Politicians*. Karachi: Royal Book Company, 1991.

Khan, Asghar. *We've Learnt Nothing from History*. Karachi: Oxford University Press, 2005

Khan, Hamid. *Constitutional and Political History of Pakistan*. Karachi: Oxford University Press, 2009.

Kizilbash, Hamid H. and Khawar Mumtaz. *Pakistan Foreign Policy and the Legislature*. Lahore: South Asian Institute, University of the Punjab, 1976.

Kukreja, Veena. *Civil-Military Relations in South Asia: Pakistan, Bangladesh and India*. New Delhi: Sage Publications, 1991.

Kux, Dennis. *The United States and Pakistan, 1947–2000: Disenchanted Allies*. Karachi: Oxford University Press, 2001.

Mahmood, Safdar. *Pakistan Political Roots and Development 1947–1999*. Karachi: Oxford University Press, 2002.

Malik, Abdullah. *Dastan Khanwada-i-Mian Mahmood Ali Kasuri*. Lahore: Jang Publishers, 1995.

Malik, Iftikhar H. *State and Civil Society in Pakistan: Politics of Authority, Ideology and Ethnicity*. London: Macmillan Press, 1997.

Maluka, Zulfikar Khalid. *The Myth of Constitutionalism in Pakistan*. Karachi: Oxford University Press, 1995.

McGrath, Allen. *Destruction of Pakistan's Democracy*. Karachi: Oxford University Press, 1996.

Menhennet, David and John Palmer. *Parliament in Perspective*. London: The Bodley Head, 1967.

Mezey, M.I. 'Legislatures: Individual Purposes and Institutional Performance.' In *Political Science: The State of Discipline II*, ed. A.W. Finifter. Washington, D.C.: The American Political Science Association, 1993.

Morris-Jones, W.H. *Parliament in India*. London: Longmans, 1957.

Muhammad, Hasan. *General Elections in Pakistan*. Lahore: Mavra Publishers, 2012.

Nawaz, Shuja. *Crossed Swords: Pakistan its Army, and the Wars Within*. Karachi: Oxford University Press, 2008.

Naz, Huma. *Bureaucratic Elites and Political Development in Pakistan (1947–1958)*. Islamabad: National Institute of Pakistan Studies Quaid-i-Azam University, 1990.

Niaz, Ilhan. *The Culture of Power and Governance of Pakistan 1947–2008*. Islamabad: Oxford University Press, 2010.

Noman, Omar. *The Political Economy of Pakistan 1947–1985*. Taylor & Francis, 1988.

Norton, Philip. 'Introduction: The Institutions of Parliaments.' In *Parliaments and Governments in Western Europe*, edited by Philip Norton, 1–15. London; Portland, OR: Frank Cass, 1998.

Parveen, Kausar. *The Politics of Pakistan Role of the Opposition 1947–1958*. Karachi: Oxford University Press, 2013.

Pirzada, Sayyid A.S. *The Politics of the Jamiat Ulema-i-Islam Pakistan 1971–77*. Karachi: Oxford University Press, 2000.

Porte, Robert La. *Power and Privilege: Influence and Decision-Making in Pakistan*. New Delhi: Vikas, 1976.

Qalb-i-Abid, S. *The Muslim Politics in Punjab 1923–1947*. Lahore: Vanguard, 1992.

Rahim, Jallaluddin Abdur. *Outline of a Federal Constitution for Pakistan*. Lahore: Pakistan Peoples Party Political Series, 1969.

Rais, Rasul Bakhsh. *State, Society, and Democratic Change in Pakistan*. Karachi: Oxford University Press, 1996.

Rehman, Taiabur. *Parliamentary Control and Government Accountability in South Asia*. Oxon: Taylor & Francis e-Library, 2007.

Rizvi, Hasan Askari. 'The Military: Role Enhancement and the Political Process.' In *Pakistan Perspectives on State and Society*, ed. Abbas Rashid, 117–140. Lahore: Society for the Advancement of Education, 2004.

———. *The Military & Politics in Pakistan 1947–1997*. Lahore: Sang-e-Meel Publications, 2000.

Saleem, Ahmad. *Tootati Banti Assembelian aur Civil Military Bureaucracy*. Lahore: Jang Publishers, 1990.

Salik, Siddiq. *State and Politics: A Case Study of Pakistan*. Lahore: Al-Faisal Nashran, 1997.

Samad, Yunas. *A Nation in Turmoil Nationalism and Ethnicity in Pakistan, 1937–1958*. New Delhi: Sage Publications, 1995.

Sayeed, Khalid bin. *The Political System of Pakistan*. Kingston: Queen's University, 1966.

Shafqat, Saeed. 'Democracy and Political Transformation in Pakistan.' *Pakistan the Contours of State and Society*, eds. Soofia Mumtaz, Jean-Luc Racine, and Imran Anwar Ali, 209–235. Karachi: Oxford University Press, 2002.

Shafqat, Saeed. *Civil-Military Relations in Pakistan*. Lahore: Westview Press, 1997.

Shah, Nasim Hasan. *Constitution, Law, and Pakistan Affairs*. Lahore: Wajidalis, 1986.

Siddiqa, Ayesha. *Military Inc.: Inside Pakistan's Military Economy*. Karachi: Oxford University Press, 2007.

Sohail, Massarrat. *Partition and Anglo-Pakistan Relations, 1947–51*. Lahore: Vanguard, 1991.

Syed, Anwar. H. *The Discourse and Politics of Zulfiqar Ali Bhutto*. New York: St. Martin's Press, 1992.

Talbot, Ian. *Pakistan: A Modern History*. Lahore: Vanguard Books, 1999.

Taseer, Salmaan. *Bhutto: A Political Biography*. New Delhi: Vikas Publishing House, 1980.

Umar, Badruddin. *The Emergence of Bangladesh: Vol. 2: Rise of Bengali Nationalism (1958–1971)*. Karachi: Oxford University Press, 2006.

Wasaya, Allah. *Parliament mein Qadiani Shikast*. Lahore: Ilm-o-Irfan Publishers, 2000.

Waseem, Mohammad. 'Functioning of Democracy in Pakistan.' In *Democracy in Muslim Societies: The Asian Experience*, ed. Zoya Hasan, 177–218. New Delhi: Sage Publications, 2007.

_____. *Democratization in Pakistan: A Study of the 2002 Election*. Karachi: Oxford University Press, 2006.

_____. *Politics and the State in Pakistan*. Lahore: Progressive Publishers, 1989.

Weber, Max. *On Charisma and Institution Building*, ed. E.S. Eisenstadt. Chicago; London: The University of Chicago Press, 1968.

Wilcox, Wayne Ayres. *Pakistan: The Consolidation of a Nation*. New York: Columbia University Press, 1963.

Williams, L.F. Rushbrook. *Pakistan under Challenge*. London: Stacey International, 1975.

Wolpert, Stanley. *Zulfi Bhutto of Pakistan: His Life and Times*. Karachi: Oxford University, Press, 2008.

Yusuf, Hamid. *The Return of the Politicians*. Lahore: Afrasia Publications, 1980.

_____. *Pakistan: A Study of Political developments 1947–97*. Lahore: Sang-e-Meel Publications, 1999.

Ziring, Lawrence. *Pakistan: The Enigma of Political Development*. Boulders, CO: Westview Press, 1980.

Articles

Afzal, M. Rafique. 'Constitutional Development in Pakistan, 1958–1969.' *Journal of Research Society of Pakistan* 19 (1982): 61–81.

Alavi, Hamza. 'Army and Bureaucracy in Pakistan.' *International Socialist Journal* 14 (March–April 1966): 140–181.

Al-Mujahid, Sharif. 'The Assembly Elections in Pakistan.' *Asian Survey* 5 (November 1965): 538–551.

Baxter, Craig. 'Constitution Making: The Development of Federalism in Pakistan.' *Asian Survey* 14, no. 12 (1974): 1074–085, doi: 10.2307/2643201.

_____. 'Pakistan Votes—1970.' *Asian Survey* 11, no. 3 (1971): 197–218, doi: 10.2307/3024655.

Bhutto, Zulfikar Ali. 'Bilateralism: New Directions.' *Pakistan Horizon* 29 (Fourth Quarter 1976): 3–59.

Chaffey, Douglas C. 'The Institutionalization of State Legislatures: A Comparative Study.' *The Western Political Quarterly* 23 (March 1970): 180–196.

Choudhury, G.W. 'New Pakistan's Constitution, 1973.' *Middle East Journal* 28 (Winter 1974): 10–18.

Feldman, Herbert. 'A Survey of Asia in 1973: Part II.' *Asian Survey* 14 (February 1974): 136–142.

Hibbing, J.R. 'Legislative Institutionalization with Illustrations from British House of Commons.' *American Journal of Political Science* 32 (August 1988): 681–712.

Lodhi, Maleeha. 'Pakistan in Crisis.' *The Journal of Commonwealth and Comparative Politics* 16 (March 1978): 60–78.

Long, Roger D. *Pacific Affairs* 64, no. 3 (1991): 427–28, doi: 10.2307/2759499.

Mahoney, James. 'Path Dependence in Historical Sociology.' *Theory and Society* 29 (2000): 507–548.

McGuire, Kevin T. 'The Institutionalization of the U.S. Supreme Court.' *Political Analysis* 12 (Spring 2004): 128–142.

Opello Jr., W.C. 'Portugal's Parliament: An Organizational Analysis of Legislative Performance.' *Legislative Studies Quarterly* 11 (Aug 1986): 291–320.

Polsby, Nelson W. 'The Institutionalization of U.S. House of Representatives.' *The American Political Science Review* 62, no. 1 (March 1968): 144–168.

Qureshi, Saleem M.M., 'Party Politics in the Second Republic of Pakistan.' *Middle East Journal* 20, no. 4 (Autumn, 1966): 456–472.

Rashiduzzaman, M. 'National Assembly of Pakistan under the 1962 Constitution,' *Pacific Affairs* 42, no. 4 (1969): 481–93, doi: 10.2307/2754129.

Sayeed, Khalid B. 'The Political Role of Pakistan's Civil Service.' *Pacific Affairs* 31, no. 2 (1958): 131–46, doi: 10.2307/3035208.

Squire, Peverill. 'The Theory of Legislative Institutionalization and the California Assembly,' *The Journal of Politics* 54, no. 2 (1992): 1026–1054, http://www.jstor.org/stable/2132107.

Tepper, Elliot L. 'The New Pakistan: Problems and Prospects,' *Pacific Affairs*, 47 (Spring 1974): 56–68.

Ziring, Lawrence. 'Pakistan: A Political Perspective.' *Asian Survey* 15, no. 7 (1975): 629–44. doi: 10.2307/2643345.

Dissertations

Kokab, Rizwan Ullah. 'Pakistani Leadership and Separatist Movement in East Pakistan.' PhD diss. University of the Punjab, 2012.

Malik, Rahat Zubair. 'Working of the National Assembly of Pakistan, 1971–1977.' MPhil diss. Quaid-i-Azam University, 2004.

Samad, Yunas. 'South Asian Muslim politics, 1937–1958.' PhD diss. University of Oxford, 1991.

Newspapers

Dawn (Karachi)

Jang (Lahore)

Nawa-i-Waqt (Lahore)

The Pakistan Times (Lahore)

Washington Post (Washington)

Websites

http://www.na.gov.pk/history.html

http://www.seamonitors.org/id37.html

http://www.senate.gov.pk/

Annexures

Annex I
Party Position in Legislatures

First Constituent Assembly (1947–1954)

Muslim League	62
Pakistan National Congress	10
Azad Pakistan Party	3
Independent	1

Second Constituent Assembly (1955–1956)

Muslim League	36
United Front	25
Awami League	13
Independent	5

National Assembly (1956–1958)

Republican Party	27
Awami League	15
United Front	12
Muslim League	11
Pakistan National Congress	4
Scheduled Caste Federation	3
United Progressive Party	2
Independent	5

Source: Muneer Ahmad, *Legislatures in Pakistan, 1947–1958* (Lahore: Department of Political Science, University of the Punjab, 1960), pp. 130–2; K.K. Aziz, *Party Politics in Pakistan 1947–1958* (Lahore: Sang-e-Meel Publications, 2007), p. 275; Safdar Mahmood, *Muslim League ka Daur-i-Hakoomat* (Lahore: Jang Publishers, 2002), p. 290.

Annex II
List of Candidates returned to the National Assembly of Pakistan from National Constituencies, 1970

NOTIFICATION
Islamabad, 29 December 1970

No. F.13(1) 77-Elsx (I).—In pursuance of the provisions of sub-section (4) of section 39 of the National and Provincial Assemblies (Elections) Ordinance, 1970 read with the states and Frontier Regions Division Notification No. S.R.O. 188(I)/70, dated 10 August 1970, as amended from time to time, the Election Commission, Pakistan is pleased to publish the names of the candidates returned to the National Assembly of Pakistan from the under mentioned national constituencies:

Sr. No.	Number of Constituency	Name of Constituency	Name	Father's Name
1	NW-2	Peshawar-II	Ghulam Farooq	Mir Aslam Khan
2	NW-3	Peshawar-III	Abdul Wali Khan	Khan Abdul Ghaffar Khan
3	NW-4	Peshawar-IV	Maulana Abdul Haq	Maulana Maaruf Gul
4	NW-5	Hazara-I	Maulvi Abdul Hakeem	Wali Mohammad
5	NW-6	Hazara-II	Maulana Ghulam Ghaus	Maulana Said Gul
6	NW-7	Hazara-III	Sardar Inayatur Rehman	Sardar Allah Dad Khan
7	NW-8	Hazara-IV	Abdul Qayyum Khan	K.S. Abdul Hakim Khan
8	NW-9	Mardan-I	Abdul Khaliq Khan	Deputy Rahim Dad Khan
9	NW-10	Mardan-II	Amirzada Khan	Khoidad Khan

Sr. No.	Number of Constituency	Name of Constituency	Name	Father's Name
10	NW-11	Mardan-cum-Hazara	Khan Abdul Qayyum Khan	K.S. Abdul Hakim Khan
11	NW-12	Kohat	Maulvi Niamatullah	Azizullah
12	NW-13	D.I. Khan	Maulvi Mufti Mahmud	Khalifa Mohammad Sadeeq
13	NW-14	Bannu	Sadarushahid	Maulvi Abdur Rahim
14	NW-17	Swat-II	Miangul Aurangzeb	Miangul Jahanzeb
15	NW-18	Dir	Safiullah Sahib	Almaruf Babaji Sahib
16	NW-19	Tribal Area-I	Akbar Khan	Haji Ali Khan
17	NW-20	Tribal Area-II	Haji Saleh Khan	Nawab Khan
18	NW-21	Tribal Area-III	Niamatullah	Malik Murad Khan
19	NW-22	Tribal Area-IV	Malik Jahangir Khan	Malik Arsalla Khan
20	NW-23	Tribal Area-V	Abdul Malik	Haji Pir Rahman
21	NW-24	Tribal Area-VI	Major General Jamal Dar	Gulab Shah
22	NW-25	Tribal Area-VII	Abdul Subhan Khan	Mohammad Jan Khan
23	NW-26	Rawalpindi-I	Khurshid Hassan Meer	Mir Khurshid Ahmad
24	NW-27	Rawalpindi-II	Malik Mohammad Jaffar	Niaz Ali
25	NW-28	Rawalpindi-III	Col. Habib Ahmad	Allah Dad Khan
26	NW-29	Rawalpindi-IV	Abdul Aziz Bhatti Advocate	Allah Ditta
27	NW-30	Campbellpur-I	Sardar Shaukat Hayat Khan	Sardar Sikandar Hayat Khan
28	NW-31	Campbellpur-II	Syed Safi-ud-Din	Syed Mohy-ud-Din Lal Badshah
29	NW-32	Jhelum-I	Ghulam Hussain	Akbar Khan
30	NW-33	Jhelum-II	Mohammad Amir Khan	Ch. Shah Niwaz Khan
31	NW-34	Jhelum-III	Mohammad Sadiq	Malik Khan
32	NW-35	Gujrat-I	Ch. Zahoor Elahi	Ch. Sardar Khan

Sr. No.	Number of Consti- tuency	Name of Constituency	Name	Father's Name
33	NW-36	Gujrat-II	Ch. Fazal Elahi	Ghulam Mohammad
34	NW-37	Gujrat-III	Ch. Manzoor Hussain Dodhra	Ch. Shah Mohammad
35	NW-38	Gujrat-IV	Ghulam Rasul	Khuda Dad
36	NW-39	Sargodha-I	Ch. Jehangir Ali	Ch. Ilam Din
37	NW-40	Sargodha-II	Anwar Ali Malik	Sultan Ali Malik
38	NW-41	Sargodha-III	Hafeezullah	Mohammad Abdullah
39	NW-42	Sargodha-IV	Karam Bakhsh Awan	Maula Bakhsh
40	NW-43	Sargodha-V	Mian Mohammad Zakir	Late Nawab Mohammad Hayat
41	NW-44	Mianwali-I	Nawabzada Malik Muzaffar Khan	K.B. Malik Amir Mohammad Khan
42	NW-45	Mianwali-II	Ghulam Hassan Khan	Ali Mohammad Khan
43	NW-46	Jhang-I	Mehr Ghulam Haider Bharwana	Mehr Shamsul Haque Bharwana
44	NW-47	Jhang-II	Maulana Mohammad Zakir	Mohammad Abdul Ghafoor
45	NW-48	Jhang-III	Nazeer Sultan	Sultan Noor-ul-Hasan
46	NW-49	Lyallpur-I	Mohammad Mukhtar Rana	Hamid Khan Rana
47	NW-50	Lyallpur-II	Mian Mohammad Attaullah	Mian Mohammad Abdullah
48	NW-51	Lyallpur-III	Ahsan-ul-Haq	Noor Mohammad
49	NW-52	Lyallpur-IV	Mohammad Bashir Ahmad	Abdul Rahim
50	NW-53	Lyallpur-V	Ch. Mohammad Aslam	Hafiz Ghulam-ur-Rehman
51	NW-54	Lyallpur-VI	Rai Hafeezullah Khan	Rai Saadullah Khan
52	NW-55	Lyallpur-VII	Ch. Mohammad Anwar Ali Khan	Ch. Asghar Ali Khan

Sr. No.	Number of Consti-tuency	Name of Constituency	Name	Father's Name
53	NW-56	Lyallpur-VIII	Ghulam Nabi	Haji Khuda Bakhsh
54	NW-57	Lyallpur-IX	Mohammad Khan	Abdul Rahim
55	NW-58	Lahore-I	Mohammad Akhtar	Khuda Bakhsh
56	NW-59	Lahore-II	Mubashar Hasan	Munawar Hassan
57	NW-60	Lahore-III	Zulfiqar Ali Bhutto	Late Sir Shah Nawaz Bhutto
58	NW-61	Lahore-IV	Sh. Mohammad Rashid	Mehr Din
59	NW-62	Lahore-V	Malik Meraj Khalid	Malik Mahi
60	NW-63	Lahore-VI	Ahmed Raza Khan	Sardar Mohammad Ahmad Khan
61	NW-64	Lahore-VII	Shafaat Khan	Dhundal
62	NW-65	Lahore-VIII	Mahmood Abbas Bukhari	Syed Nazir Hussain Bukhari
63	NW-66	Sheikhupura-I	Mumtaz Ahmad	Ch. Ghulam Qadir
64	NW-67	Sheikhupura-II	Mian Hamid Yasin	Mian Zafar Yasin
65	NW-68	Sheikhupura-III	Ch. Mohammad Iqbal	Khan Bahadar
66	NW-69	Sheikhupura-IV	Rai Shahadat Khan	Rai Bakhtawar Khan
67	NW-70	Gujranwala-I	Manzoor Hassan	Ghulam Hassan
68	NW-71	Gujranwala-II	Zulfiqar Ali Bajwa	Mohammad Sharif Bajwa
69	NW-72	Gujranwala-III	Ghulam Haider Cheema Major	Hayat Mohammad
70	NW-73	Gujranwala-IV	Shahadat Khan	Mohammad Nawaz
71	NW-74	Sialkot-I	Mian Masood Ahmad	Mian Mohammad Hussain
72	NW-75	Sialkot-II	Kausar Niazi	Fateh Mohammad Khan Niazi
73	NW-76	Sialkot-III	Nasrullah Khan	Attaullah Khan
74	NW-77	Sialkot-IV	Mohammad Suleman	Khuda Bakhsh
75	NW-78	Sialkot-V	Sultan Ahmad	Khan Bahadur

Sr. No.	Number of Constituency	Name of Constituency	Name	Father's Name
76	NW-79	Multan-I	Zulfiqar Bhutto	Sir Shah Nawaz Khan Bhutto
77	NW-80	Multan-II	Sadiq Hussain	Major Nawab Ashiq Hussain
78	NW-81	Multan-III	Abbas Hussain Shah	Altaf Hussain Shah
79	NW-82	Multan-IV	Zafarullah Khan Chaudhary	Ch. Allah Dad Khan
80	NW-83	Multan-V	Ch. Barkatullah	Ch. Nawazish Ali
81	NW-84	Multan-VI	Mian Mumtaz Mohammad Khan	Ahmad Yar Khan
82	NW-85	Multan-VII	Khan Irshad Ahmad Khan	Jang Baz Khan
83	NW-86	Multan-VIII	Syed Nasir Ali Shah	Syed Ali Shah
84	NW-87	Multan-IX	Taj Ahmad	Sultan Ahmad
85	NW-88	D.G. Khan-I	Dr Nazir Ahmad	Haji Allah Bakhsh Khan
86	NW-89	D.G. Khan-II	Sardar Sher Baz Khan	Mir Murad Bakhsh Khan
87	NW-90	Muzaffargarh-I	Manzoor Hussian	Qadir Bakhsh
88	NW-91	Muzaffargarh-II	Ghulam Mohammad Mustafa	Malik Mohammad Yar
89	NW-92	Muzaffargarh-III	Mian Mohammad Ibrahim	Mohammad Ghaus Bakhsh
90	NW-93	Sahiwal-I	Abdul Aleem Sardar	Hafiz Mohammad Shafi
91	NW-94	Sahiwal-II	Mohammad Hanif	Nawab Khan
92	NW-95	Sahiwal-III	Haji Mohammad Sadiq	Saleh
93	NW-96	Sahiwal-IV	Khurshid Ali Khan Rao	Rao Niaz Mohammad Khan
94	NW-97	Sahiwal-V	Mian Mohammad Hasan Khan	Mian Ilyas Mohammad
95	NW-98	Sahiwal-VI	M. Hashim Khan	Mohammad Ali Khan

Sr. No.	Number of Constituency	Name of Constituency	Name	Father's Name
96	NW-99	Sahiwal-VII	Nur Mohammad	Hafiz Abdul Wahid
97	NW-100	Bahawalpur-I	Mian Nizamuddin	Ghulam Hussain
98	NW-101	Bahawalpur-II	Saeed-ur-Rashid Abbasi	Sir Sadiq Mohammad Khan
99	NW-102	Bahawalnagar-cum-Bahawalpur	Mohammad Shafi	Shah Mohammad
100	NW-103	Bahawalnagar-I	Syed Rafiq Mohammad Shah	Syed Fateh Mohammad Shah
101	NW-104	Bahawalnagar-II	M. Mohammad Rafiq	Ch. Ali Mohammad
102	NW-105	Rahim Yar Khan-I	Jamal Mohammad	Ghulam Rasool
103	NW-106	Rahim Yar Khan-II	Abdul Nabi	Abdul Khaliq Khan
104	NW-107	Rahim Yar Khan-III	Noor Mohammad	Akhtar Hussain
105	NW-108	Jacobabad	Mir Darya Khan	Mir Hassan Khan
106	NW-109	Sukkur-I	Haji Moula Bakhsh	Mohammad Umar
107	NW-110	Sukkur-II	Ali Hassan	Mohammad Ibrahim
108	NW-111	Sukkur-III	Noor Mohammad Khan	Sardar Dadan Khan Lund
109	NW-112	Nawabshah-I	Hakim Ali	Mohammad Hussain Zardari
110	NW-113	Nawabshah-II	Ghulam Mustafa Jatoi	Haji Ghulam Rasool Khan Jatoi
111	NW-114	Khairpur-I	Syed Qaim Ali Shah	Ramzan Ali Shah
112	NW-115	Khairpur-II	Pir Syed Abdul Kadir Shah	Pir Syed Ahmad Shah
113	NW-116	Larkana-I	Zulfiqar Ali Bhutto	Late Sir Shah Nawaz Bhutto
114	NW-117	Larkana-II	Mumtaz Ali Khan	Nawab Nabi Bux Khan
115	NW-118	Hyderabad-I	Syed Mohammad Ali	Syed Mubarak Ali

Sr. No.	Number of Consti- tuency	Name of Constituency	Name	Father's Name
116	NW-119	Hyderabad-II	Mir Aijaz Ali Khan Talpur	Mir Ghulam Ali Talpur
117	NW-120	Hyderabad-III	Makhdoom Mohammad Zaman	Makhdoom Ghulam Mohammad
118	NW-121	Hyderabad-IV	Zulfiqar Ali Bhutto	Late Sir Shah Nawaz Bhutto
119	NW-122	Tharparkar-I	Mir Ali Bux Khan	Nawab Mir Allah Dad Khan
120	NW-123	Tharparkar-II	Pir Ghulam Rasool Shah	Pir Jahan Shah
121	NW-124	Dadu-I	Khan Sahib Abdul Hamid	Qadir Bux
122	NW-125	Dadu-II	Malik Sikander Khan	Malik Sardar Khan
123	NW-126	Sanghar	Rais Atta Mohammad Khan	Haji Ali Mohammad Khan
124	NW-127	Thatta	Zulfiqar Ali Bhutto	Sir Shah Nawaz Khan Bhutto
125	NW-128	Karachi-I	Abdul Mustafa	Amjad Ali
126	NW-129	Karachi-II	Abdul Pirzada	Abdul Sattar Pirzada
127	NW-130	Karachi-III	Abdul Sattar Gabol	Sardar Allah Bux Gabol
128	NW-132	Karachi-V	Ghafoor Ahmad	Shaikh Khuda Bakhsh
129	NW-133	Karachi-VI	Mohammad Zafar Ahmed Ansari	Fazulr Rehman
130	NW-134	Karachi-VII	Shah Ahmad Noorani	Maulana Shah Mohammad Abdul Alim
131	NW-135	Quetta-I	Maulvi Abdul Haq	Mullah Ahmad
132	NW-136	Quetta-II	Sardar Khair Bakhsh Khan Marri	Nawab Mehrullah Khan Marri
133	NW-137	Kalat-I	Abdul Hayee	Pir Bakhsh
134	NW-138	Kalat-II	Mir Ghaus Bux Khan Bizenjo	Haji Mir Safar Khan Bizenjo

Sr. No.	Number of Constituency	Name of Constituency	Name	Father's Name
135	NW-139	Women's Constituency-I	Shireen Wahab	W/o Qazi Abdul Wahab
136	NW-140	Women's Constituency-II	Mrs Nargis Naeem	W/o Mohammad Naeem
137	NW-141	Women's Constituency-III	Nasim Jahan Begum	D/o Mohammad Shah Nawaz
138	NW-142	Women's Constituency-IV	Zahida Sultan	D/o Abdul Salam
139	NW-143	Women's Constituency-V	Dr Mrs Ashraf Khatoon	W/o Haji Khan Mohammad
140	NW-144	Women's Constituency-VI	Mrs Jenniffer Jehanzeba Qazi	Late Qazi Musa

Source: Election Commission of Pakistan, https://www.ecp.gov.pk/Documents/GE%20 07-12-1970.pdf

Annex III
Facsimile: Memorandum of Settlement
PPP, ANP, JUI

MEMORANDUM OF SETTLEMENT ARRIVED AT BETWEEN
PAKISTAN PEOPLE'S PARTY, NATIONAL AWAMI PARTY
AND JAMIAT-UL-UIMA-E-ISLAM ON MARCH 6, 1972.

The following participated in the discussions which began
on March 4 and concluded on March 6, 1972:

P.P.P.

President of Pakistan	Chairman PPP
Mr. Hayat Mohd Khan Sherpao	
Mr. Ghulam Mustafa Jatoi	
Mr. Abdul Hafeez Peerzada	
Maulana Kausar Niazi	
Mr. Rafi Raza	

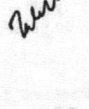

N.A.P.

Khan Abdul Wali Khan	President NAP
Mir Ghous Bakhsh Bizenjo	
Mr. Arbab Sikander	
Mr. Khair Bakhsh Mari	

J.U.I.

Maulana Mufti Mahmood	General Secretary JUI
Maulana Ghulam Ghous Hazarvi	

1. (a) The Pakistan Peoples Party (PPP) proposed that a short
session of the National Assembly should be convened on April 21,
1972, for a period not exceeding three days.

(b) The NAP/JUI proposed that the National Assembly session be
convened on March 23, 1972.

(c) It was settled that the summons to the members should be
issued on March 23, 1972, and the National Assembly Session should
be convened on April 14, 1972, for a period not exceeding three

... 2

273

- 2 -

days during which time the matters specified at paras 2, 3 and 4 below will be voted upon.

2. (a) The PPP proposed that the National Assembly should meet for the purpose of endorsing an interim Constitution on the basis of the Government of India Act, 1935, read with the Independence Act, 1947 with consequential amendments, or on the basis of the 1962 Constitution with consequential amendments.

(b) The NAP/JUI proposed that the interim Constitution should be passed on the basis of the Government of India Act, 1935, read with the Independence Act, with consequential amendments.

(c) It was settled that an interim Constitution would be prepared on the basis of the 1935 Act read with Independence Act 1947 with consequential amendments and that there should be a debate not exceeding 3 days at which only party leaders or their nominees would speak. The parties for this purpose would be : Pakistan People's Party, Pakistan Muslim League (Qayum Group), Jamiat-UL-Ulma-e-Islam, National Awami Party, Jamiat-ul-Ulma-e-Pakistan, Pakistan Muslim League (Council), Jamaat-e-Islami, Pakistan Muslim League (Convention), one representative from the independent MNAs of Tribal areas, and one representative of the remaining independent MNAs.

3. (a) The PPP secondly proposed that the National Assembly on being convened on the 21 April, 1972, pass a vote of confidence in the Government and approve and confirm the continuation of Martial Law till August 14, 1972.

(b) The NAP/JUI proposed that Martial Law should be continued till June 7, 1972.

(c) It was settled that there would be a vote of confidence in the Government and approval of continuation of Martial Law till August 14, 1972.

... 3

- 3 -

4. (a) The PPP thirdly proposed that the National Assembly on being convened for the short session should appoint a Committee of the House to draft a Constitution to be presented on August 1, 1972.

(b) The NAP/JUI proposed that the draft Constitution should be presented by July 1, 1972, and that the National Assembly should be re-convened on July 7, 1972.

(c) It was settled that the report of the Committee on the Constitution should be submitted by August 1, 1972, and that the National Assembly be reconvened on August 14, 1972.

5. (a) The PPP proposed that when the National Assembly was reconvened on August 14, 1972, it should act only as a constitution-making body to ensure the early framing of the Constitution.

(b) The NAP/JUI proposed that when the National Assembly meets on August 14, 1972, it should also act as a legislative body after August 14, 1972.

(c) It was settled that after August 14, 1972, the National Assembly should act both as a constitution-making body and as a legislative body till the permanent Constitution comes into force. It was reiterated that the powers of the President in pursuance of the Declaration of Emergency will continue till the Emergency is lifted.

6. (a) The PPP proposed that the Provincial Assemblies should be convened after the passing of the interim Constitution i.e. on May 1, 1972.

(b) The NAP/JUI proposed that the Provincial Assemblies should be convened on April 10, 1972.

(c) It was settled that the Provincial Assemblies would be convened on April 21, 1972.

... 4

- 4 -

7.   It was accepted that the Government both at the Centre and
in the Provinces would be formed on the basis of parliamentary
majority.

8.   It was accepted that till the new Constitution comes into
force, a person elected as a Member of more than one Assembly would
be permitted to retain his both seats in both the Houses till the
Constitution is finally passed. Similarly, the President, the
Vice-President, Governors, Ministers and Advisers both at the Centre
and the Provinces will retain their seats in their respective
Assemblies.

9. (a) The PPP proposed that the present Governors should continue
till the new Constitution is passed, but after the interim
Constitution is passed they would cease to be Martial Law
Administrators.

(b) The NAP/JUI proposed that after the Provincial Assemblies
are convened, the Governors may be appointed in consultation with
the Chief Minister. Meantime from today till the convening of the
Provincial Assemblies the Governments in NWFP and Baluchistan should
be given to the NAP/JUI.

(c) It was settled that until the permanent Constitution is framed
by the National Assembly, the Central Government should continue to
have the right, as in the past, to appoint Governors in the Provinces
but by way of compromise the Central Government would, during the
interim period, also appoint the Governors in consultation with the
majority in the two aforesaid Provinces.

10.   It was accepted that in the North West Frontier Province and
the Province of Baluchistan, the majority parties are NAP and JUI and
they will be entitled to form the Governments in these two
Provinces.

... 5

- 5 -

11. The PPP proposed that the date for Local Bodies Elections should be fixed as early as possible after the Provincial Assemblie are convened and that the Elections in all the Provinces should be on the same date. This was agreed to and the Elections would be he on an agreed date soon after the convening of the Provincial Assemblies.

12. The President said that he would announce today that Martial Law would be lifted on August 14, 1972.

SIGNED by MR. ZULFIKAR ALI BHUTTO,   )
President of Pakistan and Chairman   )
of the Pakistan People's Party   )

SIGNED by KHAN ABDUL WALI KHAN,   )
President of the National Awami   )
Party.   )

SIGNED by MAULANA MUFTI MAHMOOD,   )
General Secretary of the   )
Jamiat-ul-Ulma-e-Islam.   )

Rawalpindi,
March 6, 1972

Source: The PPP-NAP-JUI, The Tripartite Accord, 6 March 1972. Basic Document and background material. Islamabad Directorate General of Films and Publications, Ministry of Information & Broadcasting, 1972.

Annex IV
Facsimile: Signatures of the Constitution Committee, December 1972

Source: Gazette of Pakistan. Extra, 31 December 1972 (Part-III).

Annex V
List of Bills Passed in the Senate of Pakistan, 1973–1977

Session	Duration	Bills passed
	1973	
1	6 August	Only elections were held
2	4–15 September	9
3	1–22 December	4
	1974	
4	16 January–16 February	15
5	28 March–25 April	21
6	25 July–5 September	12
7	7 September	1
8	18 November–21 December	9
	1975	
9	16 January–16 April	34
10	30 June–12 July	10
11	6–23 August	7
12	12 November–24 December	19
	1976	
13	27 February–21 May	36
14	17 June–8 July	5
15	2 August–8 September	11
	1976/77	
16	10 November 1976–8 January 1977	30
17	26 April–17 May 1977	20
Total number of sessions: 17		
Total bills passed: 243 [28 bills introduced in the senate]		

Source: Government of Pakistan, *The First Senate of Pakistan* (Islamabad: Senate Secretariat, 1980).

	QUESTIONS						
Session	Duration	Received	Number of Questions Asked by		Replied	Disallowed	Lapsed
			Opposition	Treasury			
	1973						
1	6 August	-	-	-	-	-	-
2	4–15 September	11	9	2	15	-	6
3	1–22 December	56	44	12	31	7	18
	1974						
4	16 January–16 February	61	53	8	58	3	-
5	28 March–25 April	52	46	6	41	2	9
6	25 July–5 September	174	145	29	117	18	39
7	7 September	-	-	-	-	-	-
8	18 November–21 December	136	129	7	98	14	24
	1975						
9	16 January–16 April	103	103	-	84	11	8
10	30 June–12 July	22	14	8	14	-	8
11	6–23 August	6	3	3	6	-	-
12	12 November–24 December	155	76	78	115	12	28
	1976						
13	27 February–21 May	181	105	76	125	35	21
14	17 June–8 July	48	23	25	21	4	23
15	2 August–8 September	50	26	24	37	6	7
	1976/77						
16	10 November 1976–8 January 1977	79	60	19	68	7	4
17	26 April–17 May 1977	2	-	2	-	2	-
18	Session could not be held	35	-	35	-	-	35
	Total	**1171**	**836**	**334**	**820**	**121**	**230**

Session	Duration	Received	Ruled Out	Referred to the Committee	Withdrawn	Not Pressed	Lapsed	Fell Through
PRIVILEGE MOTIONS								
	1973							
1	6 August	-	-	-	-	-	-	-
2	4–15 September	-	-	-	-	-	-	-
3	1–22 December	9	3	1	1	4	-	-
	1974							
4	16 January–16 February	-	-	-	-	-	-	-
5	28 March–25 April	1	1	-	-	-	-	-
6	25 July–5 September	6	4	1	-	1	-	-
7	7 September	-	-	-	-	-	-	-
8	18 November–21 December	6	4	1	-	1	-	-
	1975							
9	16 January–16 April	5	2	2	-	-	-	1
10	30 June–12 July	-	-	-	-	-	-	-
11	6–23 August	-	-	-	-	-	-	-
12	12 November–24 December	8	2	-	2	-	-	4
	1976							
13	27 February–21 May	8	4	1	1	1	-	1
14	17 June–8 July	-	-	-	-	-	-	-
15	2 August–8 September	-	-	-	-	-	-	-
	1976/77							
16	10 November 1976–8 January 1977	-	-	-	-	-	-	-
17	26 April–17 May 1977	-	-	-	-	-	-	-
	Total	43	20	6	4	7	-	6

Source: Government of Pakistan, *First Senate of Pakistan* (Islamabad: Senate Secretariat, 1980).

LEGISLATIVE BUSINESS IN THE SENATE

Session	Date	Total Days of Session	Net Sittings	Average Daily Attendance	BILLS					
					Received from NA	Introduced in Senate	Referred to the Standing Committee	Amendments suggested by Standing Committee	Passed with amendments	Passed (Total)
1973										
1	6 August	1	1	45	-	-	-	-	-	-
2	4–15 September	12	5	20	9	-	1	-	-	9
3	1–22 December	22	13	27	6	-	4	1	-	4
1974										
4	16 January–16 February	32	19	22	14	4	7	-	1	15
5	28 March–25 April	29	20	24	15	3	6	1	4	21
6	25 July–5 September	43	20	25	10	2	11	1	3	12
7	7 September	1	1	32	1	-	-	-	-	1
8	18 November–21 December	34	30	25	8	8	11	-	2	9

1975									
9	16 January–16 April	46	26	20	25	2	7	1	2	34
10	30 June–12 July	13	11	25	14	1	12	1	-	10
11	6 August–23 August	18	10	25	1	1	2	1	2	7
12	12 November–24 December	43	25	20	18	3	6	1	1	19
1976									
13	27 February–21 May	84	49	28	33	2	23	-	3	36
14	17 June–8 July	22	13	19	5	1	2	1	1	5
15	2 August–8 September	38	21	17	8	1	2	-	1	11
1976/77									
16	10 November 1976–8 January 1977	47	31	18	30	-	21	-	-	30
17	26 April–17 May 1977	22	10	41	20	-	-	-	-	20
	Total	**507**	**305**	**25**	**217**	**28**	**115**	**8**	**20**	**243**

Source: Government of Pakistan, *First Senate of Pakistan* (Islamabad: Senate Secretariat, 1980).

Annex VI
List of Acts Passed by the National Assembly, 1972–1977

Acts 1972

1. Agricultural Produce (grading and marking) (Amendment) Act
2. Banking Companies (Amendment) Act
3. Board of Industrial Management *see* Development of Industries (Federal Control) Act
4. Civil Commotion Compensation Fund (Repeal) Act
5. Code of Civil Procedure (Amendment) Act
6. Companies (Appointment of Trustees) Act
7. Criminal Law (Amendment) (Special Court) Orders (Amendment) Act
8. Development of Industries (Federal Control) Act
9. Diplomatic and Consular Privileges Act
10. Discontinuance of Medical Reimbursement Act
11. Displaced Persons *see* Evacuee Property and Displaced Persons Laws (Amendment) Act
12. Drugs (Generic Names) Act
13. Evacuee Property and Displaced Person Laws (Amendment) Act
14. Extradition Act
15. Foreign Exchange (Prevention of Payment) Act
16. Generic Names *see* Drugs (Generic Names) Act
17. *Katchi Abadi see* Transfer of Evacuee Land (*Katchi Abadi*) Act
18. Labour Laws (Amendment) Act
19. Law Reforms (Amendment) Act
20. National & Provincial Assemblies (Qualification for the Membership) Act
21. National Book Foundation Act
22. National Press Trust (Appointment of Chairman) Act
23. National Sports Trust Act
24. Naval Academy *see* Pakistan Naval Academy (Award of Degrees)(Amendment) Act
25. Pakistan Citizenship (Amendment) Act
26. Pakistan Mujahid Force (Amendment) Act
27. Pakistan Naval Academy (Award of Degrees) (Amendment) Act
28. Pakistan Red Cross Society (Amendment) Act
29. Patents and Designs (Amendment) Act
30. Peoples Finance Corporation Act

31. Settlement Commissioners (Validation of Orders) Act
32. Small Industries Corporation *see* West Pakistan Small Industries Corporation (Dissolution) Act
33. State Bank of Pakistan (Amendment) Act
34. Transfer of Evacuee Land (*Katchi Abadi*) Act
35. War Risks Insurance (Amendment) Act
36. West Pakistan Small Industries Corporation (Dissolution) Act

Acts 1973

1. Agricultural Development Bank (Amendment) Act
2. Assistant Settlement Commissioner (Validation of Orders) Act
3. Chemical Fertilizers (Development Surcharge) Act
4. Civil Servants Act
5. Code of Criminal Procedure (Amendment) Act
6. Companies (Amendment) Act
7. Companies (Managing Agency and Election of Directors (Amendment) Act
8. Companies Profits (Workers Participation) (Amendment) Act
9. Copyright (Amendment) Act
10. Cotton (Amendment) Act
11. Criminal Law (Amendment) Act
12. Development of Industries (Federal Control) (Amendment) Act
13. Displaced Persons (Compensation and Rehabilitation) (Amendment) Act
14. Drugs (Generic Names) (Amendment) Act
15. Economic Reforms Order (Amendment) Act
16. Economic Reforms Order (Amendment) Act
17. Electoral Rolls (Amendment) Act
18. Equity Participation Fund (Amendment) Act
19. Evacuee Property and Displaced Persons Laws (Amendment) Act
20. Factories (Amendment) Act
21. Federal Public Service Commission Act
22. Federal Security Force Act
23. Finance Act
24. Foreign Exchange Regulation (Amendment) Act
25. Funds Vesting in the President (Transfer) Act
26. High Treason (Punishment) Act
27. Holy Quran *see* Publication of the Holy Quran (Elimination of Printing Errors) Act
28. House Building Finance Corporation (Amendment) Act
29. Hydrogenated Vegetable Oil Industry (Control and Development) Act
30. Industrial Development Bank of Pakistan (Amendment) Act
31. Industrial Relations (Amendment) Act
32. Islamabad University *see* University of Islamabad Act
33. Land Reforms (Amendment) Act

34. Law Reforms (Amendment) Act
35. Legal Practitioners and Bar Councils Act
36. Legal Practitioners and Bar Councils (Amendment) Act
37. Legal Practitioners and Bar Councils (Amendment) Act
38. Life Insurance (Nationalization) (Amendment) Act
39. Loans for Agricultural Purposes Act
40. Medical Council (Amendment) Act
41. Mines (Amendment) Act
42. National Bank of Pakistan (Amendment) Act
43. National Council of the Arts *see* Pakistan National Council of the Arts Act
44. National Development Finance
45. National Development Volunteer Programme Act
46. National Guards Act
47. National Registration Act
48. Pakistan Science Foundation Act
49. Pakistan Tobacco Board (Amendment) Act
50. Newspapers Employees (Conditions of Service) Act
51. Nursing Council *see* Pakistan Nursing, Council Act
52. Pakistan Army (Amendment) Act
53. Pakistan Broadcasting Corporation Act
54. Pakistan Citizenship (Amendment) Act
55. Pakistan Citizenship (Second Amendment) Act
56. Pakistan Coast Guard Act
57. Pakistan Council of Scientific and Industrial Research Act
58. Pakistan National Council of the Arts Act
59. Pakistan Nursing Council Act
60. Pay-As-You-Earn Scheme Act
61. Payment of Wages (Amendment) Act
62. Pharmacy (Amendment) Act
63. Port Qasim Authority Act
64. Publication of the Holy Quran (Elimination of Printing Error) Act
65. Railways (Transport of Goods) (Amendment) Act
66. Removal of Accused Persons Act
67. Service Tribunal Act
68. Short Title Act
69. Social Security *see* West Pakistan Employees' Social Security (Amendment) Act
70. State Bank of Pakistan (Amendment) Act
71. Supreme Court and High Court Extension of Jurisdiction to Certain (Tribal Areas) Act
72. University of Islamabad Act
73. West Pakistan Arms (Amendment) Act
74. West Pakistan Employees Social Security (Amendment) Act
75. West Pakistan Industrial and Commercial Employment (Standing Orders) (Amendment) Act

76. Workers Children (Education) (Amendment) Act
77. Workmen Compensation (Amendment) Act

Acts 1974

1. Administrator General (Amendment) Act
2. Bank (Nationalization) Act
3. Bank (Transfer of Assets and Liabilities) Act
4. Centres of Excellence Act
5. Civil Aviation (Amendment) Act
6. Companies (Appointment of Legal Aviator) Act
7. Constitution (First Amendment) Act
8. Constitution (Second Amendment) Act
9. Criminal Procedure (Amendment) Act
10. Dangerous Cargoes (Amendment) Act
11. Delimitation of Constituencies Act
12. Development of Industries (Federal Control) (Amendment) Act
13. Displaced Person (Land Settlement) (Amendment) Act
14. Dock workers (Regulation of Employment) Act
15. Economic Reforms (Amendment) Act
16. Electoral Rolls Act
17. Employees Cost of Living (Relief) Act
18. Employees Cost of Living (Relief) (Amendment) Act
19. Finance (Supplementary) Act
20. Finance Act
21. Foreign Exchange (Prevention of Payments) (Amendment) Act
22. House Building Finance Corporation (Amendment) Act
23. Import of Goods (Price Equalization Surcharge) (Amendment) Act
24. Income Tax (Amendment) Act
25. Karachi Port Trust (Amendment) Act
26. Marketing of Petroleum Products (Federal Control) Act
27. Members of Parliament (Salaries and Allowances) Act
28. Passport Act
29. Pakistan Atomic Energy Commission (Amendment) Act
30. Pakistan Maritime Shipping (Regulation and Control) Act
31. Pakistan Maritime Shipping (Regulation and Control) (Amendment) Act
32. Pakistan Red Cross Society (Amendment) Act
33. Peoples Open University Act
34. Post Office (Amendment) Act
35. Prevention of Anti-National Activities Act
36. Private Military Organizations (Abolition and Prohibition) Act
37. Provincial Service Tribunal (Extension of Provisions as the Constitution) Act
38. Service Tribunals, (Amendment) Act
39. Succession (Amendment) Act

40. Sukkur Barrage (Validation Orders) Act
41. Tariff (Amendment) Act
42. Transfer of Property Ordinance Repeal Act
43. University Grant Commission Act
44. Weight and Measure (Metric Systems) (Amendment) Act
45. West Pakistan Arms (Amendment) Act
46. West Pakistan Industrial and Commercial Employment (Standing Orders) Act
47. West Pakistan Industrial Development Corporation (Transfer of Projects and Companies) Act

Acts 1975

1. The Abandoned Properties (Taking over and Management) Act
2. The Airport Security Force Act
3. The Archival Material (Preservation and Export Control) Act
4. The Area Study Centres Act
5. The Associated Cement (Vesting) Act
6. The Balochistan Constabulary Act
7. The Banking Companies (Amendment) Act
8. The Banks (Nationalization) (Amendment) Act
9. The Boilers (Amendment) Act
10. The Capital Development Authority (Abatement of Arbitration Proceedings) Act
11. The Central Employees Benevolent Fund and Group Insurance (Amendment) Act
12. The Chairman and Speaker (Salaries, Allowances, and Privileges) Act
13. The Chief Election Commissioner (Salary, Allowances, and Privileges) Act
14. The Code of Criminal Procedure (Amendment) Act
15. The Companies (Appointment of Legal Advisers) (Amendment) Act
16. The Companies (Managing Agency and Election of Directors) (Amendment) Act
17. The Constitution (Third Amendment) Act
18. The Constitution (Fourth Amendment) Act
19. The Law Reforms (Amendment) Act
20. The Legal Practitioners and Bar Council (Amendment) Act
21. The Legal Practitioners and Bar Council (Second Amendment) Act
22. The Life Insurance (Nationalization) (Amendment) Act
23. The Malaria Eradication Board (Repeal) Act
24. The Members of the National Assembly (Exemption from Preventive Detention and Personal Appearance) (Amendment) Act
25. The Members of the Provincial Assemblies Privileges (Amendment) Act
26. The National Guards (Amendment) Act
27. The National Registration (Amendment) Act
28. The Newspaper Employees Conditions of Service (Amendment) Act
29. The North-West Frontier Province Bus Stand and Traffic Control (Peshawar) Act
30. The North-West Frontier Province Public Service Commission (Amendment) Act
31. The North-West Frontier Province Suppression of Crimes Act

32. Criminal Law Amendment *see* Pakistan Criminal Law Amendment Act (Amendment) Act
33. The Criminal Law (Special Provision) (Amendment) Act
34. The Cutting of Trees (Prohibition) Act
35. The Dangerous Drugs (Amendment) Act
36. The Decorations Act
37. The Deputy Chairman and Deputy Speaker (Salaries, Allowances, and Privileges) Act
38. Deputy Speaker (Salaries, Allowances, and Privileges) Act
39. The Employees Cost of Living (Relief) (Amendment) Act
40. The Evacuee Property and Displaced Persons Laws (Repeal) Act
41. The Evacuee Trust Properties (Management and Disposal) Act
42. The Exclusive Fishery Zone (Regulation of Fishing) Act
43. The Explosive Substances (Amendment) Act
44. The Federal Board of Intermediate and Secondary Education Act
45. The Federal Investigation Agency Act
46. The Federal Ministers and Ministers of State (Salaries, Allowances, and Privileges) Act
47. The Finance Act
48. Fishery Zone (Regulation of Fishing) *see* The Exclusive Fishery Zone (Regulation of Fishing) Act
49. The Foreign Cultural Associations (Regulation of Functioning) Act
50. The Frontier Crops (Amendment) Act
51. The General Statistics Act
52. The House Building Finance Corporation (Amendment) Act
53. The Hydrogenated Vegetable Oil Industry (Control and Development) (Amendment) Act
54. The Imports and Exports and Exports (Control) (Amendment) Act
55. The Import of Goods (Price Equalization Surcharge) (Amendment) Act
56. The Income Tax (Amendment) Act
57. The Industrial Relations (Amendment) Act
58. The Insurance (Amendment) Act
59. The Labour Laws (Amendment) Act
60. The Land Reforms (Amendment) Act
61. The North-West Frontier Province Urban Planning Act
62. The Opium (Amendment) Act
63. The Pakistan Army (Amendment) Act
64. The Pakistan Coinage (Amendment) Act
65. The Pakistan Commissions of Inquiry (Amendment) Act
66. The Pakistan Criminal Law Amendment Act (Amendment) Act
67. The Pakistan Insurance Corporation (Amendment) Act
68. The Pakistan Standards Institution (Certification Marks) (Amendment) Act
69. The Pakistan Tobacco Board (Amendment) Act
70. The People's Finance Corporation (Amendment) Act

71. The Political Parties (Amendment) Act
72. The Ports (Amendment) Act
73. The President's Pension Act
74. The President's Pension (Amendment) Act
75. The President's Salary, Allowances and Privileges Act
76. The Preventive Detention Laws Amendment Act
77. The Prime Minister's Salary, Allowances, and Privileges Act
78. The Road Transport Workers (Amendment) Act
79. The Senate (Election) Act
80. The Speaker (Salaries, Allowances, and Privileges) Act
81. The State Bank of Pakistan (Amendment) Act
82. The Suppression of Terrorist Activities (Special Courts) Act
83. The Telegraph (Amendment) Act
84. The Validation of Laws Act
85. The West Pakistan Rangers (Amendment) Act
86. The West Pakistan Water and Power Development Authority (Amendment) Act

Acts 1976

1. The Abandoned Properties (Taking over and Management) (Amendment) Act
2. The Antiquities Act
3. The Auqaf (Federal Control) Act
4. The Balochistan Land Revenue (Amendment) Act
5. The Centres of Excellence (Amendment) Act
6. The Civil Servants (Amendment) Act
7. The Code of Civil Procedure (Amendment) Act
8. The Code of Criminal Procedure (Amendment) Act
9. The Code of Criminal Procedure (Amendment) Act
10. The Co-operative Farming Act
11. The Conformity with Fundamental Rights (Amendment of Laws) Act
12. The Conformity with Fundamental Rights (Baluchistan Amendment of Laws) Act
13. The Constitution (Fifth Amendment) Act
14. The Constitution (Sixth Amendment) Act
15. The Contempt of Court Act
16. The Compulsory Service in the Armed Forces (Amendment) Act
17. The Cost and Industrial Accounts (Amendment) Act
18. The Cotton Ginning Control and Development Act
19. The Cotton Ginning Control and Development (Amendment) Act
20. The Criminal Law (Amendment) Act
21. The Criminal Law Amendment (Special Court) Act
22. The Criminal Law Amendment (Special Court) (Second Amendment) Act
23. The Criminal Law Amendment (Special Court) (Amendment) Act
24. The Defence of Pakistan (Amendment) Act

25. The Defence of Pakistan (Second Amendment) Act
26. The Defence of Pakistan (Third Amendment) Act
27. The Defence of Pakistan (Fourth Amendment) Act
28. The Divorce (Amendment) Act
29. The Dowry and Bridal Gifts (Restriction) Act
30. The Drugs Act
31. The Emigration Act
32. The Employees Old-Age Benefits Act
33. The Esso Undertaking Act
34. The Federal Supervision of Curricula, Text-Books and Maintenance of Standards of Education Act
35. The Fee-Charging Employment Agencies (Regulation) Act
36. The Finance Act
37. The Flour Milling Control and Development Act
38. The Flour Milling Control and Development (Amendment) Act
39. The Foreign Private Investment Promotion and Protection) Act
40. The Industrial Relations (Amendment) Act
41. The Labour Laws (Amendment) Act
42. The Land Reforms (Amendment) Act
43. The Land Reforms (Second Amendment) Act
44. The Land Reforms (Balochistan Pat Feeder Canal) Regulation (Amendment) Act
45. The Law Reforms (Amendment) Act
46. The Legal Practitioners and Bar Councils (Amendment) Act
47. The Legal Practitioners and Bar Councils (Second Amendment) Act
48. The Members of Parliament and Provincial Assemblies (Exemption Advisers from Disqualification) Act
49. The National and Provincial Assemblies (Elections to Reserved) Act
50. The National Guards (Amendment) Act
51. The National Insurance Corporation Act
52. The National Registration (Amendment) Act
53. The Newspapers Employees (Conditions Service) (Amendment) Act
54. Gas Development Corporation (Amendment) Act
55. Pakistan Arms (Amendment) Act
56. Pakistan Arms (Second Amendment) Act
57. Pakistan Army (Amendment) Act
58. Pakistan Engineering Council Act
59. Pakistan Hotels and Restaurants Act
60. Pakistan International Airlines Corporation (Amendment) Act
61. Pakistan Shipping Corporation Act
62. Pakistan Plant Quarantine Act
63. Pakistan Study Centers Act
64. Pakistan Tourist Guides Act
65. Provincial Motor Vehicles (Amendment) Act
66. Provincial Service Tribunals of Provisions of the Constitution (Amendment) Act

67. Publication of the Holy Quran (Elimination of Printing Errors) (Amendment) Act
68. Quaid-i-Azam's Mazaar (Protection Maintenance) (Amendment) Act
69. Railways (Amendment) Act
70. Regulation of Mines and Fields and Mineral Development (Amendment Control) (Amendment) Act
71. Presentation of Peoples Act
72. The Rice Milling Control and Development Act
73. The Rice Milling Control and Development (Amendment) Act
74. The Seed Act
75. The State Bank of Pakistan (Amendment) Act
76. The Suppression of Terrorist Activities (Special Courts) (Amendment) Act
77. The Suppression of Terrorist Activities (Special Courts) (Amendment) Act
78. The System of Sardari (Abolition) Act
79. The Territorial Water and Martine Act
80. The Travel Agencies Act
81. The University if Islamabad (Amendment) Act
82. The West Pakistan Press and Publication (Amendment) Act
83. The Withdrawal of Remission of Sentences Act

Acts 1977

1. The Antiquities (Amendment) Act
2. The Constitution (Seventh Amendment) Act
3. The Criminal Law Amendment (Special Court) (Amendment) Act
4. The Defence of Pakistan (Amendment) Act
5. The Emigration (Amendment) Act
6. The Employee's Cost of Living (Relief) (Amendment) Act
7. The Establishment of the Federal Bank for Cooperatives and Regulation of Cooperative Banking Act
8. The Finance Act
9. The Finance (Supplementary) Act
10. The Holders of Representatives Offices (Prevention of Misconduct) Act
11. The Jammu and Kashmir (Administration of Property) (Amendment) Act
12. The Labour Laws (Amendment) Act
13. The Land Reforms (Balochistan Pat Feeder Canal) (Amendment) Act
14. The Land Reforms Act
15. The Members of Parliament (Salaries and Allowances) (Amendment) Act
16. The Negotiable Instruments (Amendment) Act
17. The Organization of the Islamic Conference (Immunities and Privileges) Act
18. The Pakistan Army (Amendment) Act
19. The Pakistan Railways Police Act
20. The Parliament and Provincial Assemblies (Disqualification for Membership) Act
21. The Political Parties (Amendment) Act

22. The Prevention of Corruption Laws (Amendment) Act
23. The Prevention of Gambling Act
24. The Prevention of Smuggling Act
25. The Price Control and Prevention of Profiteering and Hoarding Act
26. The Privileges and Members of the National and Provincial Assemblies (Amendment) Act
27. The Prohibition Act
28. The Representation of the People (Amendment) Act
29. The Services Tribunals (Amendment) Act
30. The Transfer of Evacuee Land (*Katchi Abadi*) (Amendment) Act

Annex VII
A Chronology of Events related to Parliament, 1972–1977

1972	
23 March	The National Assembly (Short Session) Order is promulgated.
14 April	First meeting of the National Assembly; all elected members take oath.
17 April	National Assembly adopts Interim Constitution, to come into effect on 21 April.
21 April	President Bhutto issues proclamation, ends martial law and is sworn in as President of Pakistan.
2 July	President Bhutto and Prime Minister Indira Gandhi sign the Simla Agreement.
9 September	Mahmud Ali Kasuri, Minister for Law and Parliamentary Affairs, states that the ruling PPP is opposed to any constitutional scheme, which envisages Pakistan as a confederation or a combination of four semi-independent states.
29 September	Mahmud Ali Kasuri, Minister for Law and Parliamentary Affairs, declares that the PPP and its chairman are committed to give the country a federal parliamentary constitution, which will enshrine two pivotal principles, i.e. provincial autonomy and a parliamentary system.
17 October	Leaders of various political parties in the National Assembly—invited by President Bhutto—meet in Rawalpindi to evolve a consensus on the permanent constitution of Pakistan.
20 October	The leaders of parliamentary parties reach a unanimous agreement on the basic framework of the permanent constitution of Pakistan.
2 December	The Constitution Committee receives the draft of the permanent constitution for its consideration. Details of the draft remain undisclosed, but according to the official announcement, it has been prepared in the light of the constitutional accord between the political parties in the National Assembly.

21 December	The Constitution Committee of the National Assembly of Pakistan completes its deliberations on the permanent draft constitution.
31 December	Law Minister Abdul Hafeez Pirzada presents the report of the Constitution Committee and the draft constitution to the National Assembly.
1973	
2 February	Draft Constitution Bill introduced into the National Assembly.
15 February	The governors of Balochistan and the NWFP, Ghaus Bakhsh Bizenjo and Arbab Sikandar Khan Khalil respectively, removed from office by President Bhutto. President's Rule imposed for thirty days in both the provinces.
21 February	Mufti Mahmud's NWFP government resigns.
10 April	National Assembly unanimously adopts the permanent constitution of the Islamic Republic of Pakistan.
12 April	President Bhutto authenticates the constitution of the Islamic Republic of Pakistan.
1 June	National Assembly passes Federal Security Force Bill.
4 June	Aziz Ahmed, Minister of State for Defence and Foreign Affairs, tells the National Assembly that Pakistan has made it clear to India that the repatriation of Pakistani POWs has to be settled before the implementation of other provisions of the Simla Agreement.
6 July	In response to the Constitutional Reference made by the President, the Supreme Court of Pakistan expresses, unanimously, that the National Assembly can consider/adopt a resolution allowing the government to recognise 'Bangladesh' formally.
10 July	National Assembly passes a resolution empowering the government to accord formal recognition to Bangladesh at a time when such recognition is in the best national interest of Pakistan.
7 August	Habibullah Khan Marwat elected first Chairman of the Senate of Pakistan.
10 August	Fazal Elahi Chaudhry elected President of Pakistan—under the new constitution—at a joint session of the Parliament.
12 August	Z.A. Bhutto elected Prime Minister under the new constitution by the National Assembly.

13 August	The President and the Prime Minister of Pakistan take their oaths under the new constitution.
14 August	The Constitution of 1973 comes into force.
16 August	Top leadership of the National Awami Party arrested in Balochistan.
14 September	National Assembly passes High Treason Bill.

1974	
22 January	Government announces an exclusive sitting of the National Assembly, on 31 January, to debate the Balochistan situation and discuss the report of the committee which was appointed by the House.
22 February	Organisation of Islamic Cooperation conference held in Lahore. Pakistan officially recognises Bangladesh.
15 April	Abdul Hafeez Pirzada (law minister) introduces the first Constitutional Amendment Bill in the National Assembly.
7 June	National Assembly starts discussion on the repercussions of the underground nuclear explosion carried out by India.
13 June	The Prime Minister of Pakistan says that he would place the Ahmadiyya issue before the National Assembly immediately after the budget session.
30 June	As a result of a motion moved by the law minister, which was carried unanimously, the National Assembly sets up a special committee (comprising the entire House) to discuss and make recommendations on the issue relating to 'Khatam-e-Nabuwat' and matters relating to it.
3 July	J.A. Rahim officially removed as Central Minister for Production and Commerce by the Prime Minister under Article 92 Sub-section 3 of the constitution. Rafi Raza appointed minister in his place.
24 August	The Azad Kashmir Assembly unanimously passes the Interim Constitution of Azad Jammu and Kashmir providing for a parliamentary system of government.
26 August	The Parliament at a joint session approves the official move for continuance of the State of Emergency for a further period of six months.

7 September	National Assembly and the Senate pass the Constitution Second Amendment Bill declaring that anyone who does not believe in the 'absolute and unqualified finality' of the Prophethood of Muhammad (PBUH) was not a Muslim.

1975

17 January	Dr Mubashir Hasan appointed Secretary General of PPP.
11 February	Malik Meraj Khalid introduces the Third Amendment in the Constitution Bill in the House.
11 November	Government introduces Fourth Amendment Bill in the National Assembly.
14 November	Federal Security Force personnel in plain clothes throw Opposition members out of the House.
26 December	A Presidential Ordinance provides a five-year disqualification, for office-bearers of a party dissolved under the Political Parties Act, from the membership of Parliament and the provincial assemblies.

1976

26 February	A joint session of the Parliament extends the President's Rule in Balochistan for another two months.
1 March	General Mohammad Ziaul Haq appointed Chief of the Army Staff of Pakistan.
30 March	National Assembly and Senate unanimously pass resolutions condemning Israeli actions against the Arabs and the desecration of the Islamic holy places in Jerusalem and other parts of the occupied West Bank territories.
5 April	National Assembly passes the Defence of Pakistan (Amendment) Bill which would empower a provincial government to also constitute Special Tribunals under the Defence of Pakistan Rules.
26 April	A joint session of Parliament approves the ruling party's resolution thereby extending, for the third time, Governor's Rule in Balochistan for another two months.
9 May	In Lahore, the general council of the opposition United Democratic Front (UDF) unanimously re-elects Pir Sahib of Pagaro and Prof. Ghafoor Ahmad as President and Secretary of the UDF respectively, and appoints a joint Central Parliamentary Board.

11 May	National Assembly passes the Dowry and Bridal Gift (Restriction) Bill, incorporating several amendments, including one which makes it applicable to all citizens of Pakistan—Muslims and non-Muslims. The Bill restricts the aggregate value of the dowry, present and gifts given to the bride or bridegroom to a maximum of Rs5000, and restricts the total of other marriage expenses to a maximum of Rs2500.
12 May	National Assembly passes a bill abolishing *Sardari* system in the country.
17 May	The Political Parties Ordinance 1976, (which was due to expire on 24 May), was replaced by a new Presidential Ordinance, the Political Parties (Second Amendment), which provides for a five-year disqualification.
5 September	National Assembly passes the Constitutional (Fifth Amendment) Bill.
16 December	Government introduces a Bill in the National Assembly providing for the declaration of the territorial waters and maritime zones of Pakistan.
21 December	National Assembly of Pakistan unanimously adopts a motion which acclaims and endorses the nation's tribute to Quaid-i-Azam Mohammad Ali Jinnah on his birth centenary.
1977	
7 January	Z.A. Bhutto announces in the National Assembly that general elections will be held in March 1977. The National Assembly unanimously passes the two bills relating to land reforms announced by the Prime Minister on 5 January 1977.
16 January	At a press conference in Lahore, Mufti Mahmud, the president of the newly formed Pakistan National Alliance declares that the alliance would not contest elections to the seats of the national and provincial assemblies in Balochistan.
17 January	PPP issues the list of its candidates for the 200 seats of the National Assembly.
18 January	Pakistan National Alliance announces its list of candidates for the National Assembly.

Index